AF328700

BACKLASH PRESIDENTS

Backlash Presidents

FROM TRANSFORMATIVE
TO REACTIONARY LEADERS
IN AMERICAN HISTORY

JULIA R. AZARI

PRINCETON UNIVERSITY PRESS

PRINCETON & OXFORD

Published by Princeton University Press
41 William Street, Princeton, New Jersey 08540
99 Banbury Road, Oxford OX2 6JX

press.princeton.edu

All Rights Reserved

ISBN 978-0-691-24695-6
ISBN (e-book) 978-0-691-24697-0

Library of Congress Control Number 2025935248

British Library Cataloging-in-Publication Data is available

Editorial: Bridget Flannery-McCoy and Alena Chekanov
Production Editorial: Jill Harris
Jacket Design: Katie Osborne
Production: Erin Suydam
Publicity: James Schneider
Copyeditor: Cynthia Buck
Jacket images: Adobe Stock / Alamy Stock Photo

This book has been composed in Arno

Printed in the United States of America

10 9 8 7 6 5 4 3 2 1

CONTENTS

Acknowledgments   vii

1   Introduction: Race and Presidential Impeachment   1

2   A New Birth of Freedom: George Washington to
Abraham Lincoln   21

3   "The Constitution as It Is": Andrew Johnson's
Impeachment   50

4   "Patience and Moderation": Theodore Roosevelt
to Lyndon Johnson   75

5   Law and Order: Nixon and Watergate   110

6   "The Content of Their Character": Ronald Reagan
to Barack Obama   140

7   "Hostile Takeover": The Two Impeachments
of Donald Trump   174

8   Conclusion: The Choices We Face: Rethinking
Presidential Impeachment   207

Afterword: We Are Going Back   213

Notes   219

Index   259

THIS BOOK began as a kernel of an idea—a conference memo intended to be provocative—and it took me several years, and the grim weeks following the 2020 presidential election, to be convinced that the full argument needed a book-length treatment. I hope the following pages leave the reader convinced that was the case. If not, please consider these acknowledgments my effort to spread the blame around, though I take full responsibility for the shortcomings of the book itself.

Bridget Flannery-McCoy, in her capacity as an editor at Princeton University Press, was among the most persuasive and patient voices as I developed my ideas. Alena Chekanov, Eric Crahan, and Jill Harris made sure that the project came to fruition. I am grateful to the reviewers of the proposal and the full manuscript—their expertise has made the final product much stronger.

I am grateful to the Bright Line Watch Conference hosted at Yale University and the Korbel School at the University of Denver for inviting me to present early versions of the project. At these events, I was fortunate to receive feedback that encouraged me to keep going. Daniel Stid, Brendan Nyhan, Anna Grzymala-Busse, and Seth Masket were especially encouraging at these events. Other early supporters include Didi Kuo, Alexandra Filindra, David Mayhew, and Alvin Tillery. A Kluge Fellowship at the Library of Congress gave me time to think and read, even if I didn't yet know I was going to write this book. I am also grateful to workshops and speaker series at the University of Minnesota–Morris, Bates College, and Fordham University for the opportunity to present this work at various stages. Stephen Skowronek, as always, provided the intellectual foundation for all work on American political development and the presidency, shaping my thoughts throughout the project. I am also indebted to Michael Koncewicz for inviting me to be on an all-star panel at the 2022 American Political History Conference, where I got to share my Watergate opinions with the top experts in the field.

Being part of the Marquette University Political Science Department has also afforded me a level of intellectual and personal support that makes me feel very fortunate. Phil Rocco and Pat Sobkowski read draft chapters. Jessica Rich, Noelle Brigden, and Sam Harshner helped me talk through ideas. Paul Nolette and Amber Wichowsky have been my American politics support system for many years. Numerous others—especially Lowell Barrington, Mark Berlin, Sue Giaimo, and Amanda Heideman—cheered me on, pushed me to take lunch breaks, and took on other tasks so that I could have some space and time to work. Last but certainly not least, Will Monk and Melanie Reiner provided excellent research assistance.

Beyond Marquette, Milwaukee's amazing political science community was of great help. The Milwaukee Area Political Science Seminar offered valuable feedback. Lilly Goren of Carroll University remains among the most steadfast professional friends I could ask for, asking tough questions and cheering me on in equal measure.

I benefited greatly from the friendship and advice of a group of political scientists collectively known as the "Klugies"—Christopher Federico, Kris Kanthak, Greg Koger, Seth Masket, Joanne Miller, Hans Noel, Kathryn Pearson, Dave Peterson, Kyle Saunders, Darren Schreiber, Anand Edward Sokhey, Jennifer Nicoll Victor, and Christina Wolbrecht. Seth, in particular, provided feedback on various ideas and snippets of text while also enduring very detailed updates on the highs and lows of my writing process and my mental state throughout and keeping our collaborative projects afloat. William Adler, Lee Drutman, and James Wallner picked up the slack on our shared projects and encouraged me to keep focused on this book. Shamira Gelbman has been a better writing partner than I could ever have imagined deserving, reading multiple drafts, checking in regularly, and talking me through the writing process. Jonathan Bernstein, Matt Glassman, Anne Pluta, Andy Rudalevige, Colleen Shogan, and Mary Stuckey also gave crucial feedback. Kelly Clancy's AcWriMo group in 2023 was essential to my completion of the manuscript.

I could not have completed this project without the support of my "Sister Bay" knitting family—Kiersten Berger, Lilly Goren, Lauren Hackerott, Jenna Hoard, and Colleen Woods-Frerichs—or my friends Abbey Cohn, Tara Daly, Kim Frerichs, Natalie Knazik, Laura Mele, Kevin Miller, Sameena Mulla, Ericka Tucker, Drew Tompkins, and Tipan Verella. Katy Nicketakis, Allison O'Mahen Malcom, and Steve Malcom offered their enthusiasm for this book idea and, perhaps more importantly, let me go on about it at length during our first dinner out in 2021. Each of these individuals brought joy, encouragement, and support at times when they were deeply needed.

My husband, Todd Osterman, cheerfully allowed this book to engulf our lives for a few years, providing both support and distraction—and not an insignificant number of home-cooked meals delivered directly to my desk—and asked some great questions about the work along the way. Throughout the process, I was inspired by the example of my mother-in-law, Nancy Hathaway, who never stops learning, and by the focus and drive of my sister-in-law, Christine Chiou. The need to serve as a good example for my nephew and five nieces also kept me going— so hopefully they get the message. My brothers Nasim and Cyrus have kept me humble and been steady supporters. And my first and best readers—the only people, to my knowledge, to have a shelf dedicated to my writing—remain my parents, Sarah and the late Mahmood Azari. They are the foundation of this book and all that made it possible for me to write it. This book is for them.

BACKLASH PRESIDENTS

1

Introduction

RACE AND PRESIDENTIAL
IMPEACHMENT

"I'M NOT the president of Black America. I'm the president of the United States of America."[1] Barack Obama said this directly in an interview published in *Black Enterprise* magazine in April 2012. At other times, this distinction was implied. Obama emphasized tropes about Black fatherhood and hard work, talking on the campaign trail with Black and white communities alike about bigotry. The forty-fourth president knew his racial background was part of the story that made him so appealing. This awareness could also make him especially cautious about what he said and how he said it.

Sometimes Obama talked about life in America as a Black man, or his connection with Black history through his wife and daughters. Sometimes he talked about his own family, from Kansas and Kenya. He attempted to bring both history and complexity to the subject. Despite treading carefully and judiciously with the subject, Obama could not dodge racist attacks from opponents.

A certain strain of commentary on the right suggested that Obama was antagonistic toward white Americans, even that he hated them. "Shock jock" Rush Limbaugh connected the first Black president to a school bus fight, suggesting that "in Obama's America the white kids now get beat up with the black kids cheering."[2] Former House Speaker Newt Gingrich accused the president of "Kenyan, anti-colonial" thinking.[3] By the summer of 2016, one-third of white Americans reported that they thought Obama had "made race relations worse."[4]

Alongside these accusations were the conspiracy theories surrounding Obama's birth certificate and eligibility to serve as president. These rumors circulated in right-wing media to the point that, by 2016, a majority of Republican voters doubted or disbelieved that Obama was a natural-born citizen.[5]

This angry response to the Obama presidency culminated in the election of Donald Trump, one of the main purveyors of the "birther" conspiracy, in 2016. Trump clinched the nomination and then an Electoral College victory by talking about "making America great again," denouncing immigrants and promising a forceful brand of law and order. The latter seemed especially aimed at the recently formed Black Lives Matter movement, which had organized with a particular focus on police violence against Black Americans.

The formation of Black Lives Matter also illustrated the other side of Obama's cautious racial presidency. Activists voiced frequent frustration with the Obama administration's lack of attention to issues like violence, especially police violence, and economic inequality across racial lines.[6] Throughout his time in office, some critics alleged that Obama was doing too much for racial minorities while others said he was doing too little.

Nevertheless, the backlash forces, not those calling for greater change, were the ones that seemed to more immediately influence politics. Shortly after election day, Michael Tesler's analysis at the political science blog the *Monkey Cage* touted a stunning finding: Racial attitudes had been more important in determining the 2016 vote than they had been in 2008 or 2012, when Obama himself was on the ballot.[7]

Trump's 2016 bid for the presidency was not just about attacking Obama's legacy. It was also about pushing the boundaries of what was acceptable in politics. Mocking women, disabled people, and even war hero Senator John McCain and talking about immigrants in derogatory terms, Trump famously maintained that he could shoot someone on Fifth Avenue and not lose support.

In an essay called "The First White President," journalist Ta-Nehisi Coates explores the connection between Trump's often brazen violation of the written and unwritten rules and racial politics:

> The mind seizes trying to imagine a black man extolling the virtues of sexual assault on tape ("When you're a star, they let you do it"), fending off multiple accusations of such assaults, immersed in multiple lawsuits for allegedly fraudulent business dealings, exhorting his followers to violence, and then strolling into the White House. But that is the point of white supremacy—to ensure that that which all others achieve with maximal effort, white people (particularly white men) achieve with minimal qualification. Barack Obama delivered to black people the hoary message that if they work twice as hard as white people, anything is possible. But Trump's counter is persuasive: Work half as hard as black people, and even more is possible.[8]

Despite this description, we might not see the story of Trump's first term as "even more"—those four years were not entirely filled with political triumph and success (though perhaps Trump's reelection in 2024 counts as the fulfillment of this possibility). Though not convicted, Trump became the first president to be impeached twice. Both times were for some form of election interference—once for asking the Ukrainian government to investigate the son of his eventual 2020 election rival, Joe Biden. The second time was after Biden won the election and Trump, refusing to accept the results, encouraged an angry mob to march to the Capitol, this time interfering with the peaceful transfer of power.

The president of the United States, Donald J. Trump, delivered a speech that morning encouraging his supporters to march on the Capitol and prevent the certification of what he alleged was a fraudulent election, then watched the violent spectacle unfold on television. A week later, the US House of Representatives approved one article of impeachment against him. Nearly twelve years after the election of the nation's first Black president, another historic first occurred: A president was impeached a second time after a violent, largely white mob stormed the Capitol in response to his words.[9]

This book explores how the Obama-Trump pairing fits into a larger historical narrative. Obama, as the first African American president, was a racially transformative leader, despite his best efforts to soften the impact of this sharp break with precedent. Trump was a classic backlash president, talking about law and order and promising a return to a mythical American past. This populist rhetoric, with its disregard for norms and institutions, culminated in not one but two impeachments.

Obama and Trump were not the first such pair of presidents. This combination has occurred twice before in American history. The first such instance reaches back into the nineteenth century—Abraham Lincoln was also a racially transformative president. He was neither perfect nor always enthusiastic about the scope and depth of the changes he brought about. Nevertheless, Lincoln stood fast for the Union in the face of the secession of the slave states. He eventually evolved from a cautious Republican who opposed the expansion of slavery to the Great Emancipator who issued the Emancipation Proclamation and championed the Thirteenth Amendment.

Lincoln's successor, Andrew Johnson, came to office after Lincoln's death. Johnson's selection as vice president had been part of an effort to move forward and reunite the nation by persuading Democrats who had stayed in the Union to support Lincoln over his Democratic opponent, General George McClellan. Johnson, like Nixon and Trump, took an expansive view of his own power, especially when it came to using the executive branch to curb the Reconstruction laws passed by Congress in order to limit federal protection of freed people. Johnson's racism and desire to set up a hierarchical social structure in the South made him a backlash president, even if he was not elected in his own right. His presidency became synonymous with restoring white supremacy in the vanquished former Confederacy.[10]

And Johnson was the first president to be impeached. His impeachment was a mix of clear legal violations that could be demonstrated, assertions about the limits of executive power, and an accusation of interfering with an election by denouncing members of Congress in advance of the 1866 midterms. Such a mix would also characterize subsequent impeachments.

TABLE 1.1. Overview of Race, the Presidency, and Impeachment

Racial Order	Transformative President	Backlash Successor	Populist Politics	Impeachment Charges
Slavery	Abraham Lincoln	Andrew Johnson	Economic populist; objected to slavery; used rhetoric to delegitimize Congress; undermined executive branch responsibility to enforce laws	Violated the 1867 Tenure of Office Act in making federal appointments; interfered in the midterm elections ("swing around the circle")
Jim Crow	Lyndon Johnson	Richard Nixon	Used language about law and order and the silent majority	Obstructed justice, abused power, defied congressional subpoena (passed by the House Judiciary Committee)
Colorblindness	Barack Obama	Donald Trump	Used anti-institution rhetoric like "drain the swamp"; spoke of the "forgotten Americans"; used anti-immigrant and anti–Black Lives Matter rhetoric	2020: obstructed Congress and abused power 2021: incited insurrection on January 6, 2021

Lyndon Baines Johnson (LBJ), at the behest of a growing civil rights movement, also falls into this category of a racially transformative president. The laws he signed enhanced the political power of nonwhite Americans (the Voting Rights Act of 1965) and asserted federal power to ensure equal treatment of all, even in the realms of private business and life (the Civil Rights Acts of 1964 and 1968). His successor, Richard Nixon, taking advantage of the charged political environment, ran a law-and-order campaign in 1968. Throughout his presidency, he showed a shaky commitment to the idea of political opposition, threatening to use the government to pursue his political foes, including anti–Vietnam War and civil rights activists. The House brought charges against him in 1974 for his part in the Watergate scandal—also, in essence, for interfering with the election process—but he resigned before he could be impeached.

The Relationship Between the Presidency and Race Politics

One of the main arguments in this book is that racially transformative presidencies are both rare and highly disruptive to the political system. An important question is why this seems to be the case. We often think of presidents as the movers and shakers of the political system, but that's not always true. Their charge—as formally written in the US Constitution—to "preserve, protect, and defend" has sometimes been translated into very cautious action when the stakes are high. In describing how most presidents have gingerly approached the topic of racial equality, Russell Riley characterizes the president as a "nation-keeper, a protector of the inherited social and political order and a preserver of domestic tranquility."[11] Furthermore, presidents rely on the kinds of compromises that have kept race off the political agenda or accommodated the most racially conservative forces, including compromises over legislation and presidential nominations themselves. Presidents have strong political incentives to avoid explosive issues like race, and most of them do.

Nevertheless, the presidency is also powerful, and when presidents break away from the established racial order, the results for the political system are profound.

Three periods of time define presidential approaches to race. The first runs from the early days of the American republic through the Civil War. These years saw a great deal of change in American politics, economics, and even the territory of the nation. What all presidents of this period shared, across geography and ideology, was a general unwillingness to take a stand against slavery. As the tensions between North and South intensified, presidents became especially invested in pursuing compromise, driven by the political pressures to hold together party coalitions that depended on votes from both slave and free states. Presidents from both the Whig and Democratic Parties kept this up even as those compromises increasingly tended toward accommodating the slaveholding South and, unsuccessfully, avoiding severe crisis. Lincoln's presidency, the Civil War, and the Johnson impeachment punctuated this era.

A new, post-slavery era eventually shared many of the political features of the previous period. The politics of Reconstruction eventually gave way to forces in the South that subjected Black citizens to violence and poverty, claiming that states' rights gave them the authority to do so. The Republican Party had been founded in the 1850s to halt slavery's expansion, but its vision became murky in the postwar years. The Democratic Party of the 1870s and beyond reasserted itself as the party of white supremacy. The Republicans often responded tepidly. Presidential statements on federal protections for civil rights, or even on the general subject of racial inequality, were infrequent and hard-won.[12] Even as much about American politics changed in the twentieth century, African Americans continued to face exclusion from public places, from employment and, eventually, from many federal programs, and the mob violence that terrorized Southern Black citizens remained undisturbed by federal intervention.

It is especially striking that presidents remained cautious, preserving the racial status quo, despite the changes they made in many other areas. Leaders from Theodore Roosevelt to Woodrow Wilson to Franklin Roosevelt expressed few qualms about expanding the presidency and breaking with past practices in other ways. Yet a reluctance to disturb the racial status quo when it came to the Jim Crow South manifested in both parties.

If we assume that presidential action on race is about personal beliefs and character, then it might be somewhat puzzling to consider that Franklin Roosevelt, Harry Truman, Dwight Eisenhower, and John F. Kennedy each has a complex and ambivalent racial legacy. This is less puzzling if we think about presidential action as a response to the formidable political forces that kept the parties divided over civil rights and to the expectation that presidents would maintain, rather than transform, the racial status quo. As with slavery, this era of compromises and injustice was not sustainable and eventually ended with the civil rights legislation enacted during Lyndon Johnson's presidency. Pressure to act on civil rights legislation built in the early years of Kennedy's presidency, and after his assassination in 1963, Johnson continued on the same path, eventually signing landmark civil rights bills. The civil rights revolution enhanced the political power of African Americans and portended major shifts in social and economic life. It also began a shift in the party system that gradually sorted civil rights opponents into the Republican coalition and civil rights supporters into the Democratic one, ending over a century of internal party divisions over race.[13] Because of changing party politics, the imperative to hold together diverse coalitions on race questions had greatly diminished compared to earlier periods. Nixon's rise and fall occurred in the aftermath of these changes.

Yet after Watergate, a similar pattern reestablished itself, with presidents reluctant to rock the boat of the social order too much. This new conservative era established new norms about being "colorblind" and focusing on individual rather than group rights.[14] Unwritten rules circumscribing conversations about race reflected formal standards of nondiscrimination. Violating these norms brought accusations of "bringing race into it" or being "divisive."[15] When Barack Obama's historic status as the first African American president threw these norms and practices into disarray, along came Donald Trump.

The Connection Between Racial Transformation and Impeachment

The second question this book considers is: What explains the connection between backlash politics and presidential impeachment?

When I told people that I was writing about race and presidential impeachment, I often got puzzled looks. Impeachment, after all, is about arcane and legalistic arguments over what the term "high crimes and misdemeanors" means and whether the president committed them.[16] But if we peer beneath the surface—even just a bit—we see that each of the three impeachment crises covered in the book are linked to race and public anxiety about changes to society and politics as well as to populism and the breach of norms and rules.

Obviously, any account of presidential impeachment has to start with presidential wrongdoing. Importantly, the politics of racial backlash does not exactly cause presidents to behave lawlessly and violate the law, nor does it directly prompt members of Congress to begin contemplating impeachment. But the explosive racial politics of the periods under consideration did create the conditions under which these events could unfold.

Constitutional language about "high crimes and misdemeanors" doesn't draw a clear road map for what impeachment is supposed to look like. Over time, the process has taken on a more legalistic character.[17] Impeachment uses language taken from the legal world—"trials" and "charges"—even though holding a president to account for things like "abuse of power" is obviously not only different but also political as well as legal.[18]

Several factors in the political context of presidential impeachment seem to matter: the level of conflict between the president and Congress, and, relatedly, the level of animosity between the parties. No president has ever been impeached by his own party. Still, divided government and even extreme polarization are not sufficient conditions. George W. Bush and Barack Obama held office during some of the most partisan periods in our country's history, but despite occasional rumblings, neither was impeached, not even under divided government. Something else, something significant, has to push members of Congress to overcome their misgivings about such a major disruption in the normal practice of government.

No presidential impeachment process has resulted in a conviction and removal from office. When the House Judiciary committee began looking into the process during Watergate, they were relying on century-old precedents to guide them. Bill Clinton's 1998 impeachment was widely understood as a political liability for the Republicans who pursued it, and it would serve as a cautionary tale for two more decades.[19] Polarization alone, no matter how rancorous, has not been enough on its own to overcome these legacies.

The party question also presents some puzzles. We sense intuitively that presidents would be impeached when the divisions between parties are sharpest and the partisan disagreements between the president and Congress are the clearest. In some ways this is true—there's no denying the depth of the disagreements between Andrew Johnson and congressional Republicans, especially radicals, or between Richard Nixon and a new contingent of liberals in Congress. As the following chapters will show, these disagreements, as well as the more familiar strife between Donald Trump and congressional Democrats, were specifically tied to race. Impeached presidents have also tended to be political hybrids who built political identities based on their personal appeals rather than party or ideological affiliations.[20]

Thinking about what propels these figures into office in the first place brings us to the question of "national crisis or social upheaval" as a factor in presidential impeachment.[21] When a president upends the racial status quo, new questions enter the political arena, and new divisions (as well as new alliances) emerge. Out of these periods of extraordinary politics come figures like Andrew Johnson, Richard Nixon, and Donald Trump.

Populism

The first point of connection is populism, a political approach that attacks institutions and claims victimhood on behalf of the "true people."[22] As such, populism is a logical connective tissue between racial backlash and presidential lawlessness, and it helps explain how these kinds of leaders find themselves in power. It also sheds light on how they use presidential power.

Identifying themselves as the real representatives of the deserving people, populist leaders often connect to racial or anti-immigrant backlash. And once they have identified the problem as laws and institutions, it follows that it is acceptable to break them, in the name of defending the people.[23]

Andrew Johnson, Richard Nixon, and Donald Trump all fit this pattern. An early version of populism guided the politics that landed Johnson on the 1864 presidential ticket. His opposition to slavery was rooted in an opposition to an "economic elite" who owned large numbers of slaves.[24] Once Johnson had taken office as president, his decisions reflected this sense of victimhood and oppression not only by elites but also by former slaves. His veto of the civil rights measures passed by the Reconstruction Congress suggested that white Americans were the true victims of the post–Civil War period.

For Nixon, populist appeals were a way of navigating the new political landscape after Lyndon Johnson. To win both the Republican nomination and the general election, Nixon needed to thread the needle of racial backlash response, drawing on voters from the suburban border South and attracting the support of those who saw civil rights progress as potentially disruptive to their lives. At the same time, Nixon needed to distance himself from George Wallace and other louder and more direct opponents of civil rights. Redirecting the focus to the plight of "ordinary" Americans, the so-called silent majority, allowed Nixon to strike this balance, at least temporarily. Nixon's populism was informed by his dislike for those he perceived as intellectual and economic elites but fell short of outright disdain for political institutions.

Donald Trump's 2016 statements targeted the established power structures in both parties, as well as the media and others he depicted as part of the Washington elite. While it is important to distinguish between populist claims and outright nationalist or racist statements, part of Trump's rhetorical strategy was to cast whites as victims of modern politics. As Ashley Jardina demonstrates, "many whites have described themselves as outnumbered, disadvantaged, and even oppressed," and these perceptions shaped their support for Trump.[25] Although Trump turned out not to be much of an economic populist once in office, this language helped him shore up votes among those who preferred more government intervention in the economy. Trump's perceived populism also fueled a narrative about "economic anxiety" that provided cover for racial backlash in 2016.

After a racially transformative presidency, politicians can cultivate feelings of white victimhood. Presidential populism connects these feelings to broader critiques of institutions, especially those associated with "out-of-touch elites" or moves toward racial progress. It has proven to be a short leap from those anti-elite, anti-institution ideas to presidential lawlessness and abuse of power. Leaders who have convinced themselves and their supporters that they represent the true people and that the institutions that limit them are illegitimate are less likely to be respectful of the boundaries formally and informally established to limit their power. Abuse of power, in turn, plays a crucial role in the impeachment process, especially for more recent presidents.

Populism, by insisting on the existence of a "true people," also creates space for politicians to levy critiques against the idea of legitimate opposition, raising the stakes for the political system overall. After raising doubts about the right of their opponents to participate in politics, all three backlash presidents in this account engaged in some form of election interference, undermining the process. Andrew Johnson did this by denouncing his opponents on a speaking tour, flouting the norms of the time. Richard Nixon did this by covering up the Watergate break-in and engaging in various efforts to use state power against activists he deemed threatening. Donald Trump's efforts to undermine the 2020 election began with weaponization of a foreign power against presumptive opponent Joe Biden and culminated, after its conclusion, in the January 6, 2021, insurrection.

With a president who denies legitimate opposition in word or deed, political opponents become all the more fervent. The words and behavior of backlash presidents are perceived—not without reason—as a threat to the fabric of American democracy. This sense of threat and preservation shapes not only impeachment politics but also the aftermath of these crises.

Norms and Institutions

The Trump years opened up new conversations about the role of norms in a democratic society. Scholars have argued that informal rules are a crucial part of lawful, republican forms of government.[26] One of the arguments of this book, however, is that norms can also help to preserve unjust arrangements, such as racial hierarchies.[27] The norm by which presidents would not interfere with the politics of slavery in the South prior to the Civil War and would defer to Southern legislators in the twentieth century powerfully shaped expectations about how parties would work and how presidents would behave. After the civil rights era, a strong norm of colorblind rhetoric emerged, constraining how parties and presidents addressed the topic of race. Racially transformative presidents each transgressed these norms and in turn shifted the entire system into flux, where the informal rules were no longer clear. This lack of clarity not only opened up opportunities for populist backlash presidents but also created the conditions for pushing the boundaries of acceptable rhetoric and behavior in ways that undermined shared understandings of the limits.

Norms also play a role on the congressional side. For House members to consider starting the impeachment process, they have to get past the informal barriers that usually place that process out of reach. When the informal rules no longer apply, new possibilities open up. We have limited clues about how the founders intended impeachment to be used, but norms have evolved to proscribe it in most cases, even when presidents have engaged in corrupt behavior, overstepped boundaries, or made unpopular decisions. As Trump supporters were quick to say in 2020, impeachment removes the chief executive selected by the people, and as Clinton supporters hastened to point out in 1999, removal by impeachment would fundamentally alter the relationship between the executive and legislative branches. The potential for partisan retaliation and electoral fallout is very high. The informal rules of the game have suggested that this tool is mostly off-limits for Congress. The following chapters trace how this norm has been challenged in the Johnson, Nixon, and Trump cases.

Norms help us account for an important outlier in this story: the impeachment of Bill Clinton, which demonstrated that racial transformation is not the only force that can lead to the breakdown of norms. Clinton's impeachment was conducted by a newly elected Republican majority. Given that Republicans had not controlled the House of Representatives since the 1950s, the group that gained control came from a conservative movement that had been pushing back against informal norms and practices for some time by that point. The Clinton impeachment was an example of this new congressional majority pushing the boundaries of what was possible under the new political circumstances. What is more, the defeat of the Republicans in the 1998 midterms made politicians even more hesitant about impeachment, deepening anti-impeachment norms in Congress and ultimately shaping impeachment politics during the Trump administration.

Shifting Dynamics in Congress

Discussions of presidential impeachment tend to focus on the president, but the House of Representatives plays the most pivotal role in the process. The scanty guidance provided by the Constitution about the conditions under which presidential impeachment should occur has made members of Congress generally cautious about employing the procedure. The political consequences of overreach appear to be severe, while the rewards seem far from guaranteed.

One goal of this book is to look at how the politics of racial transformation and backlash alter the environment for members of Congress. When backlash presidents take office, they tend to face intense opposition from the other party in Congress, with a few members unable to accept the new president. Chapters 3, 5, and 7 trace the racial dimension of this opposition—from radical Republicans opposed to Johnson's Reconstruction actions to Congressional Black Caucus members suspicious of Nixon's commitment to civil rights, to Black Democrats and their allies taking immediate issue with Trump's statements. Members of Congress invested in racial transformation are among the early advocates for impeachment, often dismissed in their initial claims.

The Politics of Racial Transformation and Backlash and the Study of American Political Development

The book's third area of inquiry is the relationship between the politics of racial transformation and backlash and how we study American political development. The term used here to describe periods marked by transformative leaders is "racial order," a term that is perhaps most strongly associated with the work of Desmond King and Rogers Smith. They define racial institutional orders as "ones in which political actors have adopted (and often adapted) racial concepts, commitments, and aims in order to help bind together their coalitions and structure governing institutions that express and serve the interests of their architects."[28] They describe the functions of racial orders insofar as they "seek and exercise governing power in ways that predictably shape people's statuses, resources, and opportunities."[29] King and Smith's influential article, as well as some related work, advocates for understanding American political development as the product of two persistent and competing racial orders—one egalitarian and focused on change, and the other steeped in what they call "ascriptive hierarchy," or different legal and political circumstances for individuals based on traits like race and gender. This book builds on the idea of racial orders but differs from their approach in several key ways. While their analysis covers US institutions in a more comprehensive way, I zero in here on the presidency, where less evidence is found of competing racial orders. Instead, most presidents are influenced most heavily by the political pressures that hold the racial hierarchy in place; in the face of these pressures, a more egalitarian order breaks through and reshapes presidential politics only infrequently.

This analysis adds up to a rethinking of patterns in presidential history. It builds on, and breaks away from, one of the most influential theories in this field of study, Stephen Skowronek's "political time" formulation.[30] This approach, which links presidential legacy and political impact to a leader's positioning in the dominant "political order," suggests that presidents' fates are shaped by what comes before them, especially by their immediate predecessors. Scholars have mainly used this work to apply a four-part typology that assesses the potential for a successful, even transformative, presidency based on whether the leader is "affiliated" with the dominant party in power or "opposed" to it and on the health of that party's ideas and coalition. But the argument offers much more than that.

A crucial intervention of Skowronek's pathbreaking book is its attempt to redirect the attention of presidential studies to the impact of a president's actions on politics and policy and away from endless assessments of legislative success. Most presidents, even those considered failures, come away from their time in office boasting significant accomplishments, legislative and otherwise. What distinguishes a Jimmy Carter or a Herbert Hoover from a Lyndon Johnson, Theodore Roosevelt, or FDR is their place in the larger political context, which in turn shapes what their actions do for their successors and beyond. "Reconstructive" presidents create new coalitions, dominant ideas, and even institutional arrangements that their successors articulate by attempting to "change policy without changing politics"—usually without much success.[31]

The argument in this book rests on this idea that presidents can change politics in powerful ways, and that we can understand a lot more about presidential politics by thinking about how much a given presidency is shaped by its predecessor. However, my analysis departs from the claim that the presidency is necessarily a "battering ram" against existing arrangements. Skowronek argues that "presidents cannot help but be politically catalytic." What we will see in the forthcoming chapters is that they can certainly try, but that in the area of race, they have every incentive to carefully avoid upsetting existing arrangements. I am not the first to raise this caveat: Russell Riley also suggests that when we emphasize the racial dimensions of the presidency, we see a much less disruptive office most of the time. Whereas presidents have been eager to carve out distinct political identities on many issues—foreign policy, westward expansion, tax cuts, social programs—the dominant pattern has been avoidance when it comes to directly facing the nation's challenges on race, especially activist demands. This pattern extends to a particular asymmetry: Presidents whose actions deepened racial hierarchy or enhanced the power of racially conservative forces had a different impact than did those few who pushed the nation in the direction of equality.

Another important contention is that presidents do not make this determination on their own. The story of presidential politics is a story of changing presidential coalitions. In describing the rise and fall of party orders, Skowronek details how Jacksonian Democrats brought together North and South through party procedures, and then the inadequacy of these procedures in the 1850s to address the nation's moral and political crisis around slavery. A similar coalition came back together with the Democratic resurgence in the New Deal era, only to disintegrate once again around the issue of civil rights. The rise and fall of Lincoln's Republicans is described mostly without respect to the structural dynamics around race after the conclusion of the Civil War, though this order saw the end of Reconstruction and the beginning of a Jim Crow order. It is true that race did not play a central role in cleaving the party coalition the way that it did for Northern and Southern Democrats. However, factional shifts, especially between "black-and-tan" Republicans and proponents of a "lily-white" party, drove developments in Republican politics as well.[32]

If we look at race as the central fault line, the cause of the nation's great conflict, and the anchor weighing down our democracy until (at least) 1965, then coalition politics and the pivotal presidencies look different. Importantly, as we shall see in chapter 4, this view highlights the continuities that persisted through the rise of the New Deal order and Franklin Roosevelt's presidency. It also helps to explain why Barack Obama's presidency had such significant and destabilizing effects on politics, despite his careful efforts at what Skowronek describes as "interest management." Obama carefully tended to the different groups within the Democratic Party's governing coalition rather than offer a bold new vision around which to organize a new era of politics.[33]

The third relevant piece of the political time formulation is its approach to presidential impeachment by linking it to the "politics of preemption," which places a leader in opposition to the party that controls the main ideas of the era, as well as—usually—Congress. These leaders tend to be vulnerable to character criticisms—up to and including impeachment—because they pursue more individualistic and candidate-centric politics, unmoored from political coalitions. Skowronek uses this insight to describe the fates of Andrew Johnson and Richard Nixon, as well as the impeachment articles drawn up against John Tyler in the 1840s and the political "convulsions" that Woodrow Wilson experienced around the Treaty of Versailles.[34] In the 1997 book

The Politics Presidents Make, these concepts also presciently describe the dynamics of Bill Clinton's impeachment. This analysis provides some of the foundation for digging into impeachments in this book. Like Skowronek, I view the tenuous coalitions cobbled together by Andrew Johnson, Nixon, and Trump as central to the dynamics leading to their impeachment. One contribution of this book is to explore the parallels across the politics that drove these presidencies. This further refines the political time approach by narrowing down the broad category of preemptive leadership. The emphasis Skowronek places on the highly personal politics of preemption means that his theory does an excellent job of explaining why popular generals like Zachary Taylor and Dwight Eisenhower succeed at getting elected to the presidency. But while Johnson, Nixon, and Trump may have benefited from broadly similar politics—the ability to exploit weaknesses in the dominant party—they are undoubtedly a distinct political breed. What I aim to add is some deeper scrutiny of how impeachment emerges from unstable politics, particularly destabilization caused by shifts in norms and by the responses of ascendant political forces to backlash figures. By looking at the role of elections, Congress, and political movements, I hope to open up new avenues in the American political development conversation about presidential impeachment.

The Implications for American Democracy

Finally, the book poses the question: What are the implications for American democracy? What does the cycle of racial maintenance and avoidance, transformation, and backlash tell us about the possibilities and flaws of the American experiment? This story offers both hope and caution and highlights the potential for institutions to be both a hindrance and an important tool in the pursuit of a more racially just society.

In addition to the importance of institutions, critiques of contemporary US politics point to partisan polarization as a threat, suggesting that moderation and compromise are inherently laudable goals. This may be the case much of the time, but moderation and compromise also have important costs. In the story of American politics, one long-term and recurring cost has been racial progress and equality.

The term "backlash" has fallen out of favor with experts on race and American politics, and with good reason. One critique is that the backlash framework treats racism as episodic rather than woven into many aspects of politics and identity.[35] In this book, I use "backlash" to denote those periods when race drove politics more overtly. The evidence here presents the case that some periods are different, precisely because racism and racial hierarchy are built, sometimes tacitly, into so many elements of American politics—from political language to assumptions about the roles of the state and federal governments, to the policy questions that are kept off of party and congressional agendas.

Another criticism is that "backlash" is an imprecise term. Political scientist Vesla Weaver writes, "Much like the ambiguity around its origins and motivation, it is equally unclear what the ultimate aim or target of backlash is—repeal of an advance, desert a party who has gone too far to the extreme, revert to some prior status quo condition, or simply to register anger."[36] It's exactly this ambiguity that creates the conditions for presidents like Andrew Johnson, Richard Nixon, and even Donald Trump. They are elected to turn back the clock, or alter the direction, or . . . something. In 1864, Republicans sought the preservation of the Union and chose a Southern politician and former Democrat as Lincoln's running mate. After the war, Andrew Johnson devoted his presidency to reestablishing white supremacy in the South.[37] In 1968, Nixon won office through a law-and-order campaign that identified the Democrats with social disorder. In 2016, Trump promised to "make America great again." The pursuit of such vaguely described ends spurs lawless behavior and ensures that the goals of at least some of a president's support coalition are primarily about destruction and moving backward.

The third problem with backlash is that it can sometimes be taken to imply that racial progress is bad or dangerous. While this is a possible interpretation of the dynamics described in this book, it is hardly my intention to suggest as much. When the dust settles after an impeachment and a backlash presidency, Americans, especially those in power, have a choice. If this book has a prescription for politics, it is to take seriously the painful lesson of a transformative period. That is, to create political institutions, formal and informal, that break more decisively with the hierarchies of the present and past. Such a move would require facing problems and tough questions directly. Historically, the impulse so far has been to retreat from those difficulties, in both the Reconstruction era and the years following the civil rights movement. But such avoidance is far from inevitable.

The period since Trump's election has brought a great deal of introspection in the United States about the health of democracy here. Much of it has zeroed in on institutions and norms. However, not all norms and institutions are equally just, and we can learn a great deal about our democracy from the periods that followed backlash and impeachment as the country settled into a new routine. The trappings of impeachment have the effect of distracting from the major national issues at hand. And the ideology fueling the backlash has a way of entering the political mainstream. Allowing it to do so is also a choice.

American democracy is a work in progress, and that progress has not always been linear. The chapters to come show that racial hierarchy is built into the political foundations of the American system through compromises and unspoken agreements. They also show that these features of politics are reasserted and rebuilt even after a racially transformative president has altered the status quo. Backlash presidents like Andrew Johnson, Nixon, and Trump eventually prove to be vulnerable and unpopular. Yet some of their ideas outlive their presidencies, taking hold especially at the state level, where they are once again beyond the reach of national—presidential—policy jurisdiction. The cycle repeats. It looks different each time, but after each period of transformation, there have been important political figures who were unable to take the risks necessary to prevent backsliding. There are lessons here for twenty-first-century Americans as this history continues to unfold.

2

A New Birth of Freedom

GEORGE WASHINGTON
TO ABRAHAM LINCOLN

ABRAHAM LINCOLN WAS NO believer in racial equality, or so he said for the public record in a debate with Stephen Douglas in 1858: "I will say then that I am not, nor ever have been in favor of bringing about in any way the social and political equality of the white and black races."[1] The sixteenth president was also known to enjoy "darky jokes" that rested on the premise that African Americans were "thick-headed, stubborn, and not terribly bright."[2] By contemporary standards, these views are abhorrent. Even by the standards of the time, Lincoln was hardly on the cutting edge of thought about racial equality.[3]

Yet Lincoln was also the Great Emancipator, the president who marshaled the tools of the executive branch to bring about the end of slavery, if gradually and incrementally at first. Presidents bring their power to the work of transformation after others have done much of the heavy lifting. But Lincoln, over the course of his presidency, fulfilled this role while also harnessing presidents' capacity to provide moral leadership, play a persuasive role in the legislative arena, and carry out wartime prerogatives to help bring a legal end to slavery in the United States. Frederick Douglass confronted this tension in his "Oration in Memory of Abraham Lincoln" in 1876: "Viewed from the genuine abolition ground, Mr. Lincoln seemed tardy, cold, dull, and indifferent; but measuring him by the sentiment of his country, a sentiment he was

21

bound as a statesman to consult, he was swift, zealous, radical, and determined."[4]

How to think about early presidents and race presents a real dilemma for modern Americans. Most conventional wisdom about which presidents were "great" glosses over important and painful history.[5] Some heralded among the greats—Washington, Jefferson, and Jackson—owned slaves, along with nine more of the nation's first eighteen presidents.[6] Beyond this, even presidents who did not claim ownership over other human beings were complicit in maintaining the peculiar institution, and most held deeply racist views. One approach is to write off these facts as simply reflective of a time when slavery was legal throughout the South and the country had not yet developed the more egalitarian attitudes about race that would come later.

But the presidency is a political institution, and individual attitudes and beliefs are not the whole story. Regardless of their ideas or their slave-owning status, presidents in the years leading up to the Civil War responded to political influences. Political pressures differed for Democrats and Whigs and evolved with changing circumstances. The push to find compromise that would stave off existential conflict ultimately deepened that conflict. Tracing each of these compromises through the decades that led up to the war also reveals that, in seeking to preserve the nation, presidents took action that ultimately strengthened the pro-slavery side, even when they intended to do otherwise.

Two strong forces limited what presidents could do. The first was the need to be electorally competitive in both the North and the South. After the 1830s, this became an especially prominent feature of the party system. The Democratic Party created by Andrew Jackson and Martin Van Buren depended on harmony between its Northern and Southern factions.

The Whig Party, too, drew from both parts of the country and balanced a variety of views on the slavery issue. Both Lincoln and the eventual vice president of the Confederacy, Alexander Stephens, started their political careers as Whigs. Henry Clay, one of the party's most important leaders, took a view of slavery that rejected "extremists" across the spectrum.[7] Clay's compromise spirit led him to favor the colonization approach—that is, sending formerly enslaved people to Africa or the Caribbean.

The second factor was the Constitution. As the anti-slavery movement grew in the 1830s and 1840s, most Americans came to see it as impossible under the Constitution for Congress to "simply legislate slavery out of existence."[8] For presidents, this posed an even trickier problem: Their role, as laid out in the Constitution, was understood to be protecting and defending the document. One element of the debate was federalism—the ongoing discussion about what the federal government could do about slavery in states and newly acquired territories. Not only did the Constitution issue lay the foundation for how presidents would approach the issue before the Civil War, but it also created the basis for conflict in the first years of Lincoln's presidency about how to approach slavery within the bounds of the Constitution. This widespread interpretation of the Constitution shaped the degree to which Lincoln's presidency disrupted the political system. Making the war about abolishing slavery, even if gradually achieved, required a complete rethinking of the Constitution, even before it was formally amended to end the practice. And for the future of the former enslaved, now freed, people as well as the political, social, and economic structures in the rest of the nation, it also left open the deep and wide question: Now what?

In other words, we have to look at the political environment—the party system, the state of development of the presidency as an institution, the way people understood the Constitution—in order to grasp the impact of presidential action on the issue of slavery. Leading up to the Civil War, party politics and constitutional politics were deeply bound up with compromises that preserved slavery. Knowing this helps us understand why Lincoln's actions had such a profound impact on the political system, and how they shaped the conditions for Andrew Johnson's lawless presidency and subsequent impeachment. This approach also directs us away from simply evaluating presidents' personal racial attitudes and gives us the tools to evaluate how they affirmed existing principles of compromise, or challenged those principles, and, as a result, the principles of the entire political system.

Lincoln, as the nation's first Republican president, rejected the compromises that drove politics for his predecessors. Lincoln also took affirmative steps to end slavery, using the war powers and the rhetorical powers of the presidency to upend the status quo and ultimately to free enslaved people. Regardless of his views about slavery and about African Americans—which have been the source of great debate among scholars—Lincoln broke dramatically with his predecessors in the actions he took as president.

Presidents, Slavery, and the Early Republic

Revelations about some of the earliest and most revered founders have shaken up perspectives about them somewhat. In the late 1990s, historian Annette Gordon-Reed chronicled the relationship between Thomas Jefferson and a very young enslaved woman he owned, Sally Hemings. Hemings was the sister-in-law of Jefferson's late wife, further demonstrating how common it was for white men to father children with women they legally owned.[9] George Washington was not one of those men, as far as we know. But twenty-first-century historians have documented his relentless pursuit of Oney Judge, who escaped to freedom and lived out her life in the North.[10] Historian Alexis Coe begins her irreverent biography of Washington by pointing out that his mouth was filled with the teeth of slaves he owned, further highlighting the visceral and violent nature of an institution often sanitized in public narratives about beloved presidents.[11]

Presidents are products of their time, and presidencies are products of the political environment and the incentives that it creates. For every era in US history—but especially early on—this starts with the Constitution. Debates about the Constitution's precise relationship to slavery will probably never be resolved. Its text is ambiguous on a variety of important issues that would come up later—and especially on the expansion of slavery to new territories. But we do know something about the political structures created by the Constitution.

The word "slavery" never appears in the US Constitution, but many of its hallmark compromises accommodate the role of slavery in the

Union. The Three-Fifths Compromise was reached after debate on the question of how the enslaved population would be represented in Congress. This in turn shaped the Electoral College, which gives each state a number of votes equal to the size of its congressional delegation. This structural decision had profound effects on the era's balance of political power and, as a result, on presidential politics. What is more, in answering this representation question, the framers of the Constitution found compromise where basic logic would have seemed to prohibit it. Humanity is not determined as a matter of degrees, yet they created an institutional framework that accommodated this view by treating enslaved people as both people and property.

In the debates over the Constitution, an asymmetry between the interests represented often arose: Those critical of slavery were frequently less ardent and more willing to compromise.[12] The perspective that slavery was a moral stain on the nation—as well as a practical impediment to a functional Union—was present at the Constitutional Convention and perhaps accounts for the document's silence on the issue. But the structures, taken in total, "protected" slavery, ensuring that the South's political power would remain substantial.[13]

James Monroe and the Missouri Compromise

The story of compromise, presidential involvement, and slavery in the pre–Civil War South starts with the Missouri Compromise of 1820, negotiated during the presidency of James Monroe. Monroe, like most of the early presidents, was a slave owner. But facing other pressures on the issue, he regarded it perhaps more than others not only as immoral but as a threat to national unity.[14]

The issue of admitting Missouri to the Union highlighted the basic conflict: Southern legislators feared that their Northern counterparts wanted to limit the expansion of slavery and facilitate its gradual disappearance, and some Northerners did in fact want exactly that.[15] Monroe's involvement in the passage of compromise legislation implied his support for a congressional role in slavery's expansion into the territories, a position that riled some on the pro-slavery side. Overall, however, Monroe favored compromise; his eventual stance was to push the anti-slavery side to accept the compromise that Maine would be admitted as a free state and Missouri as a slave state.[16] From Southerners, a major concession was also extracted: the adoption of the Thomas Proviso preventing the expansion of slavery above the 36°30 parallel.[17] In the words of historian Robert Pierce Forbes, the proposal went from being framed as a "clear-cut northern victory" to a "miraculous escape from the imminent threat of northern domination" over the South.[18] The Missouri Compromise set the stage for the later conflicts over slavery that became intractable once bills repealing it were signed into law. Monroe's involvement in the issue also foreshadowed much about how presidents would approach slavery debates: avoiding the major moral confrontations while keeping a careful eye toward compromises that would preserve the Union. Monroe also hoped, as would so many of his successors, that the agreement reached on his watch would be the last compromise on slavery and take the issue of the national agenda for good.[19]

Andrew Jackson, Martin Van Buren, and the New Party System

Andrew Jackson's expansive attitude about presidential power would make him a perennial, and contested, fixture on lists of great presidents. There is no doubt about the impact of his assertion of the right to direct national policy from the White House even when Congress and the courts disagreed with him. If the definition of presidential greatness is someone who acts decisively and pushes institutional boundaries aside, then Jackson belongs at the top of the list.

But Jackson's harmful actions toward nonwhites, which have now become well known, have made his presence on the list of greats a controversial matter in recent years. The lasting impact of his treatment of Native Americans rightly tops the list of concerns.[20] His actions toward Native Americans are also relevant to the economic development of slavery, as the need for land for larger plantations drove the push for the removal of Native Americans from the South.[21]

Jackson's attitudes toward slavery also illustrate elements of his presidency. He was a slave owner and did not consider the practice immoral, in contrast to previous slave-owning presidents like Jefferson and Madison.[22] His attitudes informed how Jackson responded to policy issues related to slavery when they came up. As an architect of both a stronger presidency and the first mass-based political party in the United States, Jackson also contributed to the political conditions that shaped subsequent compromise politics. He and Van Buren created a party system that balanced the preferences of Northern and Southern politicians.

Jackson believed in both the Union and limits on federal power.[23] His overall approach to slavery and to the major policy issue he faced on the subject—the question of sending abolitionist material through the mail—reflected this sensibility. While Jackson was not invested in moral debates over slavery, he was concerned about the divisiveness of the issue and its potential to undermine the Union.[24] Accordingly, he saw the emerging abolitionist movement as a threat to national stability and unity, a theme that would recur during pre–Civil War presidencies.

The issue was the circulation of abolitionist literature through the US mail. Jackson undermined the abolitionist effort both passively and actively by providing quiet cover to Postmaster General Amos Kendall's decision to allow local postmasters in the South to refuse to deliver anti-slavery materials addressed to "prominent citizens" in South Carolina.[25] Jackson communicated to Kendall that the national obligation to deliver mail was "from city to city," and that local postmasters could make the final decision about what was appropriate for public delivery in specific areas.[26] Besides passive reliance on federal structures to prevent the delivery of abolitionist literature, Jackson looked the other way as "vigilante intolerance" also interfered with such communications. Violent mobs destroyed anti-slavery pamphlets and even interfered with travel from free states to slave states because of the presumption that some travelers were engaged in abolitionist activity.[27]

Jackson also advocated for federal action against abolitionism and publicly identified it with instability. In his seventh message to Congress, Jackson described the dangers of abolitionist material and asked Congress to pass a law prohibiting it in the US mail. Before asking for legislation, Jackson highlighted that the tranquility, even the existence, of the Union depended on the ability of the federal government and the free states to avoid interfering with slavery:

> Our happiness and prosperity essentially depend upon peace within our borders, and peace depends upon the maintenance in good faith of those compromises of the Constitution upon which the Union is founded. It is fortunate for the country that the good sense, the generous feeling, and the deep-rooted attachment of the people of the non-slaveholding States to the Union and to their fellow-citizens of the same blood in the South have given so strong and impressive a tone to the sentiments entertained against the proceedings of the misguided persons who have engaged in these unconstitutional and wicked attempts, and especially against the emissaries from foreign parts who have dared to interfere in this matter, as to authorize the hope that those attempts will no longer be persisted in.[28]

Jackson's successor, Martin Van Buren, differed from "Old Hickory" in many crucial ways. He was from New York, not the Western frontier, and he was a designer of systems, whereas Jackson was reactive and quick-tempered. Van Buren was the politician most widely credited with creating the convention system and assembling a Democratic Party that could be electorally competitive in both the North and the South.

Because of the need to navigate these political dynamics, Van Buren was an early proponent of the approach to compromise that tilted toward accommodating the South's position and calming fears about efforts to pass anti-slavery legislation.[29] Under these circumstances, Van Buren responded to considerable political pressure in the 1836 election to maintain the truce between the two factions.[30] He did so by disavowing abolitionism and maintaining his support for the position that "slavery was subject to the exclusive control of the states."[31] Van Buren's political allies underscored this position and extended it to the question of slavery in the District of Columbia. It was in the context of this presidential campaign, in which these positions needed to be spelled out because there was a prominent Northern candidate, that Van Buren and his campaign surrogates advanced the idea that "agitation" on slavery ran the risk of undermining national unity.[32]

Van Buren's 1837 inaugural address made this political stance clear. In his framing we can see the ideas that shaped how presidents would talk about slavery over the ensuing decades. Echoing his campaign themes, Van Buren promised not to give "constitutional sanction" to any bills that would threaten the "slightest interference with it [slavery] in the States where it exists," or that would abolish slavery in the District of Columbia.[33] The logic behind these promises stemmed from the fear that slavery had no less potential to undermine national unity in the 1830s than it had in the 1780s. A commitment to keeping the party together by sidestepping the issue of slavery was evident not simply in Van Buren's rhetoric. In his capacity as party leader, Van Buren had also promoted the "gag rule," which for nearly a decade had been used to keep the issue off the national agenda by banning petitions on slavery in the House of Representatives.[34]

Through the 1840s and 1850s—and, indeed, well into the twentieth century—the party that Jackson and Van Buren created depended on an alliance between Northern and Southern interests. Groups and individuals advocating for the abolition of slavery were presented as threats to delicate national unity. As president, both had deployed the power of the office to support this view, using words, informal party influence, and the federal bureaucracy to discourage anti-slavery changes while overlooking lawbreaking by the pro-slavery side. They set a precedent that would inform not only how pre–Civil War presidents thought about the politics of slavery but also the dynamics of the Democratic Party well into the twentieth century.

James K. Polk and the Pressures of Expansion

The White House would be in slave-owning hands for the next decade. After William Henry Harrison's brief tenure in office in 1841, he was succeeded by John Tyler, who brought to the office the sensibilities of a "Virginia aristocrat" and slave owner.[35] After Tyler came James K. Polk, a slave owner from Tennessee. In addition to their personal investment in slavery, both also faced political pressures that pushed them toward the South—in ways that had significant political consequences.

In some sense, Polk owed his nomination to Tyler, who was the incumbent president in 1844. As a vice president who had taken office after William Henry Harrison's death, Tyler found his very authority contested; was "His Accidency" a lawful president or simply a placeholder? He had also by that point been a member of and subsequently left both major parties. Though Tyler was in many ways a political enigma—a president highly constrained by his lack of either electoral legitimacy or a personal support base—he was consistent in his defense of the South.[36] During his presidency, his pro-Southern sentiments manifested as support for the annexation of Texas.

Tyler, hemmed in by his political circumstances, was unable to carry out his desire to annex a large slaveholding state that could considerably enhance the political power of the South. Nevertheless, his emphasis on the issue made it an important question at the 1844 Democratic Convention.[37] Lack of support for the Texas issue became a liability for the presumed favorite, former President Martin Van Buren.[38] Van Buren fell short of the necessary two-thirds of delegate votes to receive the nomination, paving the way for Polk to succeed on the ninth ballot.[39] In the general election, Polk's cross-regional coalition—Michigan, Indiana, Illinois, Missouri, Arkansas, Louisiana, Mississippi, Alabama, Georgia, South Carolina, Virginia, Pennsylvania, New York, New Hampshire, and Maine—beat perpetual Whig candidate Henry Clay by only a narrow margin in the popular vote.

The electoral and party politics of the moment informed Polk's presidency in two distinct ways. First, despite a narrow victory margin, Polk interpreted the authority of his office in broad terms in order to push expansionist politics through the annexation of Texas and, eventually, war with Mexico. Second, Polk saw preserving the balance of factions within his party as a key imperative for a successful presidency.[40]

On May 11, 1846, after conflict in a disputed border area, Polk issued a message informing Congress that "war exists" with Mexico and asking for a formal declaration from the legislature.[41] This move earned the ire of Whigs (including a young Illinois Whig named Abraham Lincoln), who saw this as an overly broad use of presidential power. Polk's war also advanced the sectional crisis by opening up new questions about slavery and national expansion.

By pursuing a war with Mexico aimed at acquiring more territory, Polk set the stage for an intractable debate about slavery. As previously explained, compromise over slavery was from the beginning a crucial factor in envisioning national harmony. Slave states and their representatives had the upper hand in many of these negotiations because of the imperative to preserve the Union, and compromises ultimately were oriented toward their preferences. Polk's presidency shifted this terrain somewhat, though without fundamentally altering the upper hand enjoyed by those who held national unity in the balance.

Nevertheless, anti-slavery forces began to find various ways to organize and focus their cause as the nation pursued territorial expansion. In the context of Polk's appropriations request to Congress for war funding, Pennsylvania Democrat David Wilmot introduced a resolution barring the expansion of slavery into the territories acquired through war with Mexico, known in the language of the time as the Mexican Cession. The Wilmot Proviso passed easily in the House but failed in the Senate. Although it never became law, it revealed the inability of the Polk administration to pursue its expansionist agenda while also balancing the Northern and Southern factions of the Democratic Party.[42]

The impact of the Wilmot Proviso extended beyond Polk and the Democrats. Based on its principles, the newly formed Free Soil movement welcomed a small coalition of Northern politicians who were suspicious of both Democratic nominee Lewis Cass and Whig Zachary Taylor in the 1848 election. Taylor was a Southerner and a slave owner. Cass, though from Michigan, hewed to the new Democratic compromise line of "non-intervention," or allowing territories to decide about slavery. The Democratic platform likewise promised not to interfere with "domestic institutions" in the states and asserted the party's belief in a limited federal government throughout.

The Free Soil Party, with an erstwhile Jacksonian Democrat as its nominee, did not come close to winning the presidency in 1848. But in addition to winning some seats in Congress, the party was able to alter the dynamics of the presidential race and push the Whigs in a more anti-slavery direction.[43]

Zachary Taylor and Millard Fillmore: Whig Presidents and Compromise

If Polk exemplified the competing political pressures facing Democratic presidents at the time, Zachary Taylor, a slave-owning former general, embodied the contradictions of the Whig Party. In keeping with the Whig approach to the executive branch, Taylor relied on his personal reputation as a battle hero and concealed his policy opinions during the campaign. Thus, when he took office his views about the pressing issues of the day—the Wilmot Proviso and its principles and the sectional crisis—were not known. Like the Democrats, the Whig Party encompassed both Northern and Southern wings.

Taylor's nomination and short time in office, during which the Compromise of 1850 was negotiated, highlight several important facets of this period. During the campaign, his identity as a Southerner—and a slave owner—were considered an advantage by some party leaders. Alexander Stephens of Georgia, who would go on to serve as the vice president of the Confederacy, hoped that Taylor would "safeguard" the interests of the South amid the growing influence of ideas like the Wilmot Proviso.[44]

Yet the sectional cracks—the distrust and disagreement—were already apparent. Taylor's Southern affiliation and slave-owner status opened up opportunities for accusations by Northern Democrats that he would, in fact, be primarily concerned with the interests of his own section.

The Whig approach to the rise of sectional splintering within their own coalition, and in the electorate overall, was to obfuscate the party's positions on key issues. Historian Michael Holt refers to the 1848 Whig campaign as a "deft two-faced strategy on slavery extension," with promises to the North to sign the Wilmot Proviso and to the South to look out for its interests.[45] The Whig platform was silent on the extension issue, and Taylor maintained ambiguity about where he stood on it. The nature of campaigns in this era made this kind of vacillating possible—because campaign surrogates, rather than the candidates themselves, did most of the talking, different messages could be spread in the North and in the South.

The Whig position, originally formed in response to Andrew Jackson's expansive view of the president's political role, was that the president should execute the law as passed by Congress, the true representatives of the people.[46] In other words, the Whigs rejected on principle the idea that the president spoke with the true voice of the people when it came to vital and contested policy issues.

But once Taylor took office, he had to face these questions. Maintaining the same sensibility of earlier eras, Taylor sought compromise and tried to keep the slavery issue off the agenda as much as possible.[47] One way that the Whig general attempted to do this was to advocate for California and New Mexico to be admitted as states, thus skipping the territory phase and the argument about their territorial status in order to sidestep the issues addressed by the Wilmot Proviso. However, this proposal, by opening up new questions about the process by which new territories and states might make the decision to become slave or free, served only to make the tension worse.

From a presidency perspective, the Compromise of 1850 was an important turning point. The blocking of the submission of the New Mexico Constitution for congressional approval as a free state led to Millard Fillmore becoming "the first of three pro-slavery Northerners to inhabit the White House in the 1850s."[48]

The Compromise of 1850 included concessions for both sides, as well as something to make everyone unhappy.[49] Defenders of slavery were unhappy about the admission of California as a free state and the banning of the slave trade in Washington, DC. But the language of the negotiation process highlighted the "reasonableness" of the compromise position, setting it in opposition to the abolitionist view. In other words, to the extent that the principles of the Wilmot Proviso informed the policy debate, they set up a specific kind of situation. At the risk of stating the obvious, polarization—the increasing irreconcilability of political alternatives—made it more difficult for presidents to pursue compromises. This was certainly the case for Zachary Taylor, who faced an impossible situation if the Wilmot Proviso was passed—alienating Northern Whigs if he vetoed the bill, and Southern Whigs if he signed it. Interlocking tensions between party politics and sectional politics created new political opportunities that pro-slavery politicians sought to exploit. In particular, Southern Democratic politicians like John C. Calhoun could exploit sectional conflict for partisan purposes, painting Southern Whigs as "untrustworthy" and as working in the service of Northern political dominance.[50]

With Taylor's sudden death in 1850, the questions about his commitments to specific courses of action and his attitudes on slavery-related policies more generally would remain unknown. But we do know that his general approach was to advocate for the admission of California and New Mexico in quick succession as states, in the hopes of taking the slavery issues off the agenda moving forward. By some accounts, his desire not to clutter up the legislative request with other issues, like fugitive slaves, put him at odds with Whig congressional leader Henry Clay, who had proposed a more comprehensive bill.[51]

After becoming president upon Taylor's death, Millard Fillmore signed the Compromise of 1850 into law, complete with the Fugitive Slave Law. Fillmore in this sense is perhaps even more of an enigma than Taylor. Where Taylor was a Southern slave owner whose sectional commitments were unclear, Fillmore's position was on record: He considered the Fugitive Slave Law morally repugnant[52] and also was a "proslavery Northerner."[53]

The contrast between Taylor and Fillmore conveys the constraints of the presidency at this time. Being identified as anti-slavery was politically risky, and politicians like Calhoun made clear the costs of such a stance. But appearing too sympathetic to slavery and its supporters carried political risk as well. The passage of the Fugitive Slave Law and the general tenor of the compromise debates after the Mexican War suggest that the potential for political damage was less clear to White House occupants—Whig or Democrat, Northerner or Southerner. Any legislation on the expansion of slavery was bound to kick up resentment from one or both sides, regardless of what the compromise was called and what its intentions were.

The 1850 laws deepened the compromise problem on two related fronts: The arrangements called "compromises" no longer reflected any sort of back-and-forth between North and South but rather the growing gap between sectional interests, and they served to widen that gap. Dealing with slavery and expansion was no longer about trying to reconcile sectional interests but about balancing them. Even if the former objective had never been realistic, presidents had political incentives to act as if it was and to seek common ground among partisans. In the debate leading up to the Compromise of 1850, key players—including President Zachary Taylor and Congressman Daniel Webster—could identify "extremists" and defenders of "sectional interests" as the problem.[54] But after the passage of the 1850 package of laws, it was difficult for anyone to deny that sectional interests were, in fact, growing increasingly at odds.

By challenging the foundations of the Missouri Compromise, the Compromise of 1850 opened up the system to new possibilities for instability. This increased the pressure on the next two presidents to find compromise and seek ways to maintain order.

The expansion question, as framed by the Wilmot Proviso, the Free Soil movement, and the subsequent politics surrounding slavery extension, also set the terms for how maintenance and disruption would work in the years leading up to the Civil War. If the Free Soil movement nudged the Whigs in the direction of favoring the principles of the Wilmot Proviso, this was depicted as the compromise position. Favoring non-extension was presented as compatible with leaving slavery alone where it existed and eschewing the divisive and reviled attitudes of the abolition movement.[55] These compromise dynamics outlasted the Whigs and also shaped the formation of the Republican Party. After its formation in the 1850s, the new party unified around its opposition to the extension of slavery. Within the confines of that position, the Republicans held a range of views, from those who favored a gradual end to slavery to others making a more radical and immediate demand for abolition. The Republican Party's stance would, in turn, influence early understandings of the Civil War and Lincoln's impulse toward constitutional preservation.

Franklin Pierce, James Buchanan, and the Last Compromises

Because it was not in fact a compromise but a series of laws that were at times "purposefully evasive on crucial issues," in the words of historian Sean Wilentz, the Compromise of 1850 did little to head off disaster in the next decade. Issues of expansion and slavery had not been resolved. It is possible, though not certain, that a steady moral leader in the White House could have navigated these unresolved issues. But we will never know, because instead the nation had Presidents Franklin Pierce and James Buchanan. Many have blamed these two leaders, both of whom are frequently found at the bottom of presidential rankings, for passively allowing the country to fall apart.

Their characterization as passive is not entirely off-base, though it reflects to some extent the more limited role of the nineteenth-century presidency. However, both Pierce and Buchanan actively promoted the kinds of policies they thought would address the crisis. Both presidents' sense of what it would mean to resolve the crisis and what was at stake was quite narrow.

Pierce's path to office ran through not only forty-nine ballots before he became the 1852 presidential nominee but also the increasingly difficult balance between Northern and Southern Democrats.[56] As a Northerner who had supported Southern causes, including delivering his state for the Democratic ticket in 1848 in the face of the Free Soil threat, the New Hampshire lawyer was a fitting symbol for what his party had become. Pierce's vision for his presidency involved holding the party together through patronage, with little attention to searching for policies or ideas that could bring the coalition back together once he took office in 1853.[57]

Into the void left by Pierce's lack of vision stepped Illinois Senator Stephen Douglas, another Northern Democrat whose idea for saving the nation was popular sovereignty—letting states decide whether to be free or slave "upon admission as states."[58] Pierce was under political pressure to "formally organize" the northern area from the Louisiana Purchase known as Nebraska, mostly for economic reasons.[59] However, because the land was north of the Missouri Compromise line, the prospect of bringing it into the Union as a free territory (and eventually a free state) incensed Southern Democrats. This brewing conflict endangered the confirmation of Pierce's patronage appointees from the anti-slavery faction of the party.[60]

Douglas favored westward expansion for both political and economic reasons. Because he shared Pierce's concern for keeping the party together, Douglas was willing to work on legislation to bring Southerners on board for the organization of Nebraska, which eventually became the Kansas-Nebraska Act. While Douglas favored popular sovereignty as the solution to the Nebraska question, some Southerners wanted to take things a step further. They sought a firmer rejection of the Missouri Compromise rather than the rejection only implied by the Compromise of 1850. Douglas revised the compromise version of the Kansas-Nebraska Act in response to these demands, moving away from an approach rooted in the right of territories to determine their own status and toward a stronger stance that Congress would not intervene in slavery in the territories.[61] The bill ended the Missouri Compromise, instead allowing the new territories to decide the slavery question for themselves. Pierce gave his support to the bill and made it a "test of loyalty" in the Democratic Party.[62] In doing so, Pierce and the Democrats owned the legislation, as well as all the political consequences that followed. And what followed was a strong negative response from anti-slavery forces, complete with rhetorical appeals aimed at bringing moderates onto their side. These appeals—one of which was published by newspapers critical of slavery—highlighted the power dynamics involved. Throughout the process, both North and South had been displeased with different aspects of the legislation. But Southern and pro-slavery forces more effectively held the balance of power, since they could block bills and confirmations and even occasionally made credible threats of violence and secession.[63]

Pierce's immediate and longer-term legacy was to kick off a transformation of the Democratic Party into a Southern and pro-slavery party. By prompting a sectional split among Whigs as well, the Kansas-Nebraska Act had moved the country closer to a system organized around conflict over slavery—a recipe for the kind of instability that all of the pre–Civil War compromises had ostensibly been designed to avoid.

Conflict over slavery, despite so many years of painstaking efforts to push it off the agenda, had become the focal point of the political system. Even the anti-immigrant Know-Nothing Party had become divided along sectional lines.[64] Kansas was mired in violent conflict. A day after a group of several hundred pro-slavery men attacked free-state leaders in Lawrence, South Carolina Representative Preston Brooks beat Senator Charles Sumner of Massachusetts with a cane on the floor of the Senate for giving a lengthy speech denouncing "slave power"; Brooks's attack provided a visual image of "Slave Power brutality and arrogance personified."[65] And in the wake of the Kansas-Nebraska bill, a new party, the Republicans, had formed around the idea of stopping the expansion of slavery.

It was in this political environment that Pierce sought renomination in 1856 but was weighed down by his support for the Kansas legislation and by Northern ire against him. Pennsylvanian James Buchanan, taking advantage of the circumstances that weakened both Douglas and Pierce, won the nomination on the seventeenth ballot.

Buchanan had a long but undistinguished career in public service. His willingness to eschew "extremism" from either pro- or anti-slavery forces was key to securing the nomination, but less workable once he was in office.

In his inaugural address, Buchanan anticipated the US Supreme Court's decision in *Dred Scott v. Sandford*, which, he argued, might finally turn the nation's attention to other problems by resolving the lingering issues of slavery. However, Buchanan was by all accounts no mere observer on the case. As president-elect, he pressured the Court to rule against Scott, a Black man who had lived in several free states and thus declared himself free. The Court issued such a ruling two days after his inauguration. Buchanan's urging may not have made the difference in the outcome, but persuading Northerners on the Court to vote as he wanted did cushion the sectional blow of a broader ruling.[66] In the end, the court held that African Americans could not be citizens, expressed in the chilling language of Chief Justice Roger Taney's opinion that Blacks had "no rights which the white man was bound to respect." But it also invalidated congressional control over slavery in the territories and declared the Missouri Compromise null and void. It seems a near-certainty that Buchanan knew what the ruling would be, and he urged the nation to accept the court's decision in his inaugural address.[67]

Whereas past presidents had hoped to evade the slavery question and hold together nationally competitive parties, Buchanan by 1857 was hoping to end the conflicts that had emerged and quell the activity of "geographical parties"—a direct dig at the Republicans but also an acknowledgment that the political terrain had shifted.[68] Pinning these hopes on Kansas statehood, Buchanan anticipated that resolving this question might finally put the larger questions to rest.[69]

To this end, Buchanan supported the "proslavery Lecompton Constitution, which many Northerners believed to be the result of rigged debate and ratification elections," resulting in further splintering among Democrats.[70] Still reeling from the fallout of the Kansas-Nebraska Act, Douglas chose the North, while Buchanan's political incentives drove him toward the South.[71] The Lecompton Constitution protected slavery in Kansas and excluded African Americans from any rights established there. Opponents raised the objections that the territorial document had not been ratified according to the proper process and thus did not demonstrate respect for the principle of "popular sovereignty" that had been so important to the Kansas-Nebraska debate. Those opposed included many Northern Democrats, including Stephen Douglas, and the territorial governor of Kansas. Despite this controversy and lack of broad party support, Buchanan eventually recommended that Congress approve the territorial document. Congress failed to approve the originally submitted Lecompton Constitution, but a slightly altered version, with a smaller land grant for the new territory, was submitted and passed. Buchanan had favored the pro-slavery elements of his party, further alienating other factions.

If Pierce's presidency illustrated that the slavery question was woven into many aspects of politics, from patronage to railroads, Buchanan's tenure showcased what the antebellum presidency looked like when stripped down to the studs. Buchanan saw favoring the South as the more politically advantageous course, and perhaps the one most likely to preserve order. But the other part of the equation was his lack of moral investment in the slavery question. Buchanan appreciated the political power dynamics at stake, but not the extent to which others found slavery to be a moral harm to the nation.[72]

However, these political calculations were based on faulty logic. There was the problem that, because the conflict over slavery was embedded in so many aspects of political life, it could not be resolved with a simple move. There was Buchanan's lack of appreciation for the growing power imbalance: Slave owners were wielding disproportionate influence and undercutting the nation's sense of democratic governance. These underlying factors made his own party vulnerable to further disunity and electoral retribution.

Perhaps more important, however, was the flawed and long-standing assumption in Buchanan's approach that appeasement could work. The questions of process—of minority rule, of state and federal power— could not be separated from the moral questions at the center of the issue: the impact of slavery on the enslaved, and the moral stain of a system built on human bondage. There was plenty of racist thinking across the sectional divide at that time, but one side necessarily relied on racism to justify its position and its practices. This side could not be placated with compromises or even the admission of new slave states. Lincoln's election in 1860 would prove it.

Abraham Lincoln: Moral Evasion No Longer

When it comes to race and the presidency, Abraham Lincoln has a dual status. In most standard accounts, he is the "Great Emancipator." He led the nation through a civil war that ended slavery. As the first Republican president, Lincoln represented a new political philosophy that turned away from the Whig Party's reservations about executive power and its ambivalence on slavery.[73] Lincoln's election ushered in a national realignment, which in turn brought decades of Republican national dominance, at least when it came to holding the White House. Lincoln is consistently ranked number one in a C-SPAN expert poll in both the "pursued equal justice for all" and "crisis leadership" categories.[74]

Other accounts of Lincoln have challenged his status as a national hero to some degree. In a not uncommon accusation in the sixteenth president's own time, one strain of criticism has asked if Lincoln's use of war powers tilted into tyrannical territory. Feeding this line of questioning is Lincoln's suspension of habeas corpus, seizure of ships, and even the military act of the Emancipation Proclamation.[75]

Another troubling element of Lincoln's legacy is his attitude toward African Americans. How should we deal with a "great emancipator" who laughed at racist jokes, favored the colonization of Africa by freed people rather than envisioning the races living together in the United States, and warmed slowly to the concept of national emancipation?[76]

Viewing Lincoln through the lens of compromise and disruption isn't sufficient to resolve moral dilemmas and historical debates. But it helps us reconcile these different elements of his legacy. In order to understand Lincoln, we have to appreciate both the imperative of compromise that informed the election of 1860 and the political dynamics of a system that could no longer sustain these compromises. As the first Republican president, Lincoln also led a political project that eventually could not tolerate the continuation of slavery anywhere in the United States. While past presidents had protected slavery and white supremacy, Lincoln used the power of the presidency—and the war power no less—to enhance the Union cause. And as the Union cause became fused with the end of slavery, Lincoln aligned the presidency with the anti-slavery position as no previous president had done.

But this political project was also left unfinished, and its unanswered questions remained salient to the political, social, and economic orders of the country after the war. Lincoln's cautious approach was met with anger, violence, and delegitimization by opponents, and with derision by those who felt he had not gone far enough. Pressure to solve the problems surrounding race—slavery, in this instance—were also accompanied by strain within his own party, which was fracturing over what to do next, and from corners that favored trying to accommodate and appease conservative political forces. This conundrum accompanied many of Lincoln's biggest decisions as president and intensified as the end of the war approached.

Elections and Party Pressures

Who was Lincoln politically? For one thing, he was a former Whig, a politician whose political training and socialization had occurred within that party. This experience informed his sense of presidential restraint and may help us understand both how he became the 1860 nominee and why caution and constitutional reverence characterized his disruption of the racial status quo. Lincoln had defended Zachary Taylor's refusal to campaign on the major issues of the day in 1848, and the Whig influence on his approach was evident throughout Lincoln's presidency.[77]

Even in making the transition from Whig to Republican, Lincoln was a party politician, a role that was a source of both power and constraint. Lincoln balanced a complicated coalition, and historians have praised his political skill in co-opting or defusing political rivals and managing both factions and personalities.[78] Lincoln's ability to master this system allowed him to navigate the difficult politics of the Civil War.

But a mere mechanical understanding of Lincoln as a party politician is inadequate. As historian Matt Karp has pointed out, the emergence of the Republican Party on the presidential stage in 1856, though not victorious, represented a significant shift in parties and ideas. The formation of a party dedicated to preventing the expansion of slavery was a significant break from the old "partisan alliances that kept the question of human bondage on the margins of national politics."[79] This party shake-up had a populist tinge: The Republican Party in 1856 identified a "tyranny of a slaveholding minority" and saw itself as preventing the dangerous consolidation of power of slave-owning interests. Not that all Republicans were abolitionists. Some were, while others held racist beliefs and wanted to exclude African Americans from certain areas, and still others were more concerned about the balance of political power or the preservation of the Union.[80]

The Election of 1860: Nomination and Election

In 1860, the newly formed Republican Party met for the second time to nominate a presidential candidate. William Seward of New York was the expected nominee. Although there were many reasons for his loss to Lincoln on the third convention ballot, one point of discussion among party leaders was what modern observers might call "electability"— concerns that Seward's political reputation was too forceful on the slavery issue.[81] Lincoln was seen as a more moderate alternative, a candidate who would be bound by his respect for the Constitution to favor a gradual elimination of slavery and to avoid any drastic measures.

The 1860 four-candidate presidential race election exposed the deepest irony of presidential efforts at racial maintenance. Ultimately, by tolerating and encouraging compromise after compromise—from Missouri to 1850 to the final, disastrous Kansas-Nebraska Act—the passivity and timidity of presidents on this issue had allowed for the crack-up of both parties. The Whigs no longer existed, though John Bell ran on the Constitutional Union ticket in hopes of carrying the Whig ideology on slavery forward. The Democrats split apart entirely, with John Breckinridge running in the South and Stephen Douglas in the North. The four-way race conferred some advantage on Lincoln, who could—and did—cobble together an Electoral College majority by winning free states. Breckinridge, the sitting vice president and the "strongest supporter of the extension of slavery," was not competitive in the free states and could not build a majority from only slave states.[82] Therefore, Lincoln enjoyed a substantial advantage over his competitors, but his vote share still fell well short of a majority.

The Republican platform of 1860, adopted at the convention that nominated Lincoln, conveyed both the profound shift and the continuing spirit of compromise. The platform denounced the Democratic Party for its support of various pro-slavery measures, including the Lecompton Constitution in Kansas. It also directly addressed the *Dred Scott* decision (without naming it specifically), calling it "dangerous political heresy." At the same time, even as it entirely rejected Whig-style avoidance of the slavery question, the platform still conceded—as did Lincoln—that Congress could not interfere with slavery where it existed, insisting that "the right of each state to order and control its own domestic institutions according to its own judgment exclusively, is essential to that balance of powers on which the perfection and endurance of our political fabric depends."[83]

But in the second and eighth planks of the platform, we see evidence of Lincoln's eventual disruption of the long period of racial compromises. The second plank invoked the Declaration of Independence, foreshadowing Lincoln's Gettysburg Address. The eighth plank read:

> That the normal condition of all the territory of the United States is that of freedom: That, as our Republican fathers, when they had abolished slavery in all our national territory, ordained that "no persons should be deprived of life, liberty or property without due process of law," it becomes our duty, by legislation, whenever such legislation is necessary, to maintain this provision of the Constitution against all attempts to violate it; and we deny the authority of Congress, of a territorial legislature, or of any individuals, to give legal existence to slavery in any territory of the United States.[84]

This plank, while not more radical than the 1856 platform on this issue and perhaps less so, established several key principles: By prescribing legislation to prevent the territorial spread of slavery, it communicated the ideas of the Wilmot Proviso that had incensed pro-slavery politicians more than a decade before. The platform was still not an abolitionist one, but the document, especially this eighth plank, shifted the terrain of compromise, firmly establishing the principle of nonexpansion. And like Lincoln himself, the text spelled out a stance delicately balanced between avoidance of a full abolitionist position and a quiet insistence on the immorality of slavery.

This moral conviction, expressed by Lincoln throughout his political career prior to the 1860 convention, set his arguments about slavery apart from other arguments in important ways. Some other Republicans presented the issue in terms of the relative political power of slave owners in the federal government. Others saw the issue in economic terms. But Lincoln's presentation of slavery as a moral issue made him, in the words of historian Michael Holt, "one of the most radical men in the Republican Party," despite his institutional caution and adherence to the limits of the Constitution.[85]

Lincoln's stances and those expressed in the 1860 Republican platform therefore illustrate the basic contours of all racially disruptive presidencies: They are often just as committed as others to some aspects of compromise and the maintenance of the status quo, but the adjustments they do make in policy and symbolism leave the political system with unsettled institutions and unanswered questions. In Lincoln's case, his election led immediately to the greatest political upheaval the nation has known to date: the secession of the Southern states.

Early Efforts to Compromise

Lincoln's election signaled a shift on slavery, even if the precise meaning was contested. In a fragmented Republican Party, some politicians stressed their commitment to white supremacy and deemphasized the party's anti-slavery aims.[86] But the divisions in the election around sectional and slavery-related questions were difficult to deny. Anti-slavery and even anti-Southern sentiment motivated some Republican voters.[87] Two of the candidates on the ballot, John Bell and John Breckinridge, tried to position themselves as best representing Southern interests.[88]

The period after Lincoln was elected and the early months of his presidency were characterized by a back-and-forth that centered the preferences of slave states and yet also showed how difficult it was, especially at this stage, to appease them. This response to Lincoln's election, which highlighted the perceived threat that the North would dominate the South, eliminate slavery, and cause anything from a fundamental reversal of the social order to a violent revolution, showcased a recurring feature of periods of racial disruption. More than other issues, race issues were framed politically as a zero-sum power game. Until Lincoln, the presidency had been heavily influenced by the South.[89] Presidential power, previously dedicated to forging compromise after compromise, became unacceptable when harnessed for the other side.

Early on, Lincoln stuck to the general principle that he had to follow the law: Any effort toward ending slavery had to be carried out within the confines of lawful processes. For example, he insisted that, as president, he was bound to enforce the Fugitive Slave Law, even though he disliked it.[90]

What happened between Lincoln's election and his inauguration was a more extreme version of the power balance that had characterized slavery debates for decades: The South defended its interests with violence and vigor, and the center tried to hold. Southern states, starting with South Carolina, declared their secession.[91] One of the most extensive last-ditch efforts to hold the Union together was offered by Kentucky Senator John J. Crittenden, who put together a package of proposed constitutional amendments and resolutions with the intention of stopping the secession movement.[92] Lincoln declined to give his support to these proposals, citing the principle that taking this course would be apologizing for winning the election and "buying the privilege to take possession of this government to which we have a constitutional right."[93]

Despite his rejection of efforts to placate the secessionists, Lincoln signaled his openness to compromises he considered reasonable. He maintained in his first inaugural that he would not oppose a proposed constitutional amendment limiting Congress's ability to ban slavery in the states.[94] Throughout the address, Lincoln insisted that his core purpose was not to end slavery where it existed, and his statements about the Constitution—that it did not expressly say whether Congress could ban slavery from the territories, nor who should decide the fate of fugitive slaves—implicitly rejected more radical theories that the Constitution was an anti-slavery document.[95]

When he addressed the issue of slavery itself in the first inaugural, Lincoln stressed the constraints he faced as president around ending slavery and conceded the possibility of adding the Corwin amendment to the Constitution, a last-ditch effort to stave off secession by prohibiting Congress from making laws about slavery in the states. Lincoln stated that he had "no objection" to the proposed amendment and reiterated the right of Americans to amend the Constitution through the process it laid out. In addition, Lincoln's speech laid out the argument that the cause of the war was not slavery but rather the South's refusal to allow the regular political process to resolve the issue: "If a minority in such case will secede rather than acquiesce, they make a precedent which in turn will divide and ruin them, for a minority of their own will secede from them whenever a majority refuses to be controlled by such minority."[96]

While Lincoln was not ready in March 1861 to identify the war with the moral fight over slavery, the other side did not share those reservations. A few weeks later, Alexander Stephens—like Lincoln, a former Whig—stated the values of the Confederacy plainly: "Our new government is founded upon exactly the opposite idea; its foundations are laid, its corner-stone rests, upon the great truth that the negro is not equal to the white man; that slavery subordination to the superior race is his natural and normal condition."[97] Other secession documents similarly identified slavery as the cause for withdrawal from the Union.

Disrupting the Racial Status Quo

Lincoln's early attempts at compromise lit the path for more disruptive moves. The Corwin amendment and the idea of compensating slave owners for the loss of their property after emancipation exemplified Lincoln's political dilemma: These proposals were never radical enough to satisfy the strong proponents of abolition in his own party, but they were too close to abolitionist positions to appease the status quo forces. The idea of compensating slave owners was morally noxious, yet cracked open the door to talk of emancipation. These compromises shifted the politics of the issue in fundamental ways and made emancipation seem possible in ways few had anticipated.[98]

The next steps for disrupting the status quo and ultimately fully undermining slavery were three very different political actions: the Emancipation Proclamation, the Gettysburg Address, and the Thirteenth Amendment. The most lasting and thorough of these in terms of eliminating slavery, the Thirteenth Amendment, did not fall within the president's official powers. The other two showed the president's power and influence but also his limitations.

When Lincoln became a wartime president, he assumed wartime executive powers. But these powers extended mainly to what were clearly war issues, like the suspension of habeas corpus along the mid-Atlantic and the seizure of ships headed to Confederate ports. Ending slavery remained out of constitutional reach. However, Lincoln could use his war powers to emancipate slaves in the areas of the Confederacy not under Union control. The Emancipation Proclamation was issued first on a preliminary basis in September 1862, and then on January 1, 1863. Criticisms were plentiful; for instance, some felt that it lacked the rhetorical flourish that they might have expected for such a momentous document. By focusing on areas still controlled by the Confederates, the document freed the slaves that Lincoln did not have the power to free—and kept those in Union territory in bondage.[99]

The Emancipation Proclamation demonstrated not only Lincoln's characteristic respect for constitutional boundaries but also his move away from conciliatory stances. Loyal slave states were excluded from the Proclamation as a means of keeping them in the Union, but its reach still extended to them by shrinking the market for enslaved persons and "destabilizing" the institution as a whole.[100] It had both practical and psychological impacts. For instance, bringing African American men into the Union military and arming them against Confederates made a long-standing nightmare of the South a reality.

With the Emancipation Proclamation, Lincoln had used the war powers of the presidency in a limited but forceful way. By ordering the Union army to free slaves and allowing them to join the fight on the Northern side, the document certainly hinted at a new moral aim for the war. But in order to articulate this aim more clearly, a few more words were necessary.

In November 1863, the Union had suffered a series of difficult battles and morale was low. Lincoln had traveled to Gettysburg to dedicate a battlefield and deliver a short address. The Gettysburg Address was only 272 words long, but it is widely acknowledged to have changed the nation. The speech accomplished this by redefining the war and what it meant for the relationship between the country's future and its founding ideas.

In 1858, Lincoln had disavowed equality between the races. But at the start of the Gettysburg Address, he embraced it with an opening line that set the moment of the American founding not at the adoption of the Constitution but with the signing of the Declaration of Independence, and that identified equality as the purpose of the nation. He went on to describe the purpose of the war—the cause for which the war dead had given their lives—as the survival of the principles of the Declaration. In other words, Lincoln used the rhetorical reach of the presidency—his speech was widely commented on in the press—in order to connect the war to the idea of equality, the end of slavery, and the hope for the nation's "new birth of freedom."[101]

Making a second founding reality would require changing the Constitution. Though the president plays no formal role in the constitutional amendment process, Lincoln threw his support behind the Thirteenth Amendment, which abolished slavery nationwide. The sixteenth president would not live to see it ratified, but he did see its passage in Congress. He also had the opportunity to show his sense of ownership and accomplishment over the amendment by signing it before it went to the states for approval. That opportunity did not come, however, until January 1865. First, Lincoln would have to win reelection in 1864.

3

"The Constitution as It Is"

ANDREW JOHNSON'S IMPEACHMENT

MODERN PUNDITS like to dream about a "unity ticket" featuring a president and vice president from different parties. In 1864, such a ticket became a reality. Fearing that Lincoln's reelection was in danger, the National Union Party formed and nominated a former Democrat, and loyal Southerner, to be Lincoln's running mate. This turned out to be one of the most consequential running mate decisions in American history.

Johnson's peculiar political identity shaped his approach to Reconstruction after the war was over. His perspective was that because the Union was "perpetual," the Southern states had never legitimately left. As a result, this thinking went, rebel states should be readmitted quickly and with few conditions. When Johnson also found himself excluded from the patronage networks and party loyalty structures of both the Republican and Democratic Parties, he was left politically isolated but able to take a flexible approach to the postwar environment.[1]

We don't know a lot about how Johnson ended up in this role. One theory is that Abraham Lincoln favored the choice as a means of defusing opposition by Northern Democrats and furthering his vision for what a national reconciliation should look like. But some historians have argued that Lincoln was largely detached from the process and had left its management to party leaders. However, we do know a fair amount about the political circumstances of Johnson's nomination as the vice presidential candidate for the National Union Party.

Support for the war appeared to be flagging, and criticism of the president was on the rise. Some disapproved of his use of executive wartime powers. Others were repelled by Lincoln's reinterpretation of the war's meaning as a battle to end slavery, not simply to save the Union.[2] As the 1864 election approached, Lincoln and the Republicans were acutely aware that they could lose. Lincoln wrote in a private memo that because he anticipated not being reelected, he would "have to save the union 'between the election and the inauguration.'"[3]

The war and the politics of emancipation also changed the Republican Party. Over its first decade, the platform had grown more radical, taking a more favorable stance on emancipation and becoming more inclined to punish the rebellious Confederate states.[4]

Compared with the drama of the 1860 election, which led to Southern secession, we don't hear much about the 1864 contest, in which Lincoln soundly defeated George McClellan. With the regional disintegration of the Democrats, the four-candidate election, and the secession crisis after Lincoln's victory, the 1860 contest shook things up in a much more visible way and made for a far more dramatic story. But comparing the Republican Party platforms from the two election years illustrates the case for the national transformation afoot in 1864. Republican leaders had promised in 1860 to leave the "domestic institutions" in the states alone. Four years later, they called for an end to slavery, calling it "hostile to the principles of Republican government."[5]

This call to end slavery put the party at odds with its president. Lincoln began laying out plans for a postwar reunification rooted in a spirit of reconciliation rather than punishment. The centerpiece of this planning was the "Ten Percent Plan," so called because it would allow states to choose new state governments and restore more rights if 10 percent of the adult male population had taken a loyalty oath.[6]

Lincoln's 1863 Proclamation of Amnesty and Reconstruction contrasted with the vision held by radicals in Congress, as well as the views of Black abolitionist leader Frederick Douglass.[7] The message was emblematic of Lincoln's dilemma at the end of the war: While it clarified that Southern states would be forced to accept emancipation, it also offered some assurances to moderates and conservatives about how they would be treated.[8]

Union Democrats, too, had reoriented themselves around race, slavery, and the question of what they were willing to sacrifice for their Black compatriots. As the war wore on, the answer was "not much" with increasing frequency. As civil war historian Jennifer Weber explains, the so-called Copperhead Democrats opposed the expansion of federal power that the war had necessitated. And they were also notable for their views as "harsh white supremacists" eager to blame abolitionists for their fears about what would happen to the nation.[9] While some Republicans were skeptical of Lincoln for his tempered approach to abolition and Reconstruction, Democrats were able to depict him as an "abolitionist dictator and a war criminal."[10] These accusations had boosted the Democrats to electoral success in the 1862 midterms, and some feared that they would be able to replicate this success in 1864. Lincoln, caught between two irreconcilable sets of political critiques, had begun to assume that he was facing sure defeat.

Enter Andrew Johnson. The sole Southern senator to remain loyal to the Union, Johnson had already proven a valuable figure to the war government. He had been appointed as the military governor of Tennessee and was popular in the North for his loyalty to the Union and charisma as a speaker.[11]

Johnson brought an odd mix of political qualities—he owned some slaves, but opposed slavery as an institution. He despised the Southern rebels, especially Jefferson Davis, and advocated for harsh "punishment" of those who had been disloyal. The Tennessean's defense of the Union had a deep foundation in early populist thinking. When the Southern states first seceded after Lincoln's election in 1860, Johnson pushed a line of thinking that harkened back to Andrew Jackson—the idea that the Union was more than simply a collection of autonomous states. This thinking extended to his arguments about politics: The extremists on both sides of the conflict were tearing the nation apart, he maintained, but the people would save the Union. In this line of reasoning, secessionists and abolitionists alike were to blame for the conflict.[12]

Johnson's attitudes about slavery were also rooted in economic populism. He saw slave owners as the enemies of independent small farmers. These views informed his ideas about Reconstruction, as he saw the "planter aristocracy" has having persuaded their less affluent brethren to secede.[13]

Johnson was selected as Lincoln's running mate at the 1864 National Union Party convention, which drew together Republicans, former Whigs, and others loyal to the war cause. Some historians emphasize the need for Lincoln to soften the approach toward the Confederacy and distance himself from the so-called radical Republicans, whose position had grown more punitive toward the South.[14]

The selection of a loyal, Southern former Democrat grew directly out of Lincoln's attempt to soften the impact of the changes he had brought about. The 1864 Republican platform "implicitly repudiated" the Ten Percent Plan.[15] "We approve the determination of the Government of the United States not to compromise with Rebels," it stated, "or to offer them any terms of peace, except such as may be based upon an unconditional surrender of their hostility and a return to their just allegiance to the Constitution and laws of the United States, and that we call upon the Government to maintain this position and to prosecute the war with the utmost possible vigor to the complete suppression of the Rebellion."[16] Choosing, or allowing the National Union Party to choose, a running mate like Johnson enabled Lincoln to defend his vision for national reunification.

What Would a Postwar Nation Look Like?

The National Union Party victory in 1864 clarified some questions, but not all of them. Not long after the convention, Congress passed the Wade-Davis Bill (so called after Benjamin Wade in the Senate and Henry Winter Davis in the House), which required a majority—not 10 percent—of white adult men in a former Confederate state to swear loyalty to the Union. It also established the "ironclad oath" required for participation in the formation of new state governments—an individual's promise that they had never given aid to the Confederacy at all.

Lincoln pocket-vetoed the bill while Congress was in recess, expressing reservations about committing fully to a specific course of action.[17] This move was not well received by Republicans who wished to see a stricter and more punitive approach taken toward the Confederacy.

After the 1864 election, despite these tensions between Congress and the president, members of Congress accepted the idea that the election outcome had been a popular mandate in favor of abolition. Not only had Lincoln put this idea before the electorate, but the party's two distinct platforms helped to clarify the issue. As a result, the Thirteenth Amendment abolishing slavery moved forward.[18]

Despite the resolution of this major issue—Lincoln's slow evolution toward abolition—many important questions were left unresolved, including the issue that was the subject of the Wade-Davis Bill—the conditions for rebel states to be readmitted to the Union. The bill also addressed the economic, social, and political questions about what the nation would look like after slavery. Throughout the war and the long struggle over abolition, politicians had discussed the issue of compensation and land redistribution. Resource distribution not only had symbolic implications for how punitive the federal government would be toward the South but also carried tremendous weight for the fate and prospects of freed people.

There was also the question of what a post-slavery, postwar society would look like. Soon after the war, it became clear that Southerners were unlikely to warm to racial equality. Instead, violent resistance followed the war's end. Racial terror carried out with the express purpose of establishing white supremacy became a widespread problem throughout the South.

Intimately tied to anxieties about social structure were debates about political power, which took several forms: How much control would the federal government exert over the states? What kinds of political representation would be afforded to the erstwhile rebels? And perhaps most explosively, what sort of political power would be afforded to freed Black men? Would the federal government guarantee suffrage?

These questions unfolded over the course of Johnson's early presidency. With numerous looming considerations about what the postwar nation would look like, the new president's uncertain political identity offered few clues. Johnson had a strong sense of Jacksonian nationalism that had made him a useful addition to the presidential ticket in 1864. But what did this mean in 1865 and beyond? His insistence that "the union is perpetual" and that the South did not need to be readmitted because it had never truly left naturally led to conclusions that were quite lenient toward the South. As the debates about what postwar Southern politics and society would look like, the accidental president's dedication to white supremacy became more relevant. Johnson's commitment to the white man—the common man of modest means—was no secret at any point in his political career. But there was a period during which there was some hope that he might also be able to apply his populist ideals to African Americans, as he had promised to do in a speech delivered to a Black audience in Nashville in October 1864. As historian Robert Levine describes the event, Johnson was paternalistic in his approach and did not regard his Black audience as equals. Nevertheless, his speech highlighted the "promise of Reconstruction" and offered "new ways of thinking about race relations in the South."[19]

This development did not come to pass. Instead, over the course of his presidency, Johnson increasingly saw, in the words of historian Annette Gordon-Reed, "the races as locked in a zero-sum game for racial survival."[20]

Andrew Johnson as President

Johnson wasted little time enacting what would become known as "presidential reconstruction." There were disputes about which branch—the president or Congress—had the proper authority to lead the readmission process. While Congress was in recess, Johnson chose not to call a special session of the legislature and instead took matters into his own hands.

On May 9, Johnson issued a proclamation recognizing Virginia's reentry into the Union and establishing federal offices there, including tax collection and post offices.[21] The question of state readmission opened up the issue of state versus federal control, and where that issue is argued, race is often not far behind. One of the "radical" notions of the radical Republicans was that Black suffrage should be a requirement for Confederate states to be readmitted to the Union.[22] By issuing the order reinstating Virginia, Johnson undermined the cause of Black suffrage and established that, regardless of constitutional debates, the president could and would take charge of the readmission process. Longtime Johnson skeptic Representative Thaddeus Stevens (R-PA) immediately saw the Virginia order as an indicator of what the country could expect from a Johnson-led Reconstruction. Other Republicans, like Senators Charles Sumner and Benjamin Wade, held out hope that the president would eventually defend Black voting rights.[23] The idea that the president would put in place a provisional government in the name of states' rights struck some critics as especially incongruous. Johnson defended this presidential action on the grounds that the Constitution guaranteed states a "republican form of government" in Article IV, Section 4.[24] Stevens disputed this, questioning whether the presidential appointment of a state leader could constitute a "republican form of government."[25]

A few weeks later, two important proclamations revealed more about the nature of presidential reconstruction.[26] One such proclamation declared amnesty and pardon for former Confederates who would promise loyalty to the Union. It also included the restoration of most property rights other than slaves.[27] In some ways, the proclamation was classic Johnson: It condemned the rebellion but was not especially representative of any of the other values that Lincoln had come to espouse over the course of the war. But it also adapted the rhetoric of constitutional maintenance even in the strained situation of 1865. The proclamation justified the pardons, arguing that "the authority of the Government of the United States may be restored and . . . peace, order, and freedom may be established . . ." with the changes brought by the order.

The other proclamation set up a provisional government in North Carolina, with William W. Holden appointed by Johnson as the provisional governor. Johnson also ordered the restoration of "a republican form of government." But this government upheld the same rule for voting eligibility as before the war—whites only.[28]

After the provisional governors were appointed in the former rebel states, it was still unclear what to do with the former rebels. Johnson ultimately adopted the perspective that the sooner normal life could return to the nation, the better.[29] As a result, he did little to prevent the return of Confederate sympathizers to political and economic power.

As historian Eric Foner observes, "Johnson's pardon policy reinforced his emerging image as the white south's champion." Foner points out that Confederates were not subject to "mass arrest" at the end of the war, Confederate President Jefferson Davis was never tried (though he spent two years in prison), and Confederate Vice President Alexander Stephens returned to politics in the 1870s.[30] In this sense, Johnson tried to adapt the prewar sense of order-keeping to the postwar world.

With power turned over to state governments, there was little to keep former Confederates out of power. Provisional governors, now in charge of tremendous patronage opportunities, were free to appoint sympathizers and even rebels for state and local government offices.[31] One complaint about these new governments was that many of the people appointed to office would have been unable to truthfully take the required oaths.[32]

Johnson's Reconstruction legacy is shaped not only by what he did but also by what he did not do. In this case, his inaction allowed for the spread of both new legal forms of racism and racial violence. The Johnson government did nothing about the adoption of "Black codes" in Southern states. These new rules were "ordinances designed to prevent freedmen and -women from owning property, traveling freely, making contracts, and enjoying any form of civil rights or due process."[33] The president also looked the other way and did nothing to prevent significant violence against African Americans in the former Confederacy. Johnson was as inert when it came to the concerns of Southern Black Americans as he was active in pardoning Confederate soldiers and sympathizers. When a group of Black Richmond residents presented him with a petition featuring 1,500 signatures asking for voting rights to "protect themselves from 'unjust legislation,'" Johnson responded with silence and inaction.[34]

Furthermore, the administration's efforts to "maintain order" did not include addressing violence against freed people throughout the South. Seeking to reestablish their position atop the Southern social and economic hierarchy, some white Southerners found multiple ways to torment newly freed Blacks: for instance, telling them that they were no longer emancipated after Lincoln's death, trying to capture or kill them, and subjecting them to shootings, arson, and even sexual violence.[35]

Two major incidents stood out and shaped the conflict over whether the Johnson administration was on the side of the former Confederates. In May 1866, a clash between Black Union soldiers and local police in Memphis left forty-six Black residents and two white residents dead.[36] Black soldiers were accused of bumping into four white policemen, and the situation rapidly escalated; days of chaos ensued before federal troops intervened. The Memphis riot had all the key factors in the Reconstruction politics informing Johnson's increasingly fraught presidency. There was widespread white violence—arson, rape, and shooting—against Blacks.[37] The symbolism of the conflict also pitted Lincoln, the hero of the Black soldiers, against Johnson, whose "white man's government" was cheered by the white antagonists.[38]

The reaction—or lack thereof—to these injustices at the state level sent a signal about Johnson that went far beyond his views about federalism. Allowing these abuses to continue "told Southern whites he was on their side," in the words of historian David O. Stewart. By declining to interfere with the states, the new president signaled that he would help to restore much of the social, political, and economic structure of the prewar South.

A few months later, whites, including some police officers, attacked African Americans in New Orleans who were attending a political convention. The convention had been dedicated to updating the state constitution to protect Black rights, but the event quickly dissolved into horrors that resembled what had happened in Memphis.[39] Moreover, Johnson tried to blame Congress—radical Republicans—for what had happened.[40] "New Orleans" eventually became a phrase used to signify the administration's negligence in the face of anti-Black violence and would sometimes be shouted by audiences during Johnson's ill-fated tour later that year.[41]

Deteriorating Relations with Congress

When Congress reconvened, it got to work enacting its own vision for Reconstruction, guided not by the more radical Republicans but by more moderate figures like Senators Lyman Trumbull (R-IL) and William Pitt Fessenden (R-ME). In taking this approach, members of Congress assembled legislation that they thought would receive the president's support.[42]

Instead of inviting cooperation, the first signs of the congressional blueprint for reconstruction offered up a new opportunity for conflict with the president. Johnson's vetoes of two important bills further revealed his commitment to white rule in the South and indicated that the nation was still at a perilous moment. The president with the ambiguous political affiliation was beginning to shift to a particular side: While he was nominally a member of the Republican side, Johnson objected to Black political rights, which were embraced by Republicans across factions.[43]

Johnson's drift toward full-fledged white supremacy was evident in a few ways. There was his meeting with Black leaders in the White House during which he treated his guests with racist condescension; he later referred to Frederick Douglass with a vile racial epithet and suggested that Douglass would "sooner cut a white man's throat than not."[44]

The veto of the Freedmen's Bureau Bill was another example of Johnson's hostility to Black rights. The legislation provided for the expansion and continued function of the Freedmen's Bureau. Initially created by a law passed in 1865, the bureau provided for the leasing of plots to newly freed persons and their families, thus allowing them a new measure of economic self-sufficiency and opportunity for eventual landownership.[45] Johnson had already blocked the implementation of these reforms upon the initial passage of the law.[46] The 1866 bill would have expanded federal power to punish civil rights violations by state officials in a way that constituted a "radical departure" from past practice. But these measures were intended to be temporary. As such, the bill unified the diverse Republican caucus in support.

The veto helped to clarify the president's connection with the South and with the opposition, as it seemed designed to aggravate Northern Republicans. The veto message was not just policy dissent but defiance of Congress as an institution.[47] In his veto message, Johnson cast white Americans as the hardworking victims of a lopsided policy:

[The US Congress] has never founded schools for any class of our own people, not even for the orphans of those who have fallen in the defense of the Union, but has left the care of education to the much more competent and efficient control of the States, of communities, of private associations, and of individuals. It has never deemed itself authorized to expend the public money for the rent or purchase of homes for the thousands, not to say millions, of the white race who are honestly toiling from day to day for their subsistence. A system for the support of indigent persons in the United States was never contemplated by the authors of the Constitution; nor can any good reason be advanced why, as a permanent establishment, it should be founded for one class or color of our people more than another. Pending the war many refugees and freedmen received support from the Government, but it was never intended that they should thenceforth be fed, clothed, educated, and sheltered by the United States. The idea on which the slaves were assisted to freedom was that on becoming free they would be a self-sustaining population. Any legislation that shall imply that they are not expected to attain a self-sustaining condition must have a tendency injurious alike to their character and their prospects.

A remarkable feature of this message is how much it anticipated the racial rhetoric of later debates, including those of the late twentieth century. Johnson claimed that too much government assistance would bring moral harm to Black citizens, a refrain of later anti-welfare talk. It gave a nod to the fiction of a colorblind society and appealed to white victimhood by suggesting that Blacks would receive special favors denied to their white counterparts.

In another part of the veto message, the president doubled down on his views about the readmission of former Confederate states. He argued that the bill had been passed by a Congress in which no Southerners were seated (having been denied their seats after the fall of the Confederacy). Of course, this line of thinking also cast Johnson's own election into doubt. No Southern votes had been cast for the National Union Party ticket in 1864 either. But the argument showed Johnson's intention to provoke the Republicans who had nominated him for the vice presidency and brought him to power.[48]

After vetoing the Freedmen's Bureau Bill, Johnson followed up with a bizarre and self-serving speech at the White House. Ostensibly to honor the birthday of George Washington, Johnson's speech turned into an aggrieved rant about how Congress wanted to thwart his efforts to preserve the nation. A central theme of the speech was the president's sense of victimhood. He mentioned himself two hundred times.[49] He also mentioned by name, at the audience's request, members of Congress whom he had identified as foes, among whom were Stevens, Sumner, and the editor of *National Anti-Slavery Standard*, Wendell Phillips.[50] Johnson's denunciation of Congress anticipated his eventual "swing around the circle" tour leading up to the 1866 elections.

Johnson launched this verbal assault on congressional Republicans partly to emphasize the fate of the nation. He pointed to the enormous political stakes of his fight against congressional Reconstruction: "The substance of your government may be taken from you and the shadow remain to you." He spoke of "an earthquake coming"—a groundswell of public opinion and judgment on Constitutional questions.

The seventeenth president had also not finished weighing in on constitutionality questions. His next veto was of an even bigger and more fundamental Reconstruction bill: a civil rights law that would have conferred citizenship on all persons born in the United States. Congress was able to override his veto in this case, paving the way for what would eventually become the Fourteenth Amendment.

These vetoes, especially of the civil rights bill, put Johnson firmly on a new political course. "Had he responded to their plans with a little of the give-and-take of normal politics, Johnson could have maintained a power base in the National Union/Republican Party," writes Gordon-Reed.[51] From then on, however, the prospect of cooperation with Congress was replaced with a struggle for power in which both sides treated the other as an adversary. As a result, Johnson's presidency was permanently reoriented. Common ground, or even a working relationship, with Congress no longer seemed to be his objective. Instead, he sought to score victories over Republican legislators.

His treatment of politics as a zero-sum game grew naturally from Johnson's early populist outlook. Presenting himself as a defender of the common people against the encroachment of an illegitimate elite, he needed to identify an enemy. With the "slave power" gone, congressional Republicans could be assigned this role. For Johnson, the issues at hand could be understood only in terms of winners and losers, rather than in terms of nuance and compromise.

At the core of the questions facing the country after the Civil War was the question of whether the government could transform in ways that could sustain a multiracial democracy. Johnson's brand of early populism also tied together his white supremacist views and his sense of political entitlement to act independently, often in isolation and in ways that undermined other actors in the system. Using the presidency to undermine political opponents—and to upbraid a coequal branch of government— would be the foundation of Johnson's next political move.

The Swing Around the Circle

The stated reason for Johnson's 1866 trip was to attend the laying of a cornerstone for a monument to Stephen Douglas in Chicago.[52] Forging this connection with Douglas was revealing enough—the Northern Democrat had "notoriously argued against anything that smacked of emancipation or civil rights for Black people," and he had been associated with the popular sovereignty cause during the expansion debates of the 1840s and 1850s.[53]

This event, however, was only the beginning. Johnson had already castigated Congress to audiences visiting the White House, and now he was taking his attack act on tour. The "swing" started out well enough in Baltimore and Philadelphia, where he was met by large and mostly receptive crowds.[54] As the trip progressed, more opportunities arose for Johnson to chip away at the fragile foundation of his own political legitimacy.

To contemporary observers, the idea that a presidential speaking tour leading up to a midterm election would be controversial—so controversial as to eventually end up in impeachment proceedings— seems quite alien. The era's proscriptions against a president taking such an action were taken seriously, however; they highlighted the ways in which nineteenth-century Americans still feared the potential for demagoguery to undermine the republic. But the political fallout from Johnson's "swing around the circle" was about much more than his break with accepted norms against presidents engaging in too much popular leadership. By speaking directly to the people, Johnson both acknowledged his political isolation and deepened it. In addition to being a man without a party, Johnson lacked much claim to electoral legitimacy. The National Union ticket in 1864 had been headed by Lincoln, not Johnson. And efforts earlier in the year to revive the National Union Party had not been especially successful.

Nevertheless, Johnson was determined at this point to vindicate his own vision of Reconstruction, at the expense of the Republicans. On his 1866 speaking tour he issued not only a series of insults against his opponents but also a plea for electoral vindication of what he referred to as "my policy" of Reconstruction in the South.[55]

The tour through the mid-Atlantic and the Midwest revealed a great deal about the president's political isolation and liabilities. It wasn't just that people yelled taunts, such as "New Orleans!"—referring to the massacre that Johnson had allowed to happen—and "Hang Jeff Davis!" It was that Johnson's inability to weather these taunts was now on full display as he responded with, "Why don't you hang Thad Stevens and Wendell Phillips?"[56] At another stop, Johnson blamed the New Orleans massacre on radical Republicans, "maintaining that the violence was 'substantially planned' by those whose incendiary speeches excited 'that portion of the population, the black population, to arm themselves and prepare for the shedding of blood.'"[57] In St. Louis, he repeated past lines about being treated like "Judas Iscariot."[58] The "swing around the circle" appears often in the scholarly literature as an example of a violation of early norms against presidential engagement with the public. But the story of this particular tour is just as much about what the president actually said as it is about any break with convention in form. The tone in which he depicted political opponents, the direct racial remarks, and the incendiary claims about his victimhood all made his speeches fodder for the impeachment movement to consider. Johnson came off as defensive and volatile, and he did little to dispel notions that he was antagonistic toward Congress, which was, after all, a coequal branch of government.

Andrew Johnson's Impeachment

Three years into Johnson's embattled, accidental presidency, congressional Republicans disagreed about the precise reasons for impeachment. To radical Republicans, Johnson's general approach to Reconstruction was enough—the president had "usurped" powers that rightfully belonged to Congress, used the appointment power to stack the executive branch with loyalists, and thwarted a meaningful reconstruction of Southern society. Indeed, to Johnson's harshest critics, the president had used the executive power to empower the losers of the war that had just been fought. Moderate and conservative Republicans were more cautious. They favored seeking an impeachment only under more clear-cut conditions—that is, with evidence that the president had broken the law.

In 1867, Congress had little precedent for considering these issues. Because the Constitution is unclear about what constitutes an impeachable offense, impeachment debates can reflect congressional dynamics as much as presidential offenses. Through multiple impeachment attempts, the increasingly fractured Republican Party learned about the boundaries of these claims.

At issue was the tension between impeachment as a legal process and as a political one. The legal approach required specific violations of law, as implied by the phrase "high crimes and misdemeanors." The other way of thinking about impeachment is concerned with a much more nebulous vision of presidential fitness to serve. As Gordon-Reed points out, parliamentary systems have built-in processes to remove leaders who have "lost the confidence" of their parties or their constituents, the crucial difference being that "the country is not made to endure failed, and possibly catastrophic, leadership until the clock runs out."[59] But the US Constitution makes no provision for any such procedure. Gordon-Reed poses the question of what the country can or should do about a president who "makes a series of grievous mistakes that harm large numbers of people, sometimes resulting in great loss of life."[60] But is even significant evidence of presidential incompetence, hostility, or failure to serve the interests of the whole nation grounds enough for impeachment? Every impeachment effort has featured a struggle over this question. And this and related questions tend to bubble to the surface as politicians navigate the system after a racially transformative presidency.

The first effort to impeach Johnson, pushed by longtime critic Representative James Ashley of Ohio, suggested that Johnson had been involved in Lincoln's assassination.[61] The House Judiciary Committee rejected this measure in June, opting instead to censure the president. The intensive investigation had been "tedious" and fruitless, uncovering little evidence for the specific claims advanced.[62] But it demonstrated the need to search for specific legal claims rather than proceed solely on a general sense that Johnson was unsuitable for the presidency.

The second attempt to impeach Johnson was a more direct effort to address bigger leadership issues. According to Jonathan Meacham, "the key distinction between the first [impeachment] effort and this one lay with rising Republican anxiety about Johnson's substantive obstruction on Reconstruction." For example, John Churchill of New York pointed explicitly to Reconstruction—and the president's undermining of it— as the reasoning behind his changed vote, which allowed the impeachment articles to proceed from committee to the House floor.[63] Not only had Johnson tried to veto several new Reconstruction bills, but he was now more proactively using the executive branch to undermine Congress's objectives. By appointing an attorney general, Henry Stanbery, with "impeccable conservative credentials," Johnson was able to interfere with the implementation of the new Reconstruction acts.[64] These acts divided the South into five military regions and appointed military leadership to enforce voting rights and administer elections.[65] There was little dispute that this top-down structure imposed by the federal government would be directly intended to replace local rule in order to shape the political fate of the South. But Stanbery undermined the power of the military leadership and undercut the objective of using federal intervention to protect Black voting rights. This development also marked a new phase of confrontation between the president and Congress, which would culminate in Johnson's suspension of Edwin Stanton as secretary of war. That suspension was consistent with the recently passed Tenure of Office Act, but it also signaled an escalation in the disputes between Johnson and Congress.

The second impeachment effort showed that the stakes had been raised. With the switch of a single Judiciary Committee vote, that of John Churchill (R-NY), the articles were reported to the floor of the House. Notably, Churchill cited Johnson's attempts to take control of Reconstruction, including both his public statements and his efforts to tighten control over the Department of War.[66] This switch allowed a majority report from the committee to make the case for the more expansive approach to impeachment—arguing that Johnson's overall attitude toward Reconstruction and the Congress was enough to qualify as an impeachable offense—while the more legalistic view was now confined to the committee's minority report. But in the House vote, the anti-impeachment view still won out.

At the end of 1867, Johnson did not seem chastened or alarmed by the two impeachment attempts. His third annual message, issued that December, doubled down on his favored Reconstruction themes: the dangers posed by Congress and the perceived inferiority of African Americans. Importantly, the president used this message to call on Congress to repeal the Military Reconstruction Act. His objections to it were not merely procedural—it imposed too much federal power on the states, he maintained. "In this case the end itself is evil, as is the means," Johnson said, highlighting that the acts posed the risk of "Negro domination" over "the people" in the South. From there, Johnson argued that whites, but not Blacks, had shown their capacity for self-government:

> No independent government of any form has ever been successful at their hands. On the contrary, wherever they have been left to their own devices they have shown a constant tendency to relapse into barbarism. In the Southern States, however, Congress has undertaken to confer upon them the privilege of the ballot. Just released

from slavery, it may be doubted whether they know more than their ancestors how to organize and regulate civil society.[67]

Historian Eric Foner has referred to this as one of the most racist presidential statements on record.[68] While the president's message also included some statements that were more paternalistic and indicated the intent to protect African Americans in the South, he made his position on political rights for freedmen clearer than ever.

The situation at the War Department also escalated during this time. Johnson attempted several maneuvers to remove Stanton. When he sent a lengthy justification to the Senate for Stanton's removal on December 12, the message failed to persuade that body, and a committee recommended that the suspended Stanton be reinstated as war secretary. Crucially, that message showed Johnson's understanding and acceptance of the law; as his defense would later suggest, the president had not violated the law but merely operated under a different interpretation of it.[69] Johnson had also tried to convince the popular Civil War general Ulysses S. Grant to remain interim secretary, against the Senate's wishes. Grant, who hoped to seek the presidency himself, declined to break the law.[70] In February 1868, seeing another opportunity to seek Johnson's impeachment, Thaddeus Stevens drew up an article on the basis that the president had encouraged General Grant to violate the Tenure of Office Act. The article was tabled in committee.[71]

Finally, in the middle of that month, Stevens and the other advocates of impeachment found their opportunity. After a long struggle with Stanton and the key generals tasked with enforcing the laws in the South, Johnson had appointed Lorenzo Thomas as the new secretary of war . A dramatic showdown between the two war secretaries resulted, with arrests and accusations in the press of a coup d'état.[72]

This time, the dynamics were different. Johnson's violation of the Tenure of Office Act was a specific charge, and it had real policy implications. It combined the three elements that swirled around the entire impeachment discussion. The first was the general question of Johnson's attitudes about Reconstruction and African American political rights and whether his leadership was adequate to the demands of the moment.

The second element concerned real constitutional issues over the role of the presidency. As legal scholar Keith Whittington has pointed out, Johnson pushed the boundaries of the presidency at a time of "Constitutional flux," and the impeachment process served as a tool—if an imperfect one—for navigating these boundaries.[73] The final element was what distinguished this impeachment bid: the presence of a concrete legal charge backed by evidence. Unlike James Ashley's flights of fancy about assassinations and affairs, there was no disputing that Johnson had fired Stanton and appointed Thomas.

The House passed an impeachment resolution before articles outlining the charges were presented. Republicans who had been wary of the political fallout from impeachment and preferred to wait for the 1868 election "could not ignore the executive's direct assault on the legislative branch of government."[74] But while the new circumstances overcame some of the past obstacles, the basic debate about impeachment had not progressed at all: Should it be narrow and legalistic, or should it be broadly directed at Johnson's fitness for office and the major constitutional questions at hand?

The eleven articles of impeachment approved by the House in 1868 mostly concerned the Tenure of Office Act. In one sense, these issues were all of a piece. The act had been passed in order to rein in Johnson's growing tendency to control appointments and to pack the executive branch with loyalists.[75] As such, Johnson's violation of the Tenure of Office Act had larger implications. Its passage had been motivated by his tendency to subvert the will of Congress and flout the law, and by the related questions about which branch should lead the Reconstruction efforts. His long conflict with Stanton and the generals was also about which ideas should inform the implementation of the laws.

But the impeachment articles themselves were narrow and legalistic—even tedious in their repetition. The Reconstruction subtext—the fight over the legal and political structures that would shape the fate of freed people in the South—was undeniably present, even as the articles that were eventually passed in the House and debated in the Senate were focused on Stanton and Thomas. The press covering the impeachment were certainly aware of the implications for Reconstruction, as were African

Americans, who were all too familiar with the consequences of Johnson's defiance.[76] So were the members of the Ku Klux Klan sending death threats to the Republican impeachment managers.[77] But when the Senate trial began, the presentation of the articles relied on the details and evidence of the Tenure of Office Act charges.[78] The disconnect between these two foundations of impeachment, which had been undeniable during the previous attempts, undermined the legitimacy of the impeachment enterprise.

What about the tenth article, which charged the president with "improper rhetoric"? This article has been widely dismissed, especially in light of changing norms about how presidents relate to the public.[79] Nevertheless, if a key problem with the Tenure of Office Act articles was their attenuated connection to the real issue at hand, the charges concerning Johnson's "swing around the circle" may have come closer. The complaint against Johnson was not so much that he had spoken to the people as that he had done so in a way intended to challenge a coequal branch of government. But as with all of the more substantive claims about Johnson as a racist, a usurper of power, and a person unfit for public office, this charge was nebulous and legally flimsy.

The eleventh article of impeachment dove directly into the conflict over the readmission of states. The article began:

> That said Andrew Johnson, President of the United States, unmindful of the high duties of his office and of his oath of office, and in disregard of the Constitution and laws of the United States, did heretofore, to wit: on the 18th day of August, 1866, at the city of Washington, in the District of Columbia, by public speech, declare and affirm in substance that the Thirty-Ninth Congress of the United States was not a Congress of the United States authorized by the Constitution to exercise legislative power under the same: but, on the contrary, was a Congress of only part of the States, thereby denying and intending to deny that the legislation of said Congress was valid or obligatory upon him.[80]

This article blended the two strains of impeachment charges that finally passed in the House after the previous failed attempts.[81] It drew together the interbranch element that drove the other Stanton-related charges and the accusation of "improper rhetoric."

One possible interpretation is that a more skilled team of impeachment managers could have made this work, but that the team presenting these articles at the Senate trial in 1868 did not draw out what was most compelling or persuasive. In the end, Johnson was acquitted by the margin of a single vote, cast by Republican Edmund Ross of Kansas.

The Meaning of the Andrew Johnson Impeachment

As the first American president to serve after a major disruption in the racial status quo, Johnson's trajectory shows us a great deal about the functioning of the politics of these moments.

"The Johnson case suggested that impeachment could be undertaken for reasons of political conflict but pursued only along more technical grounds," writes Meacham. Indeed, this tension hamstrung Johnson's impeachment, muddling its purpose and allowing its multiple arguments to undermine each other.

But there is another way to think about impeachments in the context of a recent racially transformative presidency. In these moments, the potential of the executive branch has been unlocked, freed from past constraints, and the president's role as a symbol of the nation looms especially large in the public mind. The possibilities for executive action to shape race policy are expanded. Johnson's impeachment demonstrates that the process questions at issue in impeachment politics are inseparable from the linkages between the presidency and race.

Arguments about the Tenure of Office Act were impossible to distinguish from Johnson's larger political project, which included the imposition of Reconstruction policies that favored states' rights over national control and allowed Southern states to enact Black codes. These aims were connected to the president's repeated willingness to look the other way in the face of anti-Black violence and efforts to deny political rights to freedmen. In other words, the Johnson impeachment was very closely related to his brand of racial backlash politics: scrambling party coalitions, taking advantage of the porous border between expansive executive power and presidential lawlessness, and allowing and even encouraging state policies that rolled back any racial progress.

Andrew Johnson's hybrid political identity got him into a position to become president. The similarities with Donald Trump, serving a century and a half later, are especially notable. Like Trump, Johnson, a politician without a real home in either party, sought to go outside the existing system and forge a new kind of conservative political party.[82] Both Trump and Johnson employed their political ambiguity to respond to the new questions that emerged in a changing political environment. As political scientists Jeffrey Tulis and Nicole Mellow note about Johnson, he had no "natural base of support" and was viewed with suspicion by both Northerners and Southerners, yet "with precariousness [came] potential."[83] Their point is that while Johnson's presidency was dogged with political setbacks, culminating in impeachment, he effectively set the direction for the post–Civil War South. What I would add to this is that impeachment emanates from the politics that follow a racial disruption, but that it has proven to be an inadequate remedy for stopping their trajectory. Instead, as we will see with Johnson, impeachment crises engage with presidential racism indirectly and divert public debate to specific inquiries about presidential wrongdoing. The public conversations around presidential impeachments are not without some value, but in focusing systemic questions on individuals, these conversations allow the systemic problems to adapt and persist.

Race and the Reconstruction Presidency

Andrew Johnson left office in 1869 and would not be a serious contender for the presidency again, although he would continue to be active in politics until his death in 1875. The nation remained in a period of difficult transition. Compared with the period before the Civil War, politicians and citizens alike could see evidence for a much wider range of political outcomes. The prospect of a radically transformed democracy, with Black representation and participation, seemed tenable. Yet at no point did this possibility appear to be free of a major threat from violence. Achieving this outcome would require significant federal action.

Although much had changed with the war and the presidencies of Lincoln and Johnson, the familiar presidential conundrum reemerged in the decades that followed. American presidents once again found themselves caught between the competing pressures to use federal power to protect the rights of African American citizens and to retreat from doing so, deferring to state authority.

The story of the presidency in this period is one of both political constraints and lack of political will and moral leadership. Both Ulysses S. Grant and Rutherford B. Hayes, who held the presidency after Johnson, were Republicans and had some belief in federal support for racial progress. But their qualified support was no match for the committed and violent resistance to racial progress that flourished in the South during their tenures.

Grant secured the Republican Party's nomination in 1868, and again in 1872. There was reason to believe that one of Lincoln's generals might carry out a serious vision of Reconstruction, but Grant was also a former slave owner and was married to a woman from a Southern, slave-owning family.[84] Beyond his personal life and beliefs, Grant's 1869 inaugural address also reflected some ambivalence, even as he expressed a commitment to protecting Black suffrage and equal treatment.[85] This democratizing impulse was tempered, however, by a promise not to push bills to address "social equality" or "social status":

> The effects of the late civil strife have been to free the slave and make him a citizen. Yet he is not possessed of the civil rights which citizenship should carry with it. This is wrong, and should be corrected. To this correction I stand committed, so far as Executive influence can avail.
>
> Social equality is not a subject to be legislated upon, nor shall I ask that anything be done to advance the social status of the colored man, except to give him a fair chance to develop what there is good in him, give him access to the schools, and when he travels let him feel assured that his conduct will regulate the treatment and fare he will receive.[86]

Grant's cabinet appointments also sent a mixed signal, as he appointed both "advocates for Black interests" and figures like former Ohio Governor Jacob Dobson Cox, who had opposed African American voting rights in his home state.[87] By most accounts, Grant did support civil and political rights for African Americans and wanted to consolidate a new political order after the war.[88] But the politics of doing so proved increasingly difficult. The major obstacle was the flourishing of white supremacy and anti-Black violence in the South, much of which was aimed at preventing Blacks from voting.[89] Grant sent federal troops in response, but his willingness and ability to address this problem was limited.[90]

Grant championed the Fifteenth Amendment, which prohibited the denial of voting rights to Black citizens. Enforcement, however, was something else entirely. The president successfully backed bills to bolster federal efforts against the Ku Klux Klan and other groups, but felt politically obligated to balance out these measures by supporting a bill to remove the "political disabilities" conferred on former Confederates by Section 3 of the Fourteenth Amendment, which prevented insurrectionists from holding political office.[91] In addition to the growing need for the president to pursue policies "fair" to both sides of the erstwhile conflict, resources were a problem for enforcement. Maintaining a regular federal presence to protect the rights of Southern African Americans was expensive, and Congress was not in the habit of appropriating enough funds for an expanded federal presence.[92]

While the challenges of Southern violence and resistance continued, the political energy behind federal intervention diminished. After the 1868 election, Republicans nervously began to suspect that being identified as the party of African Americans was a liability at the ballot box.[93] The party also continued to splinter, with a liberal Republican movement emerging to oppose the Grant administration and push for quicker reconciliation with Southern whites.[94] This group, whose ranks included Missouri Republican Carl Schurz, Representative Charles Francis Adams, and their 1872 presidential candidate, Horace Greeley, linked the issues of corruption, expanded federal power, and Black suffrage in opposing all three.[95]

Grant won the 1872 election easily, but the political situation around enforcement of the Fifteenth Amendment worsened while the anti-Black violence intensified. The 1873 stock market crash and subsequent economic downturn shifted the administration's focus and dampened its political fortunes.[96] By 1874, the country had grown tired of conflict and wary of federal activities in the South, which raised the specter of a new civil war. Voters, in particular white Northerners, blamed Blacks and the federal government acting on their behalf—not the Klan or Louisiana's White League—for the prospect of further instability. The idea that individual rights were being sacrificed in order to protect Black civil rights fueled this political resentment.[97]

A deadly confrontation in Vicksburg, Mississippi, and a clash over control of the Louisiana State Legislature intensified Grant's dilemma.[98] Sending federal troops to the South exacted a high political cost that the president found increasingly difficult to bear. But allowing violence and chaos to persist did not seem sustainable either. Grant called on the South to respect the law and, in a message to the Senate in January 1875, "expressed his extreme distaste at having to interfere in the domestic affairs of Louisiana."[99]

But as politics became increasingly inhospitable to federal military intervention in the states, Reconstruction drew to a close. Violence continued in the South, marring the results of the 1876 presidential election. Grant's Republican successor, Rutherford B. Hayes, agreed to pull back the Northern military presence in the South in the "infamous bargain" that ended the Electoral College stalemate between himself and Democratic candidate Samuel Tilden. But by that point the nominees of both parties had emphasized "reunion and reconciliation." The latter term became a watchword for Hayes's political overtures toward the South and his often reserved approach to civil rights.[100]

In the decades following the Civil War, Lincoln's Republican Party moved ever further away from the ideology that had fueled its inception. Compared with the Democratic Party, it remained the more racially liberal and the more committed to nationalist ideals. There were few incentives, however, for Republican presidents to expend political resources on race issues. The result was a return to a high degree of state autonomy in the treatment of African American citizens, including the right to vote.[101] Violence and inequality carried over into the twentieth century, setting up a challenge for presidential leadership that was at once new and familiar.

4

"Patience and Moderation"

THEODORE ROOSEVELT
TO LYNDON JOHNSON

ON JUNE 19, 1964, President Lyndon Johnson offered brief remarks on the Senate's passage of the 1964 civil rights bill. He did not confine his comments to commending the promise of the bill and the legislative work that had been done to enact it. Instead, the president also reflected on the tensions that remained and the hard work ahead:

> Lastly, this bill is a challenge. It is a challenge to men of good will in every part of the country, to transform the commands of our law into the customs of our land. It is a challenge to all of us, to go to work in our States and communities, in our homes, and in the depths of our hearts to eliminate the final strongholds of intolerance and hatred. It is a challenge to reach beyond the content of the bill to conquer the barriers of poor education, poverty, and squalid housing which are an inheritance of past injustice and an impediment to future advance.

By alluding to what the legislation did not do, Johnson issued a provocation. One of the excuses sometimes proffered by civil rights opponents was that prejudice could not be legislated away.[1] In acknowledging this, the president then asked the nation to close the gap—to change society and to address the obstacles to inequality that lay beyond what was covered in the bill.

75

Lyndon Johnson aspired to a transformative presidency. He recognized that the status quo he inherited was unjust and unsustainable, and that he was in a position to address it more directly than his twentieth-century predecessors. The presidential actions he took included signing the Civil Rights Act of 1964, the Voting Rights Act of 1965, and the Civil Rights (Fair Housing) Act of 1968 as well as numerous antipoverty measures connected to the civil rights agenda. In addition to his record on the legislation that crossed his desk, when it came to mentioning race in speeches, communication scholars Kevin Coe and Anthony Schmidt find that "Johnson stood noticeably apart from other presidents," in his references to race and "explicit statements against racism."[2]

Johnson, to be clear, was not the central driver of civil rights change; his presidency was shaped by the work of activists who exerted pressure to change the status quo. And the situation was in many ways very different from the century prior; no war had broken out, and the necessary constitutional changes were more modest. At the same time, the racial dynamics of presidential politics bore some important similarities with the period leading up to the Civil War. Both major parties were divided on civil rights and race, as they had been on slavery. These political circumstances—legislative progress on anti-lynching laws stalling out repeatedly and Southern legislators making sure that social policies from the New Deal onward excluded Blacks as much as possible—made the problem seem intractable. And the direction of compromise tended to tilt toward the preservation of racial hierarchies.

Racial hierarchies touched nearly every aspect of the lives of Black Americans. As political scientist Kimberley Johnson observes, "White supremacy was not only a social hierarchy, it reflected a political and economic hierarchy as well."[3] In the decades after the Civil War, the federal government had backed away from the task of enforcing equal rights for Black Americans, and the Fourteenth and Fifteenth Amendments, guaranteeing equal protection and voting rights, were little more than promises.

The range of problems presented to presidents in this era, as a result, was wide and included economic hardship as well lack of opportunity and access to education. The lynching crisis of the early twentieth century, in subjecting Black Americans to the terror of mob violence, threatened their basic human rights. As the civil rights movement grew, demands mounted for equal access to public spaces—public transportation and restaurants—as well as federal protection to guarantee the right to vote.

Despite the political similarities to the earlier era and the efforts to restore the prewar social order, important changes had nevertheless taken place. Despite their exclusion from many domains of politics, African Americans had built up new sources of political power during this period. The National Association for the Advancement of Colored People (NAACP), formed in 1909, had been bolstering its legal and lobbying capacities while also releasing pamphlets to inform and persuade the white public about the problem of lynching.[4] The Great Migration of African Americans to the North also altered political calculations as Blacks gained political power in Northern cities and took on a larger role in the Democratic Party.[5]

This political and legal capacity was soon applied to the struggle for civil and political rights for Black Americans. The pressure sometimes brought results from the White House. Presidents Truman and Kennedy used executive action to further some civil rights causes, and in 1957 President Eisenhower signed the first civil rights bill since Reconstruction.

Presidents in this period also began to view themselves as legislative leaders, masters of the bully pulpit, and architects of a new administrative state. The presidency expanded in response to the economic and national security challenges of the twentieth century. In one sense, this expansion deepens the puzzle: How was it that an office that amassed so much power in multiple arenas was so constrained when it came to addressing racial inequality?

Some of the answer lies in the persistent limitations of the presidency: The chief executive still depended on Congress to make lasting change through legislation. Political pressures—to tend to their coalitions, to manage the political fallout from their actions—also limited what presidents were willing to do. Federalism and a prevailing sense that states could manage their own affairs made key policy areas, like education, delicate territory for presidents.

The civil rights struggle culminated in transformative change during the Lyndon Baines Johnson presidency. LBJ made ambitious federal policy—the Civil Rights Act of 1964, the Voting Rights Act of 1965, and the Civil Rights (Fair Housing) Act of 1968—the signature objective of his presidency. Combined with the legislative initiatives of the Great Society, Johnson's presidency expanded the power of the federal government, upending the legal structures of Jim Crow. Johnson's pursuit of legislation to help Black Americans represented a temporary break from the cautious approach of past presidents, yet even Johnson tried to soften the disruptive impact of his civil rights actions, distancing himself from the civil rights movement and taking steps to limit the impact of these landmark changes. As with Lincoln and the changes to the country brought by the Civil War, Lyndon Johnson's presidency changed the policy and legal frameworks of the country. These changes altered the power structure by moving away from the default compromises that had appeased forces for racial conservatism. African Americans gained new legal and political rights, and reformers for justice claimed new political victories. But these achievements were also limited, in both cases stopping short of fulfilling promises to achieve social and economic equality.

The End of the Party of Lincoln: Theodore Roosevelt to Herbert Hoover

Theodore Roosevelt kicked off the twentieth-century racial presidency. He harbored deeply racist views that drove not only his attitudes toward Black Americans but also informed his outlook on America's role in the world.[6] Though he saw Black Americans as less than equals, he also sought the benefits of cultivating "black-and-tan" party politics as a way of pushing back on other powerful figures in the Republican Party. But the pushback and political costs of racial inclusion proved difficult for the twenty-sixth president to bear. Among Roosevelt's successors, some version of this dilemma would play out again and again. The moral and political benefits of embracing racial progress would be tantalizing, but the political incentives of the system would beat back any real efforts to make change and ensure that the status quo won out instead.

Just a few weeks after taking office, Theodore Roosevelt destroyed any political favor he had built up in the South. Or so said Southern newspapers, which asked, "White men of the South—how do you like it?" and, "White women of the South—how do YOU like it?" In a vividly violent comment, Senator Benjamin Tillman suggested that one thousand lynching deaths of African Americans would be necessary in order to ensure that they would "learn their place again."[7]

The offense? Roosevelt invited a prominent African American, educator and leader Booker T. Washington, to dine with his family at the White House in October 1901. The invitation was part of a plan to distinguish himself politically from his predecessor. Determined to break away from the politics of William McKinley and Republican operative Mark Hanna, Roosevelt began to think about cultivating the support of Black Americans.[8] One part of this strategy was engaging with leaders like Booker T. Washington; the result was a dinner invitation to the White House.[9]

Roosevelt was not exactly an advocate for racial equality. He believed in racial differences among groups and in white superiority, not only in his views about American politics but also in his imperial vision on the world stage.[10] But the twenty-sixth president viewed the race issue in the United States as a pressing problem. He also felt uniquely positioned to chart compromise, as he considered himself "half southern and half northern" and had grown up in New York with some influences from his mother's Southern family.[11]

Roosevelt saw political benefit in forming a working relationship with leaders like Washington, whose approach was to embrace incremental gains toward racial equality and encourage Black achievement.[12] The Southern response to the White House dinner came as a surprise to Roosevelt, and he was unprepared for how long the reaction would be sustained. Commentaries emphasized that Roosevelt's wife and daughter had been present, stoking the fears of interracial sex and Black sexual predators that drove the culture of violent racism that still thrived in the South and throughout the nation.[13] The response was both fierce and sustained, and the reactions from politicians and newspapers show why. Roosevelt had used the symbols and trappings of the presidency to project a small glimmer of social equality. Southerners saw this as threatening and insulting, and they had ample opportunities to express these thoughts.

Foreshadowing the actions of other twentieth-century presidents, Roosevelt's approach to race ran through the practices of party politics. Here, too, he sought to cultivate Black support by appointing African Americans to federal positions, a stance he also connected to larger principles of equality and the legacy of Lincoln's Republican Party. The prospects of confrontations with Southern Democrats over nominating highly qualified African Americans appealed to Roosevelt's penchant for confrontational politics, and he considered it "cowardly" not to make such appointments. But backlash politics, and the constraints they imposed, were ever present at the edges of such moves. Roosevelt wanted credit for appointing Black Americans to federal offices, but in an attempt to appeal to both sides of the issue, he responded to critics that he made fewer Black appointments than his predecessor William McKinley.[14] He closed the post office in Indianola, Mississippi, in response to white vitriol about the appointment of an African American woman, Minnie Cox, as its postmaster, and he defended Cox in the face of racist attacks. The Indianola incident showed that Roosevelt was willing to stand on the side of justice on race issues, even in the face of strong political opposition.[15] But it also spurred strong backlash, revealing the kinds of political consequences that presidents would have to accept for taking action on race issues. The confrontation helped James Vardaman win the Mississippi governorship on a campaign of transparently racist appeals. In the words of Roosevelt biographer Kathleen Dalton, "by standing on principle over one federal postmaster TR had inspired the triumph of racial politics in Mississippi."[16]

These repercussions stretched out over Roosevelt's presidency. In a major effort to rehabilitate relations with the region, he took a two-week Southern speaking tour in 1905. On this tour, the president appealed to white Southern sensibilities and "legitimated southern recalcitrance through Reconstruction and Redemption."[17] His speech in Richmond, the former Confederate capital, especially drove home his willingness to reframe and accommodate the South and all that it stood for in race relations. In addition to the Southern tour, Roosevelt's response to the 1906 Brownsville massacre established some of the ideas that would define how presidents approached race for decades to come.

After 167 Black soldiers were stationed in Brownsville, Texas, residents complained about the presence of the Black battalion and eventually accused the soldiers, without evidence, of attacking a white woman. Violence eventually broke out, and all 167 soldiers were discharged without pension or compensation, despite the lack of evidence of their guilt.[18] This decision brought significant criticism, especially in the North.[19] In addition to the impact of the decision itself, Roosevelt's rhetorical defense highlighted his conservatism on the subject. In the past he had expressed credulity about the notion that African Americans were lynched in response to the crime of raping white women. Furthermore, in the context of the Brownsville situation, Roosevelt sidestepped the issue of race, even as his political opponents tried to bring it to the forefront of politics.[20] A new politics of racial avoidance was born, since addressing the issue of race directly carried too much risk for politicians who wanted to move policy in a moderate direction. Highlighting the issue handed a political opportunity to demagogic racial conservatives like Vardaman and Tillman, who challenged Roosevelt's interpretation of Brownsville and used it to argue in favor of racial hierarchy.

Theodore Roosevelt was especially attuned to the rhetorical possibilities of the presidency. But in the area of race, the reformer and pugnacious political orator used the bully pulpit to affirm the power of the South and white supremacy. Roosevelt's disinterest in putting the weight of the presidency behind real changes to the country's racial hierarchy signaled a full turn among Republican presidents away from the spirit of Abraham Lincoln and the early GOP. As the "lily-white" faction of the GOP won out and the electoral incentives to appeal to Black voters declined, Republican presidents became less and less concerned about advancing Black interests.[21]

After Roosevelt's presidential term ended, Republican presidents largely veered even further away from their party's roots. William Howard Taft in particular moved away from any pretense of protecting Black rights in the South. In his 1909 inaugural address, he declared the movement for

Black voting rights a failure, stated that there would be no federal support for voting rights, praised efforts to limit the "ignorant" electorate, and announced the end of African American federal appointments in the South.[22] In some sense, Taft's approach was in keeping with what had been established: Since Hayes, Republicans had sought to build support in the white South. They had pulled back federal efforts to enforce African American rights and cultivated "moderate and conservative" Black leaders, like Booker T. Washington, who were disinclined to challenge white leadership structures to any great extent.[23] Yet, even in this context, Taft stood out for his more overt abandonment of federal action in the service of even minimal notions of racial equality.[24]

One notable feature of this period is that some of the variation in presidential behavior does appear to have been linked to personal attitudes. Edward Frantz notes that Taft saw nonwhites as inferior but capable of improvement, and these views informed his decisions. In a more promising example of Republican leadership, Warren G. Harding navigated fraught party dynamics surrounding race and anti-lynching bills and "seemed genuinely interested in the plight of African Americans," and thus receptive to NAACP leaders' requests for support on those pressing issues.[25]

Megan Ming Francis provides an account of Harding's race politics as president that encapsulates the enduring political dilemma. Harding responded to political pressure from early civil rights activists, both during the 1920 campaign and leading up to his 1921 statement to Congress against lynching. Even "small accommodations" during the campaign invited intense backlash from political opponents ready to wield racial attacks.[26] Harding remained cautious, declining to issue further statements in support of what eventually became the Anti-Lynching Bill (so-called for Representative Leonidas Dyer [R-MO] and thwarted in the Senate after passing in the House). The Republican Party's internal struggle over the "lily-white" and "black-and-tan" factions continued after Harding's death, with the political balance eventually shifting toward the lily-white faction. In other words, presidential beliefs and intent mattered, but political structures ultimately triumphed.

This period of Republican leadership ended with a pair of contrasting presidencies: Calvin Coolidge and Herbert Hoover. While Coolidge offered little in the way of truly revolutionary policy and expended little serious political capital, he did make statements against lynching (and in favor of congressional action on the matter) and in support of the argument that Black soldiers who had served in World War I deserved fair treatment as citizens.[27] He also helped direct federal support to Howard University.

Hoover, on the other hand, represented the definitive end to any idea that the GOP might be the party of African Americans. Hoover's political support among African Americans waned significantly as disappointments with the administration mounted—especially given the disproportionate effects on the Black population of the Great Depression.[28] Hoover's (unsuccessful) nomination of Judge John J. Parker, who had a track record of racist statements, created lasting distrust between Hoover and the NAACP.[29] More broadly, Hoover's approach reflected the growing power of the "lily-white" school of thought in Republican politics: Regardless of personal racial views, the party-building strategy ultimately served to foster all-white organizations in the South, at the expense of Black voices in the coalition.[30]

Moving Backward: Woodrow Wilson and Race

Political scientists Phil Klinkner and Rogers Smith describe Wilson as "probably the most racist president of [the twentieth] century," at least insofar as attitudes toward Black Americans are concerned.[31] Wilson's reputation in the Black press and among scholars of race has long reflected this concern about the twenty-eighth president, and the rest of the world has recently begun to catch on.[32] Schools, programs, and awards have been renamed as the country has wrestled with this aspect of Wilson's legacy. Wilson was a champion of economic regulation, good government, and idealist thinking about America's role in the world—all of which made him a longtime favorite of presidential historians on the left. But his attitudes about race and their manifestation in his decisions as president have rightfully tarnished this reputation.

Like Roosevelt, Wilson's early memories were from the Civil War and Reconstruction eras, with strong Southern family influence.

Reconstruction eventually became a major subject of Wilson's critique, and his writing on the subject is direct about the reasons. He viewed the period as one of rule of the South by Blacks, whom he regarded as inferior and uneducated.[33]

Wilson's path to the presidency was also connected to race in complicated ways. He owed his nomination to the Democratic Party's requirement that presidential nominees receive two-thirds of the delegates' votes at the convention, a rule that empowered the South and gave the region a veto over nominees. But in the general election Wilson made what were at the time significant inroads into Republican support among Black voters—between 5 and 7 percent, after making overtures to NAACP leaders and winning the endorsement of leading Black intellectual W.E.B. Du Bois.[34]

Once in office, however, Wilson seriously disappointed these leaders by using the power of the presidency to entrench white supremacy and bring the racial hierarchy of the South to the federal government. One of the main ways in which Wilson used the presidency to codify his own racism was to segregate the federal civil service by having it adopt Jim Crow practices. Over the objections of NAACP leaders, Wilson claimed that this segregation was for the benefit of Black workers.[35] The decision to segregate the executive branch workforce also established the linkage between Wilson's brand of Progressivism and scientific racism.[36] But the impact was not exclusively symbolic: The exclusion of African Americans from higher-ranking federal positions had material consequences in the lives of those who were denied or demoted.[37]

The other infamous instance of Wilson's racism in the White House was his decision to screen the film *Birth of a Nation*. The novel *The Clansman*, on which the film was based, "portrayed freed blacks as incapable of suppressing their animalistic instincts and unable to resist their urges for white women," and the book cast "the Ku Klux Klan [as] the hero of the story."[38]

As with segregating the civil service, Wilson was using the presidency to reintroduce and strengthen old racist themes, in this case by reimagining Reconstruction as an especially precarious time for whites.[39] Both the workplace segregation and the themes of the film built on existing notions of status and the structure of society, including the sexual threat supposedly posed to white women from proximity to Black men. Whether he intended to or not, Wilson put the power of the presidency behind those ideas.

In one area, Wilson proved to be more receptive to the concerns of Black Americans. After considerable lobbying by the NAACP, and in the wake of the 1917 massacre of African Americans in East St. Louis, Wilson became receptive to the request that he make a statement against lynching. In the words of political scientist Megan Ming Francis, "the incident highlighted the inability of states to prevent or even halt racial violence."[40] The moment to call for action from the federal government had arrived. In addition to its lobbying efforts, the NAACP organized a silent protest parade to the White House in the hope of gaining Wilson's attention.[41]

Despite Wilson's poor track record on race, these efforts were successful. Wilson made a firm statement against lynching in his Address to the Nation on July 26, 1918. Importantly, Wilson connected racial violence to the "mob spirit," making an early overture to appeals to order that would later inform presidential statements about race and school desegregation. For Wilson to condemn lynching and violence was a major step forward for racially cautious, even regressive, American presidents. But this law-and-order frame would sound less forceful decades later and appear a poor substitute for moral rhetoric about civil rights. Furthermore, "law and order" was easily turned against those who wanted to agitate against the status quo.

Nevertheless, the NAACP's success showed an important truth about how presidents handled race: Their own attitudes didn't determine everything. Political pressure could move them to act and speak in favor of racial justice, or at least against grave and blatant injustice. But it could also do the opposite—temper the impulse to embrace change.

A New Deal?

While running for the Democratic presidential nomination in 1932, Franklin Delano Roosevelt spoke about the "forgotten man" on the bottom rung of the economic ladder. With this rhetoric, he repurposed decades-old populist ideas and began to forge a new identity for the

Democratic Party. When he won the nomination, he appeared at the convention in Chicago to accept it in person—breaking one hundred years of party tradition.

Once elected, FDR continued to build his presidential reputation as a reformer and a breaker of norms.[42] His 1932 election to the presidency ended a long period of Republican dominance in the White House and built on Progressive political ideas about expanding the role of the federal government. Roosevelt "welcomed the hatred" of critics and branded opponents as "economic royalists" as he ushered in a new set of ideas about the relationships among government, business, and democracy. These ideas built on the "forgotten man" theme.

But where Black Americans were concerned, FDR was far less eager to challenge the existing order or to think about forgotten citizens. Little in Roosevelt's political and personal background suggested that he would be a champion of racial equality. His time in the South convalescing from polio had deepened his identification with the region and the priorities of its white population.[43] Moreover, in his daily life in the rarefied and patrician world he inhabited, he had little contact with African Americans.[44]

Amid sweeping policy changes, FDR sought to chart a "middle way" that would appeal to African Americans, whose influence and voting power were slowly growing, while maintaining the "fundamental shape of race relations as he inherited them."[45] As a result of this strategy, the South maintained its power in the Democratic Party. As they continued to wield veto power in the Senate, Southern Democrats retained a strong bargaining position with a legislatively ambitious president.

The racial legacy of the New Deal may be one of the fiercest areas of argument among historians of the period, and it remains contested. On the one hand, Roosevelt's economic policies did help to lift some African Americans out of poverty and provided economic opportunities through federal programs such as the Public Works Administration (PWA) and the National Youth Administration (NYA). High-ranking New Deal officials, including Interior Secretary Harold Ickes and Labor Secretary Frances Perkins, were attentive to concerns about racial inequality and sometimes willing to expend political capital to push for more equitable practices in New Deal jobs programs. These efforts, however, faced headwinds from the discriminatory practices that were widespread in the PWA, the Civilian Conservation Corps (CCC), and other New Deal initiatives.[46]

Nevertheless, the politics of the New Deal reflected the same caution that had been historically exercised by previous presidents. The scope of FDR's policy program made it even more important to keep the Democratic coalition together. Among the concessions to Southern Democrats on New Deal programs was the exclusion of domestic and farm workers from the benefits of the 1935 Social Security Act. Equally important to maintaining systemic discrimination was the administration of New Deal programs, including agricultural and job programs; by agreeing to their implementation at the state level, the federal government thus deferred to local rules and norms about race and employment.[47] In addition, federal housing programs contributed to residential segregation through their lending practices.[48]

The stymied debate over anti-lynching legislation exposed the administration's disinterest in disrupting the power arrangements in the South. An anti-lynching bill had been unable to overcome a filibuster in the Senate in 1923. For a variety of reasons, including an increase in racial violence during the Great Depression, the NAACP had turned its attention back to promoting an anti-lynching bill in Congress. The group found two consistently Progressive senators, Edward Costigan of Colorado and Robert Wagner of New York, who were willing to introduce the NAACP's preferred legislation in the Senate.[49]

Like the 1923 bill, the Costigan-Wagner bill would have created federal penalties for state officials who failed to enforce relevant state laws against mob violence. FDR declined to address the bill directly, and when he did talk about lynching, in a December 1933 speech, he talked about mob violence against a white man jailed in California.[50] Political scientist Ira Katznelson's account suggests that this neglect was strategic, with FDR finding little to be gained by addressing the race issue "head on."[51] Black activists wielded little power at this point.[52] Considerably more power was wielded by white Southerners, with the potential to unleash backlash politics. Despite urging from the NAACP's

Walter White, as well as from First Lady Eleanor Roosevelt, FDR repeatedly evaded entreaties to publicly support the anti-lynching bill. In 1934, he dismissed the bill as "unconstitutional" after conversations with Southern senators.[53] The bill came up again, over much Southern objection, after a successful filibuster in 1934. This time the president was especially reluctant to let the bill get in the way of his 1935 legislative agenda.[54] Another version languished in 1938, as did an effort to launch a Senate investigation into mob violence in the South.

Ultimately, the New Deal legislative agenda depended on a group of senators who favored the president's economic agenda but who also resisted federal involvement in Southern affairs. "States' rights" advocacy was inseparable from the racial hierarchy of Southern life. FDR and most of his inner circle were unwilling to take real political risk to address the grievous moral harm of what could have been a fairly straightforward issue—what Megan Ming Francis calls "the right to live."[55]

There were some symbolic gains. Perhaps the most successful was the administration's continued use of rhetoric about economic inequality and forgotten Americans, which resonated with Black audiences as well as it did with white audiences.[56] Certainly, efforts were made to highlight what the New Deal was doing to address the plight of Black citizens. The administration's employment of a number of visible African American advisers was not without impact, but these advisers were frequently marginalized, "quarantined" in offices dedicated to "Negro Affairs" within specific agencies or departments, and kept limited in their visibility and access to the higher levels of power.[57]

Over time, the balance of political power shifted slightly. African Americans had relocated to Northern cities, and the NAACP's Walter White liked to remind the president that Black voters held a potentially decisive number of votes in several Northern states.[58] This power worked in strange ways to shape the administration's decisions late into FDR's second term and into the third. The electoral influence of Black voters was growing, as was their disappointment with Roosevelt's shortcomings. However, the prospect of those voters returning to the GOP en masse remained remote.[59] The pressures that drove the administration went beyond electoral politics as three forces converged: Roosevelt's own moral sensibilities about race, the desire within the administration to preserve national unity and peace as the nation lurched toward war, and the general degree of comfort in the administration with growing federal power. In 1939, the Justice Department announced the creation of a new unit to enforce civil rights and liberties (eventually named the Civil Rights Section). Among other responsibilities, the Civil Rights Section would serve as a "center for testing creative legal theories that sought to halt lynchings and police brutality."[60]

After the 1940 election, the Roosevelt administration acceded to demands from Black leaders as they planned a march on Washington to make a series of economic demands. After initial opposition to an executive order targeting African American employment, Roosevelt ultimately signed Executive Order 8802, which banned discrimination in the growing defense industry and created the Fair Employment Practices Committee.[61]

In one sense, these changes were momentous. Executive Order 8802 represented the first time a president had issued a "directive on race" since Reconstruction.[62] Although such changes opened the door for further federal involvement, they also fell short of transformative change. Roosevelt did little to advocate for the idea of federal involvement in racial strife, and he was unable to use the New Deal to create truly equal opportunities for Black and white citizens.

Furthermore, Roosevelt's moral leadership on race was simply not there. He chose a liaison for African American affairs during World War II, Jonathan Daniels, who amplified the administration's instinct to place order and tranquility above other considerations.[63] Sometimes it was possible to make incremental racial progress within the confines of this priority on order, but such progress was often not enough. And sometimes the administration's priorities could not be reconciled with racial initiatives at all.

Roosevelt's presidency might have marked the ascendancy of liberalism in the Democratic Party, but Southern political power, while perhaps diminished, was far from gone. FDR's attempt to replace anti–New Deal senators was met with strong opposition to presidential meddling in local representation and party politics. The 1938 "purge" was a failure.

As federal power closed in, this group also became more protective of Southern identity and autonomy and of their right to engage in racist practices.[64]

Instead, the modern challenge for Democratic presidents took shape during Roosevelt's four years: Inaction or inadequate action on racial equality took a toll on the support from an increasingly important bloc of voters. But Southern reactions were very real and increasingly defensive. The political risks were heightened on both sides of the issue, portending the political disruption that more transformative presidential efforts would bring.

Harry Truman

Although many aspects of Harry Truman's presidency echoed the FDR legacy, it also saw bolder action and decision-making from the White House and responsiveness to the changing dynamics of party politics.

Harry Truman's lineage in a Southern, Confederate family made him an unlikely champion of civil rights, and his private comments suggested that he was skeptical about social equality and had little personal regard for African Americans.[65] However, political considerations and pressures rather than personal predilections shaped the administration's approach. Truman and his political advisers saw Black support as key to building a coalition. An increasingly well-organized and consolidated civil rights advocacy community, led by the NAACP, contributed to the pressure felt by the administration, and the Great Migration had enhanced the strategic impact of Black voters, who were now located in electorally crucial places.[66] Compared with his predecessors, Truman's efforts stand out. As Sidney Milkis and Katherine Rader note, "Truman's unprecedented attention to racial justice was attributable in no small part to the strength of the civil rights movement and its close ties to the modern executive office."[67]

The Truman White House took responsibility for the multifaceted "race problem" by forming the President's Committee on Civil Rights. The committee format placed the issue at a remove from the president and offered the opportunity to address the issue by taking into account multiple perspectives. The committee's skeptics sounded some themes typical of the era: the limits of appropriate federal power, and the idea that law could not fundamentally alter morality or social structures.[68]

Truman marshaled the symbolic power of the presidency, speaking to the NAACP on the steps of the Lincoln Memorial and forming a committee to investigate lynching and racial injustice. His 1947 State of the Union message urged Congress to pass several pieces of legislation that the Committee on Civil Rights had asked for, including "a permanent civil rights commission; federal laws against lynching, discrimination in interstate transportation, and the poll tax; and the establishment of a permanent Fair Employment Practices Commission [FEPC]."[69] He issued executive orders desegregating the armed forces and banning discrimination in federal hiring, areas where the pressure from organized activists was especially consequential.[70] These moves, which had required acknowledgment from the White House of the problems with the existing system, would earn Truman a place in history as "the president who got civil rights firmly on the nation's agenda."[71]

Two related developments tempered the transformational impact of the Truman presidency. First, the president and his political advisers—notably Clark Clifford, who had advised a strong civil rights strategy—underestimated the potential for Southern reaction.

One view within the administration was that the South was a captured constituency for the Democratic Party—one that could be counted on for support. Strife within the party, however, belied that view. The 1948 convention produced the most visible display of Southern willingness to break with party norms. Then-Senate candidate Hubert Humphrey delivered a speech urging the party to "get out of the shadow of states' rights and walk forthrightly into the bright shadow of human rights," accompanying a civil rights plank in the party platform. But Southern dissatisfaction with Truman's speeches and the FEPC was growing.[72] Democratic Party leaders did not want this fight, and Truman, along with DNC chair Howard McGrath, tried to steer the party away from a stronger civil rights platform and toward the compromise language of the 1944 platform instead.[73] But the delegates approved a platform advanced by civil rights advocates, which read:

We call upon the Congress to support our President in guaranteeing these basic and fundamental American Principles: (1) the right of full and equal political participation; (2) the right to equal opportunity of employment; (3) the right of security of person; (4) and the right of equal treatment in the service and defense of our nation.[74]

The result was shouts of protest amid celebration, and some delegates walked out of the convention.[75]

The response at the convention and in the subsequent election illustrates how disrupting the delicate balance on race issues within the party could affect the behavior of presidents and party leaders. The reaction was not limited to the symbolic act of walking out of the convention. The States' Rights ticket, which featured South Carolina Governor Strom Thurmond and Mississippi Governor Fielding Wright and replaced the regular Democratic ticket in several states, sought to deny either major-party candidate a majority in the Electoral College in the hope of forcing the decision into the House of Representatives (per the Twelfth Amendment). These moves not only broke with long-held party norms about supporting presidential tickets but showed party leaders what they were willing to do.[76] And while the Electoral College strategy was not ultimately successful, it revealed the complexity of party politics in the South—loyalty in the region to the Democratic Party was not what Truman and his associates had imagined it to be.

In turn, the Truman administration reverted to the presidential impulse to avoid further disruption. The party would move left on civil rights over time, but it also declined to inflict real procedural punishment on the 1948 defectors.[77] Both sides of the civil rights divide in the Democratic Party had flaunted their power to some degree: Civil rights advocates showed that they could stick to their principles and win in a floor fight, while Southern opponents established that they would abandon the party if it went too far.

Faced with the unanticipated intensity of Southern opposition, Truman also changed tactics. Like other midcentury presidents, Truman bumped up against the limits of what was possible in Congress.[78] There was little that the president could do to alter the legislative incentives of

Southern Democrats, and legislative efforts to establish a permanent fair employment commission failed. As a result, he turned to executive actions to pursue a civil rights agenda.

In addition to the constraints on legislative influence, Truman saw the destabilizing potential of a turn toward civil rights, even as there were political opportunities in this policy arena. The administration had made progress on a number of issues, despite the dubious background and views of the man in the White House. His administration concluded with significant accomplishments, including the desegregation of the armed forces and the inclusion of a civil rights plank in the Democratic Party platform. But the delicate compromises over race had proven to be even more tenuous than previously imagined. The potential for civil rights opponents to hold the balance of power was called into question—Truman did manage to win the 1948 election—but opponents of civil rights progress in his own party had shown what they were willing to do.

Dwight Eisenhower

Truman's second term was tumultuous, and by 1952 the Democrats' fortunes had begun to decline. Public discontent over the Korean War, combined with still-present party fissures and the fatigue associated with a party that had held the White House for two decades, created an opportunity for change. Republicans had their own internal disagreements; ultimately they nominated General Dwight Eisenhower over conservative Ohio Senator Robert Taft. Eisenhower was the kind of presidential candidate not seen since the Civil War era—a popular general with no elected experience. Eisenhower's precise ideology—including his record on race and civil rights—remains a matter of controversy to this day.

In the 1952 election, Eisenhower tried to thread the needle. The civil rights issue had divided Democrats and created opportunities to win votes in the South. But unlike other politicians who wielded "wedge" issues against opponents, Eisenhower did not emphasize civil rights, though he did clarify his opposition to federal regulations like Truman's FEPC.[79]

Despite these soft stances on federal involvement, Eisenhower expressed sympathy with those facing discrimination and, by all accounts, had a sincere sense of fairness that extended to equal treatment of African Americans in public life. As a candidate, Eisenhower expressed openness to a Black cabinet member and vowed to reject anyone opposed to racial or religious equality from his administration.[80]

Brown v. Board of Education

Eisenhower's cautious efforts to strike a middle way on civil rights by outwardly opposing both discrimination and excess federal force were thwarted by the Supreme Court's *Brown v. Board of Education of Topeka, Kansas* decision in 1954. Several of the lower-court justices whose anti-segregation views drove the legal case had been appointed by Eisenhower, as had Supreme Court Chief Justice Earl Warren.[81] The Justice Department filed a brief in support of overturning *Plessy v. Ferguson* and opposing school segregation.[82] At the same time, the administration remained skeptical of the *Brown* case and of the general idea that the federal government could enforce desegregation.[83] The president and his advisers were acutely aware of how the school desegregation case could drag them down politically, and one adviser asked whether the administration wouldn't prefer to "just stay out of it," rather than file a brief on the case.[84] Eisenhower privately bemoaned that the case had been decided during his tenure in office.[85]

With the 1954 decision, the Warren court breathed life into the Fourteenth Amendment by declaring that "separate is not equal." It also raised the stakes of civil rights politics, with the details of enforcement becoming the subject of another court case. The decision strained the detached moderation of Eisenhower's civil rights approach. What did it look like to chart a middle way on a court case that found local schools, especially in the South, in violation of the Constitution, and specifically in violation of the nation's often unfulfilled promise to treat all its citizens equally?

Despite the dire nature of the issue, Eisenhower tried to chart such a course. As "massive resistance" to school desegregation mounted,

Eisenhower called for "patience and moderation" and enlisted the assistance of pastor Billy Graham.[86] The president's search for a middle way entailed not only looking the other way as White Citizens' Councils formed and the South grew increasingly embattled but also distancing himself from civil rights leaders and refusing meetings with them and hesitating to align with the cause or the *Brown* decision at the 1956 convention and in the party's platform.[87]

In the period after *Brown*, tensions had continued to grow. Southern legislators had issued the "Southern Manifesto," which clarified that the Deep South would not accept the court's decision. The document included the line, "We commend the motives of those States which have declared the intention to resist forced integration by any lawful means."[88]

Massive resistance in the South was not confined to these kinds of documents. Crucially, school integration seemed to some Southerners to be the equivalent of social equality between white and Black, imposed from on high. Some integration opponents used these social fears to mobilize, stoking anxiety about the prospect that integrated schools would lead to racial mixing and the exposure of young white girls to the sexual threat supposedly posed by African American boys.[89] The reaction was not just about mobs and mobilizing. State and local governments passed laws cutting funding for integrated schools and even closed schools rather than comply with the new federal mandate.[90]

Racial upheaval was not confined to the school issue. In a period marked by serious violence, a bomb was planted at Martin Luther King Jr.'s residence in 1956, and the year before the murder of Emmett Till had "galvanized Black Americans in a way that *Brown* had not."[91] The brutality of the death of fourteen-year-old Till in Mississippi spurred further calls for federal action and revived earlier lynching debates. In Alabama, civil rights leaders organized the Montgomery bus boycott.

Despite pleas from civil rights leaders for a robust federal response, the Eisenhower administration regarded the situation as one to be navigated carefully. This was not for lack of pressure within the executive branch—mainly from Attorney General Herbert Brownell and White House adviser E. Frederic Morrow—to take developments in the nation's racial politics more seriously. But Eisenhower was reluctant to assert a role for the federal government or to strain relations with Southern politicians.[92] He had a fairly established political record in favor of an incremental, preservationist approach by 1957, but in September of that year, in the face of the worsening situation, the president was no longer able to duck the issue.

A potential constitutional crisis was brewing while the world watched.[93] White citizens were unwilling to accept the integration of Black students at Central High School in Little Rock, Arkansas, and a mob had gathered to prevent the enrollment of nine Black students.[94] A district court overturned a ruling delaying the integration process, but the governor of Arkansas, Orval Faubus, gave no direct indication that he would comply with the order. At the beginning of September, he had called in the state National Guard "to maintain peace," but with orders to keep Black students out of the school.[95]

Eisenhower's actions in mid-September suggest that he was frustrated with Faubus's "open defiance of the Constitution" but also reluctant to bear the political costs of a public battle of wills.[96] After all, the president had little leverage over the governor.[97] In this moment of confrontation, the implications of the federal system were on full view: There was no straightforward way for the president to make a governor comply with a federal court order. Eventually, Eisenhower did meet with Faubus and offered a "face-saving" solution to change the orders to the Guard and ask them to keep order and protect the Black students as they entered the school.[98] Faubus promised to do so, but did not deliver, and the crisis continued to worsen. Eisenhower was frustrated by everything about the clash. He wanted to publicly denounce Faubus after his failure to uphold the bargain they had made, but from early on he had doubted that there was much role for the administration to play and was skeptical about integration ordered by federal courts.[99]

Ultimately, Eisenhower signed an order to bring the Arkansas National Guard under federal control. In his televised address to the nation soon after, the president carefully sidestepped the moral issues in play. Instead, his speech pointed to the Supreme Court's decision about schools and asserted that Americans were obligated to abide by it, not necessarily because it was morally correct but because the rule of law required compliance. He also addressed federal and regional issues as he assured the nation that the people of the South "are of good will, united in their efforts to preserve and respect the law even when they disagree with it."[100] This depiction was an effort to "mollify white southerners by attributing the disorder to the actions of a few."[101] Eisenhower characterized the incident as a unique instance of extremists thwarting the rule of law and forcing federal escalation.

Presenting the situation as a law-and-order crisis rather than a civil rights issue reflected the president's true feelings, according to Brownell.[102] The political payoff of the strategy was unclear. Southerners saw Eisenhower's actions as heavy-handed, no matter how they were justified, but some civil rights activists, like King and the singer Harry Belafonte Jr., expressed their appreciation.[103] Others, like the NAACP's Roy Wilkins, were frustrated that the administration had let the post-*Brown* situation deteriorate to that point.[104]

During the Little Rock fracas, on September 9, Eisenhower had signed the Civil Rights Act of 1957, the first one since Reconstruction. The bill strengthened federal civil rights protections in several ways and turned the Civil Rights Section created under FDR into a full-fledged division in the Justice Department.[105] The bill also "empowered the federal government to seek injunctions against obstruction or deprivation of voting rights."[106]

Nevertheless, there was considerable ambivalence about the bill. Southern legislators had weakened it, adding an amendment over Eisenhower's opposition that significantly hampered any real chance of enforcement.[107] Its provisions about school integration were also limited. While the bill was a historic step forward, its limitations were readily apparent. A published comment in the *Journal of Negro Education* in 1957 called the bill "more psychological than practical" and, foreshadowing the struggles of the 1960s, lamented its lack of impact on the economic status of African Americans.[108] Eisenhower even contemplated vetoing the weakened version of the legislation. Ultimately, he concluded that the bill was better than no bill, although that was a matter of debate among civil rights leaders.[109]

Eisenhower's approach to civil rights exposed the dilemma facing presidents. Political pressure and calls for presidential direction were building throughout the country, but there was much that presidents could not control, namely the actions of the Supreme Court, of activists, and of Congress. When it came to the civil rights bill, Eisenhower's vision was limited but driven by his instincts about fairness. On the enforcement of the *Brown* decision, Eisenhower never fully came to terms with the need for stronger federal action, nor with the prospect of moral leadership on civil rights. But despite his caution, the president also paid a political price, losing Southern support after the Central High confrontation and passage of the civil rights bill. Eisenhower's presidency ultimately revealed the risks of civil rights action, even when coupled with efforts to accommodate the South. Even as demands for action grew stronger and louder, the Eisenhower administration did not succeed at providing a blueprint for managing the politics of civil rights.

The Crisis Worsens: John F. Kennedy

Kennedy's approach to the civil rights issue as he started his 1960 presidential bid was similar to the path taken by those who had come before him: He was interested in winning Northern Black votes, but also in maintaining political support among Southern whites. During the campaign, he criticized Eisenhower's civil rights policy for the absence of "moral leadership" and inattention to ending segregation in public housing.[110] Both implied and stated was that Kennedy would address the issue of inequality more directly, and he promised Black audiences that he would remedy the public housing issue "with the stroke of a pen."[111] Often using his brother Robert as a campaign surrogate, Kennedy presented himself as the more active and engaged candidate on civil rights and criticized his Republican opponent as "No Comment Nixon" for his lack of response to the jailing of Martin Luther King Jr. in Georgia during the campaign.[112]

Kennedy's narrow 1960 victory hardly seemed like a mandate for a civil rights revolution, and the new Democratic president had no real plans to pursue one. Instead, Kennedy was determined not to pursue a legislative strategy on civil rights, preferring to make changes through executive action. However, by the end of Kennedy's first year he had also neglected to sign the promised federal housing bill, prompting activists "to mail thousands of pens to the White House to pressure Kennedy to fulfill his promise."[113]

The president was not mistaken about the pitfalls of the legislative route. Like FDR before him, JFK depended on the votes of Southern Democrats in Congress to pass his top policy priorities. These included a minimum wage bill that ended up excluding some jobs that were predominantly held by Black workers, such as laundry workers in the South.[114] Nevertheless, these concessions did not buy him much capital with Southerners. Among Kennedy's more dramatic legislative defeats was his effort to create a cabinet-level urban affairs and housing department. The president had offered the rationale for creating such a department to Congress in a letter in early 1961, in which he assumed that such a bureaucratic change would be a relatively uncontroversial and "attainable" legislative victory.[115] It was also widely assumed that Robert Weaver, who led the administration's housing division and would be the country's first African American cabinet secretary, would lead the new department. This plan was too much for Southern Democrats, who sent the bill to its defeat in 1962, handing a humiliating loss to the administration in the area of civil rights and demonstrating the difficulty of passing even legislation focused on arcane matters of government structure. A bill proposed to end the "arbitrary" application of literacy tests to vote fared no better.[116]

The Kennedy White House, in sum, demonstrated much of the characteristic caution displayed by other presidents of the era. Biographer Robert Dallek observes that while Kennedy spoke in ambitious terms about civil rights in his 1962 State of the Union address, the administration did not feel politically empowered to follow up with legislation: The public's priorities continued to lie elsewhere.[117] Where the president did take action, he prioritized areas that would minimize disruption and controversy. For example, voting rights emerged as a priority because it "did not incite social and sexual anxieties," as school integration did.[118]

Voting was not the only matter that Kennedy would consider before school integration. He also showed more willingness to champion fair employment practices and viewed the school issue in a different light, privately remarking, "If I had a child there putting him [in a school with] thirty to forty percent Negro[es] when they're so far behind—that's really tough."[119]

Integration issues were impossible to avoid, however. The next major confrontation took place over the admission of a Black student, James Meredith, to the University of Mississippi in 1962. With the legacy of Little Rock looming over the administration, there was little question that it would do what was necessary to enforce the law.[120] The president delegated much of the response to the Justice Department, which responded incrementally, wanting to avoid the spectacle of Little Rock and the subsequent loss of support in the South.[121] There was, of course, no avoiding either outcome. Violent chaos ensued in Oxford, resulting in "the feel of an armed insurrection" and hundreds of arrests (though only a few criminal charges).[122] Kennedy's speech to the nation tried once again to split the difference. His words affirmed the perspective of those who disagreed with the law, while stressing the necessity of enforcing it.[123] But these words neither calmed segregationists nor conveyed that the president was in command of the situation. The right and ability of the federal government to enforce the law, over the objection of state and local officials, remained a core problem.

Scholars differ on how much Kennedy cared about racial inequality, but there is no debate about how much he cared about foreign policy. As the world started to pay attention to racial inequality in the United States, implications for Cold War global politics became evident. Embarrassing incidents like African diplomats being denied seats at Washington, DC, restaurants attracted the attention of national security officials and forced the administration to take notice of civil rights issues.[124] Viewed in this light, civil rights could be understood as a crucial aspect of foreign policy rather than a "distraction" from the main goals.[125] Civil rights leaders promoted this line of thinking, and State Department officials in particular were receptive to it.

While international pressures heightened attention to civil rights, they also made the Kennedy White House more cautious and concerned with image. This deepened the tension between administration goals and those of social movement activists, who aimed to attract media attention and create discomfort in hopes of radically changing the status quo.[126] The attacks of angry mobs on the Freedom Riders, a group of activists who had traveled to the South to challenge Jim Crow policies, revealed exactly what activists wanted to show: the violence as well as the disengaged response from the police. The Kennedy administration, however, viewed these attacks as an "embarrassment" that tarnished the US image.[127] In this sense, the image issue was a growing wedge between the administration and activists: The latter group was much less concerned about protecting international impressions of American democracy and wanted to generate upsetting media images— as happened with the Freedom Riders—in order to bolster support for major reform. The White House, in contrast, became even more invested in pursuing angles that might calm activists.[128]

In 1963, the Kennedy White House still held to its fundamental caution and fear of disruption and disorder, but by midyear its strategy had changed. The nation saw media images of confrontations between the protesters and police, including a violent scene against protesters in Birmingham, Alabama, as well as the "bombing of Black churches, homes, and establishments by white extremists."[129] As these scenes reinforced both the moral stakes of civil rights and the potential for serious, lasting social disorder, the Kennedy administration changed tactics. Reversing his original determination not to pursue legislation, Kennedy unveiled a civil rights bill that would eventually inform the legislation passed in 1964, after his death.

The other major break with past patterns was Kennedy's national address highlighting the moral concerns of civil rights:

The heart of the question is whether all Americans are to be afforded equal rights and equal opportunities, whether we are going to treat our fellow Americans as we want to be treated. If an American, because his skin is dark, cannot eat lunch in a restaurant open to the public, if he cannot send his children to the best public school available, if he cannot vote for the public officials who represent him, if, in short, he cannot enjoy the full and free life which all of us want, then who among us would be content to have the color of his skin changed and stand in his place? Who among us would then be content with the counsels of patience and delay?[130]

Though not the first to speak on this issue—Truman had done so—Kennedy addressed the nation directly on the pressing and painful questions: public accommodation, school desegregation, and the longstanding directives to be patient and accept slow, incremental progress. This speech was in some senses a clear rebuke of the Eisenhower approach to civil rights.

But the relative boldness of Kennedy's language disguised his familiar hesitance about the civil rights movement itself. The speech and the legislation were part of an effort to calm protest efforts and limit high-profile, disruptive events like the March on Washington, about which the White House had significant reservations.[131] Despite these reservations, the Kennedy State Department hoped to frame the march as a sign of racial progress, a narrative that was undermined by the horrific bombing of a Black church in Birmingham, Alabama, several weeks later.[132] The bombing, which resulted in the death of four young girls, heightened the urgent need and moral imperative for federal intervention.

Kennedy's presidency ended abruptly in November 1963 with an assassin's bullet. But his successor, Lyndon Johnson, would continue the transformative presidential politics that, however reluctantly, had been set in motion.

Lyndon Johnson and the Civil Rights Revolution

Lyndon Johnson's civil rights legacy is sometimes captured in one quotation: "We've lost the South for a generation." Though the record on whether Johnson actually said this is unclear, the sentiment offers a powerful frame for understanding. Progress is linked to backlash, and the backlash is linked to geography. Implicit in the quotation is the idea that Johnson's moral compass on the issue was strong enough to guide him past trifling issues like political repercussions.

The full story of civil rights, race, and the Johnson presidency, however, is more complicated. After Kennedy's assassination in 1963, the moral imperative for Johnson to complete that work was self-evident. Later efforts to ensure voting rights, fair housing, and more universal social supports through the Great Society and the War on Poverty were the product of multiple, conflicting political forces.

Like Democratic presidents in the recent past, Johnson was pulled toward progress by civil rights leaders.[133] Their growing clout, bolstered by the moral clarity of their messages on civil rights and voting rights, altered the political calculus for Johnson, who could go further, and more disruptively, than his predecessors in a reversal of his role as Senate majority leader during the debate about the 1957 Civil Rights Act.[134] But the political forces driving past presidents to maneuver cautiously and preserve existing arrangements also weighed on Johnson, causing him to back away from the civil rights cause at crucial moments.

The 1964 Civil Rights Act

Just one week after Kennedy's assassination, Johnson addressed a joint session of Congress and assured the nation that he would complete the work that Kennedy had begun that year. "No memorial oration or eulogy could more eloquently honor President Kennedy's memory than the earliest possible passage of the civil rights bill for which he fought so long," insisted Johnson.[135] By framing the legislation in these terms, Johnson created new moral urgency and new political cover for legislative holdouts.

Despite the compelling nature of the argument, Johnson had doubts that the bill would pass before the 1964 election.[136] And the bill was certainly shaped by conservative forces in the legislative process. In the House of Representatives, a key obstacle was the chairman of the Rules Committee, Howard Smith, who, in the words of historian Julian Zelizer, was "still fighting the Civil War"—on the Confederate side.[137]

As with so many bills before—the Dyer anti-lynching bill, the 1957 Civil Rights Act—the real test was the Senate filibuster. Southern senators—including some signatories of the Southern Manifesto nearly a decade earlier—organized to take turns holding the floor, hoping to delay the legislation. Ending the filibuster required bringing on Republican votes, and so Republican leader Everett Dirksen negotiated for a weakened Equal Employment Opportunity Commission (EEOC) and greater local control over the enforcement of job discrimination laws.[138] The dynamics of the legislature narrowed the scope of the bill, but notably, the Southern wing of the Democratic Party was no longer wielding veto power over the process.

In addition to carrying out Kennedy's legacy and responding to activist pressure, Johnson was deeply invested in leaving a legacy as a president who achieved big things. His 1964 election victory amplified this ambition. But even before that, we see how Johnson's interest in amassing legislative accomplishments helped to overcome his caution about the political fallout that would accompany major changes to the racial status quo.

And the 1964 bill did change the status quo. By enacting a federal prohibition on racial discrimination in "places of public accommodation," the bill effectively made Jim Crow illegal.[139] This was a direct rebuke to Southern lawmakers (and others) who had insisted that such discrimination was essential to local culture and autonomy. The 1964 bill asserted federal control over private businesses, as well as employers, and created mechanisms for enforcing these new rules. In other words, this legislation revived the federal intervention in the service of equality promised in the Civil War amendments one hundred years earlier.

Civil rights opponents reacted. Strom Thurmond (R-SC) called the bill "the most unreasonable and unconstitutional legislation that has ever been considered by the Congress."[140] The constitutional framing became a more prominent line of critique, as arguments about racial mixing and purity had fallen out of public favor.[141] The constitutional threat and federal overreach of the civil rights legislation became a central focus of Arizona Senator Barry Goldwater's campaign to challenge Johnson in the fall election.

The 1964 election was a political triumph for the civil rights bill and for Johnson's other achievements in the preceding year. You did not have to squint to see the seeds of what would be an eventual backlash against this approach, but for the moment those objections appeared to be contained. Goldwater made historic gains for a Republican candidate in the old Confederacy—but pretty much nowhere else. The Republican senator's principled stance against federal overreach failed to attract a serious coalition, and the election was a blowout. But Johnson's victory concealed how unsettled politics had been by the president's commitment to addressing the civil rights question head on.

Two portentous developments during the nomination process highlight the tumult in the Democratic coalition. First, in the Democratic primaries, Alabama Governor George Wallace gained a bit of traction, even outside the South. Wallace's populist message landed with audiences in Wisconsin and Indiana.[142] The other development happened in the lead-up to the Democratic National Convention. Although Johnson's renomination was not in question, tensions over delegate seating showed the extent to which race issues were not resolved. The Mississippi delegation had been selected by a process that excluded African Americans. A group calling themselves the Mississippi Freedom Democratic Party (MFDP), led by Fannie Lou Hamer, challenged the regular delegation and sought to replace them with their own, more inclusive slate of delegates. As political scientists Sidney Milkis and Dan Tichenor explain, Hamer testified to the credentials committee that "she and the MFPD viewed the delegate fight as part of a broader battle for the right to register to vote—to 'become first-class citizens.'"[143]

While the MFDP's message resonated with much of what Johnson was trying to do, the confrontation leading up to the convention highlighted the president's impulse to compromise. Negotiations between Johnson and civil rights attorney Joseph Rauh yielded two at-large seats for the MFDP, a promise that the regular delegation would be seated but had to pledge to support the Johnson ticket, and long-term changes in the rules of the Democratic Party.[144] Johnson wanted to avoid further disruption at his nominating convention, but the compromise riled the MFDP delegates, who, in the words of Hamer, "didn't come all this way for no two seats."[145]

The summer of 1964 was early in Johnson's disruption of the racial status quo—major legislation was yet to come. But already the stakes of the new circumstances were becoming clear. Johnson would have to navigate a political world in which backlash politics was ascendant, while at the same time activists were increasingly, and more vocally, dissatisfied with incremental progress. The compromises of the past would no longer suffice. In the general election, the popular civil rights bill was a political winner, and Goldwater's project showed much less promise. Johnson was emboldened to push further in his policy agenda. But the evidence for what racial disruption could do to politics was already there.

Voting Rights

The 1964 bill had included some provisions for voting rights, but activists asserted that it had not gone far enough. In practice, only about half of African Americans in the South were able to vote.[146]

Despite the apparent nature of the problem, Johnson had not wanted, initially, to push for voting rights. The country still had to "digest" a major civil rights bill, and the clash over the Mississippi delegation at the convention showed the limits of Johnson's appetite for further political disruption. Once again echoing past presidents, he saw championing voting rights as a potential threat to his larger social agenda.[147]

But pressing on, civil rights activists continued to demonstrate the need for further government action to ensure the right to vote. The march from Selma to Montgomery, Alabama, vividly showed the administration, the Congress, and the public that federal action was imperative as officials unleashed violence on peaceful marchers. As Jesse Rhodes writes in *Ballot Blocked: The Political Erosion of the Voting Rights Act*, "Facing a swelling tide of public opinion, the president finally made an irrevocable commitment to voting rights reform."[148]

When Johnson addressed a joint session of Congress on March 15, 1965, he connected the cause of voting rights to both democracy and moral righteousness. Despite his previous reluctance, Johnson had now brought the unique power of the presidency to the cause of voting rights.

His remarks echoed his statements about civil rights, and he adopted the phrase "we shall overcome," applying it to Americans' collective need to "overcome the crippling legacy of bigotry and injustice."[149]

The bill that resulted lived up to many Southern complaints and fears. Not only had Johnson brought the communicative power of the presidents to the issue, but with the passage of the Voting Rights Act, the executive branch would also have an expanded role. The administration of voting, long understood to be under state and local purview, was now subject to federal oversight. The legislation provided for some jurisdictions to be "covered" by a formula indicating potential problems, and while not all of these jurisdictions were in the South, they were sufficiently concentrated there that the South could claim to have been singled out. In other words, with the growth of federal power and the recognition that Southern distinctiveness was in fact at odds with the nation's laws and values, Johnson's presidency had upended the foundations of the received racial order.

The Civil Rights Act and the Voting Rights Act had transformed race and public policy in the United States. But they had not transformed the realities of Black life in communities across the nation. Unrest in the Watts neighborhood of Los Angeles followed an incident of police violence. Reports from the Johnson White House revealed a president dismayed that his efforts were not enthusiastically received. Amid fears of more urban rioting, Johnson's inner circle became increasingly preoccupied with the possibility of white backlash and attuned to public concerns about crime and what Vice President Hubert Humphrey deemed "extremely hostile racial attitudes" among white Americans.[150]

Moreover, major policy change did not prevent a growing divide between the president and the civil rights movement. The movement itself was increasingly split between those who favored a more radical approach and those who chose establishment politics. Civil rights leaders, including King, began to vocalize their condemnation of the Vietnam War, deepening the rift with the White House.

Although unprepared to deal with the complex response to the earlier bills, Johnson knew that the civil rights revolution was incomplete. The president championed a bill prohibiting housing discrimination, which eventually passed after three attempts in Congress. The politics of the bill were delicate, as a period of backlash had already begun. In 1967, as communication scholar Steven Goldzwig recounts, "many Americans and their representatives also anticipated another summer of violent disturbances and they were in no mood for a civil rights package that would in any way signal compromise with violent forces."[151] The assassination of Martin Luther King Jr. in April 1968 revealed exactly which forces posed the most violent threat to social tranquility, even if many voters still saw "urban riots" as the main threat. After King's murder and the resulting upheaval around the nation, Johnson presented the housing bill as "the best and most concrete mode for healing division in the social hierarchy."[152] Johnson had added another major piece of legislation to his record, but the country was still filled with both those who felt that his transformation had gone too far and those who saw it as incomplete.

Racial Transformation and the Tragedy of Lyndon Johnson

Under the rules of the Twenty-Second Amendment, Johnson was eligible to run again in 1968. Viewed from a certain angle, Johnson's presidency had been a major success: a 1964 landslide, a formidable legislative record, and breakthrough civil rights legislation. There was little doubt that Johnson's domestic record had changed the country. But the Vietnam War had distracted him, and his violation of his campaign promises not to escalate the war had divided his party. As the 1968 nominating contest drew near, war critic Senator Eugene McCarthy (D-MN) mounted a campaign to challenge the president—and attracted serious support.

On March 31, 1968, in Johnson's address to the nation on the war in Vietnam, he announced that he would not seek reelection.

Even after Johnson's announcement, the war in Vietnam continued to drive unrest in the Democratic coalition and throughout the country. It is the Vietnam War, not backlash against civil rights, that scholars associate with the downfall of Lyndon Johnson. But the two issues are closely related.

In Johnson's March 31 speech, he linked his decision to the issue of division in the nation, invoking Lincoln:

> And in these times as in times before, it is true that a house divided against itself by the spirit of faction, of party, of region, of religion, of race, is a house that cannot stand.
>
> There is division in the American house now. There is divisiveness among us all tonight. And holding the trust that is mine, as President of all the people, I cannot disregard the peril to the progress of the American people and the hope and the prospect of peace for all peoples.[153]

The division that Johnson spoke of referred not strictly to debates about the wisdom of the war itself but also about the cultural and social changes that drew war opponents, civil rights activists, and other social movements together. Johnson's presidency had opened up questions about what society would look like after old hierarchies disappeared. Lyndon Johnson himself would step off the political stage, but many other politicians would come forward to offer their answers.

5

Law and Order

NIXON AND WATERGATE

IN HER JULY 25, 1974, speech explaining why President Richard Nixon's actions in the break-in at Democratic Party headquarters in the Watergate Office Building deserved impeachment, Representative Barbara Jordan (D-TX) tied her role in the process to the racial evolution of the Constitution. When the Constitution was signed, she said, "I was not included in that 'we the people.'" Her eventual inclusion, she went on, was the reason why "my faith in the Constitution is whole; it is complete; it is total," and why she would not allow the Constitution to be abused by an errant president. Her speech went on to explain the meaning of impeachment and why the president's behavior warranted such a drastic step. This chapter brings together these three themes: the inextricable linkage between race and American institutions; Nixon's lawless behavior; and the need for members of Congress to overcome their historical reluctance to impeach.

Richard Nixon is best known as the only American president to resign in disgrace. Compared with other figures of the era, his role in the politics of racial backlash is secondary and modest. But Nixon's path to office in 1968 and the dilemmas he faced as the first post–civil rights president share common features with the presidencies of Andrew Johnson and Donald Trump: scrambled party politics, loosening norms, and populism that eventually gave way to lawlessness. This chapter draws the connection between the racial politics of Nixon's campaigns and presidency and the politics of the Watergate scandal. In considering Watergate, we look not only at administration wrongdoing but also at how an altered political environment shaped the response of Nixon's political opponents in Congress.

We begin with Nixon's 1968 nomination as his party struggled to respond to the disruption of the Johnson years. More than in the 1860s or the twenty-first century, Nixon was the product of a Republican Party torn over how to position itself in response. Party leaders wanted to avoid a repeat of 1964, in which Goldwater's "principled opposition" to federal civil rights legislation had divided the party and alienated the mainstream of the electorate. At the same time, political conditions had worsened for Johnson across a variety of dimensions, and public concern about the riots, protesters, and unrest surrounding social change provided a ripe opportunity for the opposition party— as did the defection of Southern voters and elites from the Democratic Party. More than the other backlash presidents covered in this book, Nixon sometimes veered away from the harshest backlash perspectives and choices. Nevertheless, we can find useful parallels between the eras, both in how the parties flailed in addressing a transformed political environment and in how Nixon's candidacy, even in a very different era, still reaped both the benefits and the dilemmas of post-disruption politics.

Compared with the post–Civil War struggles between Andrew Johnson and the radical Republicans, or the controversies of the Trump presidency, Watergate looks like a scandal relatively removed from racial politics. Nevertheless, scholars still debate about what Watergate really meant. Was it about an administration filled with corrupt officials, with the biggest crook at the top? Or should we look more closely at institutions and a context that featured an excessively powerful presidency as well as larger and more complex forces in a contentious political era? In this chapter, I argue that these forces—presidential corruption and lawlessness, and the political context in which Watergate unfolded—are deeply connected.

The combination of presidential lawlessness and blurred institutional norms links Nixon to Andrew Johnson and Trump. In each case, new and conflicting political imperatives about how to react to a new reality leave questions about what presidents can and cannot get away with—and what kind of behavior is subject to the ultimate presidential punishment of impeachment. With the benefit of two cases, separated by a bit more than a century, to consider in addressing these questions, this chapter also begins to theorize about the ways in which presidential lawlessness is built into racial backlash appeals. For instance, the articles of impeachment drawn up against Nixon by the House Judiciary Committee accuse Nixon of using the power of the presidency to encroach on the constitutional prerogatives of the other branches and to delegitimize the opposition. What is more, the congressional dynamics that led to impeachment derived from the racial politics of the late 1960s. The Huston Plan, an effort early in the Nixon administration to use state power against political enemies, targeted Black political movements. African American legislators were among the earliest to call for Nixon's impeachment, sometimes tying the administration's corruption to its neglect of Black communities. Watergate may not have been all or even mostly about race, but it was very much rooted in the racial politics of the day.

Nevertheless, the distinctions between Nixon and the other backlash cases explored in this book deserve serious attention. Nixon is often described as a "middle way" candidate in a party that was negotiating the post–civil rights political landscape, and this characterization factored into his downfall as well.[1] That Nixon built a political coalition within his own party in the absence of a political base puts him in a position comparable to that of party outsiders Andrew Johnson and Donald Trump. Racial politics also informed the actions of Nixon's opponents, from their initial misgivings about his presidency to the consolidation of opposition among ambitious congressional Democrats as his presidency progressed.[2] Especially important were the emergent culture war, heightened in the 1972 election, and the decline of the unspoken and unwritten rules that had governed politics for decades. This combination redefined the stakes of the conflict between the parties and opened up new possibilities for addressing presidential scandal.

The Racialized 1968 Election

The 1968 election is consistently depicted as a unique turning point in American electoral history. Scholars of partisan polarization identify the 1968 contest and its dynamics as the basis for the racial, geographic, and ideological sorting that characterizes twenty-first-century party identification. Although not all scholars agree about the origins of racial polarization—Eric Schickler and Hans Noel identify it as emerging decades earlier—the crystallization of the political system around "liberal" and "conservative" identities in the late 1960s, merging race and other policy commitments, remains a central tenet of the study of polarization.[3] Edward Carmines and James Stimson identify race as the key factor in "party transformation" in the 1960s.[4] Lilliana Mason links the phenomenon of "social sorting"—divides between racial identities and attitudes that have come to define conflict between Republicans and Democrats—to the civil rights era.[5] Although not the sole driver of such accounts, race is at the center of them. Opposition to civil rights mapped onto conservative priorities of limiting the scope of the federal government.[6] The electorate began to permanently divide along racial lines as well as racial attitudes.

What does it mean to characterize 1968 as a distinctly "racialized" election? In contrast with past elections, in which both parties tried to both edge out the other as the champion of civil rights and push race off the agenda as much as possible, the 1968 election saw race infused into an array of cultural and economic issues emphasized in the campaign. The most evident of these was law and order, which took on kaleidoscopic meaning: It could implicate crime, or protests against the Vietnam War and civil rights demonstrations, or violent urban unrest. In the campaign context, conservatives wrestled with how to frame these law-and-order arguments. Pollsters regularly classified responses about concern over "unrest" in ways that merged civil rights and antiwar demonstrations.[7]

This connection is borne out by the survey questions posed as well as the answers. In April 1967, the Louis Harris and Associates poll asked, "Do you think by his coming out against the war in Vietnam, Martin

Luther King is helping or hurting the civil rights cause or don't you think it will make much difference one way or the other?" Fifty-nine percent of respondents said that King's stance was hurting the civil rights cause, compared with just 3 percent who said that his stance would help.[8] A University of Michigan survey reported small numbers of respondents who were worried about "riots, civil disturbances, revolutions, uprisings, and rebellions (not specifically mentioned in connection with race)."[9]

One prominent explanation for Nixon's narrow 1968 victory is his successful framing of the election around law-and-order issues. Although his stances at times left him vulnerable to comparisons with Wallace, which he had hoped to avoid, Nixon's campaign was largely able to persuade large swaths of the public that (1) law and order was an important issue, and (2) the former vice president had a better vision for maintaining it than did the sitting vice president. The law-and-order issue unified the Republican Party at its 1968 convention and in the platform, whereas specific plans about how to end the Vietnam War created division.[10] As of September 1968, Nixon also led in the polls with those who were more concerned about crime and felt "personally uneasy" walking on the streets.[11]

Nixon's Path to the Nomination

After the 1964 election, the Republican Party was wary about divisive nominations. In 1968, compared with the Democrats, they looked especially unified and organized.[12] Nixon won a victory over his primary rivals that seemed as straightforward as it was decisive.

But how straightforward was it really? Several elements of the 1968 Republican nomination contest deserve our attention. First, the nature of the contest illustrates how the civil rights politics of the 1960s shaped conflict within the Republican Party. Relatedly, the mounting tensions between different visions of the party led to a turning point for Black Republicans. Finally, Nixon's nomination depended on courting the South, specifically on civil rights and social issues. Nixon proved adept at assembling a winning coalition for the nomination, and he expanded that coalition to squeak out a close victory in the general election. How does this square with not belonging to a distinct political movement, a defining characteristic of troubled post-disruption presidents? Andrew Johnson was a man without a party. Donald Trump sought the Republican nomination after also flirting with both the Democratic and the Reform Parties. Compared with these two, Nixon was a party stalwart. Closer inspection of Nixon's pathway to the nomination also illustrates that it was his mastery of the twentieth-century nomination process that enabled him to create a core of personal support within the party.[13]

The three main contenders for the 1968 nomination show how much the fissures in the Republican Party had reorganized around race. George Romney, who competed with Nixon to be the favorite of party leaders, especially moderates disheartened in 1964 by Goldwater, had a strong track record as a supporter of civil rights.[14] On the other end of the spectrum, Ronald Reagan sought to capitalize on his law-and-order record as governor of California and position himself as the conservative candidate. Nixon's efforts to position himself as the compromise candidate between these two demonstrated the growing connection between anti-government conservatism and racial conservatism.

The impossibility of Nixon's efforts to find a "middle way" on civil rights after Johnson's transformational presidency is crucial for understanding race in the 1968 election and how it shaped Nixon's presidency. The fragmentation of the Republican Party over its response to the civil rights advances of the 1960s—from embracing them to running in opposition to them—set the stage for Southern support to be pivotal in Nixon's nomination.

In the spring of 1968, Nixon agreed with Strom Thurmond to "ease" federal enforcement of desegregation policies under a Nixon administration.[15] The future trajectory of the Republican Party was unclear at this point: While moderates appeared ascendant, from Romney to the Senate victory of Edward Brooke, backlash language had already come to define party stances. Even the moderate Black Republican Brooke had run for a Massachusetts Senate seat as the candidate of law and order as well as civil rights.[16] The looming possibility of a conservative turn in the party, focused on the nexus of issues identified with civil rights, played an important role in nomination politics and the convention that year.[17] The 1968 convention was "full of contradictions," in the words of Leah Wright Rigueur; Nixon himself aimed to portray himself as the moderate choice while taking actions that suggested the anti–civil rights South would call the important shots.[18] The selection of Spiro Agnew as a running mate was an especially divisive clue in this regard. Agnew turned out to be not only an effective campaigner in the South but also a central part of the campaign's populist turn. The Humphrey campaign ran an advertisement that consisted of nothing but laughter at the idea of Agnew in the White House. As Rick Perlstein documents, these commercials could be interpreted—and were—as liberals laughing not only at Agnew but at the listener. Such impressions contributed to an overall populist tenor of victimhood that was important to the racialization of the 1968 election.[19]

The decisions by the Nixon campaign clarified the choice facing moderates, perhaps especially Black Republicans trying to carve out a place for themselves in the party coalition. Analysis of the 1968 nomination contest reveals a deep tension in the scholarly accounts of this political moment. Joseph Lowndes and others emphasize Nixon's adaptation of white backlash themes to make them more palatable for the broader electorate. Nixon was not George Wallace, and he for the most part let Wallace occupy that lane. Yet scholars writing about the internal politics of the Republican Party emphasize that Nixon's strategic moves sharpened divisions, especially between moderates and Black Republicans and the rest of the party.[20] Nixon could moderate, and he could even carve out a position "between support for and opposition to" civil rights measures.[21] But he could not resolve these differences and make himself acceptable to both groups across the civil rights divide.

This dilemma is not novel or unique; indeed, it is one of the central themes of this book. Presidents and presidential candidates, tasked with building broad coalitions, first to win the nomination and then the presidency, are routinely faced with the irreconcilability of making racial progress and satisfying the demands of racially conservative white voters.[22] Nixon, however, was able to build a tenuous presidential coalition in 1968 and expand it in 1972, while also inspiring some fervent political opponents. What is more, because his opponents were alienated on the basis of race, the legitimacy of Nixon's presidency was undermined from the outset and a sense of disapproval became pervasive on an issue that eluded compromise.

Observing the complexity of Nixon's support coalition provides a powerful correction to the standard backlash thesis. Although racial compromise is deeply baked into American political institutions and great disruption ensues when these compromises are abrogated, such disruptions haves not been entirely driven by negative responses to racial change. Reactionary forces are of course part of the equation, and the system tends to recalibrate in cautious and inegalitarian ways. But backlash language is not an automatic political juggernaut, and racist appeals, whether overt or subtle, do not confer unmitigated political advantage. What happens to the political system in these moments after transformation is not a linear correction. It is a manifestation of rules becoming fuzzy and ambiguous, creating fertile ground for lawless populism—but also for the system to push back against it.

Finding a Middle Way in the General Election

The key to understanding Nixon's 1968 campaign is yet again to appreciate the full scope of its contradictions. Nixon sought to strike the impossible political balance of "straddling" racial conservatism and the basic imperatives of existing civil rights policy. This approach was also central in driving a wedge through the Democratic coalition. At times, these objectives overlapped, but they are distinct: Pressing at divisions among Democrats sometimes required pursuing more liberal policies, like the Philadelphia Plan for racial employment quotas, which pitted organized labor against African Americans. Charting a course between racial conservatism and racial liberalism required, at times, a disparity between Nixon's speech and his actions. And knowing that it also required speaking differently to different audiences, Nixon very deliberately hired three different speechwriters.[23]

It was not only Republicans who had to figure out their path forward in a new, post–civil rights political world. As the Democratic presidential nominee, Hubert Humphrey also sought to package his campaign in a way that would appeal to "white ethnics" in key cities and offer a law-and-order sensibility.[24] This point underscores a key theme of this book: We are not looking only at racial and ideological polarization after 1968 but also at racial compromises. Democrats, as Paul Frymer and others have noted, also sought to distance themselves from the concerns of African Americans. The sorting that occurred when Southern Democrats abandoned the Democratic Party in 1968—and chose a third-party option in George Wallace—is only part of the story. Another part of the story is the transition in the wake of civil rights legislation. Once legal equality had been established, some civil rights supporters were hesitant to embrace forms of equality that more deeply penetrated American social life. The 1968 election was racialized in the sense that race was incorporated into both new and familiar national political debates. Racialization in 1968 differed from racialization in 1864, when the cause of ending slavery was embraced as it had never been in past elections, and it was different from the racialization we will see in 2016 (chapter 7), when attitudes about race and immigration drove party choice in unprecedented ways. Instead, the proliferation of the "social issue" in 1968 shows race becoming part of a larger constellation of issues concerned with traditional life and morality, crime, housing, and school policy.[25]

The third-party candidacy of George Wallace also contributed to the racialized nature of the 1968 election. Wallace ran as an explicitly backlash candidate, building on his segregationist record and his critiques of how liberal governance had upended society and social order. As Wallace biographer Dan Carter observes, "Wallace simply erased the line between antiwar and civil rights protests, between heckling protesters and street muggers."[26] The blurring of these distinctions would prove relevant to the linkage between Nixon's abuses of power and the politics of race. The presence of a Southern segregationist in the campaign forced Nixon to navigate his position around race issues and distance himself from the Wallace positions that might be most off-putting to mainstream voters. But the Wallace campaign also gave Nixon an opportunity to make himself look moderate and measured by comparison, even as the two candidates sometimes competed for the same votes.[27]

A turning point for Nixon's attempt to configure his position on civil rights came in September 1968, less than two months from the general election. In a televised speech in North Carolina, Nixon's attempt to have it both ways began to unravel, at least according to some audiences. An editorial in the *Washington Post* titled "Law and Disorder" criticized the presidential candidate for advocating a position ripe for disorder: supporting civil rights law but opposing its enforcement.[28] Other responses to Nixon's line of argumentation were even harsher, suggesting that Nixon had clarified where he would come down on school integration debates by promising voters he would handle the issue, in the words of Roy Wilkins, with a "Wallace touch."[29] Nixon's statements about the enforcement of the law through the US Department of Health, Education, and Welfare, in North Carolina and elsewhere, attracted criticism from Black opinion leaders. An article in the *Chicago Daily Defender* suggested that any questions about Nixon's stances had "been resolved," and that the presidential candidate appeared to hope that Black voters would not notice the contradiction in his stance supporting the law but opposing its enforcement.[30]

Nixon's televised Charlotte speech and the response to it, combined with the role played by the South (especially the influence exerted by Thurmond) in Nixon's nomination and running mate selection, marked a turning point for the campaign. Nixon's comments were received, especially in the Black press, as affirmation that when a choice had to be made, he would tilt toward the needs of the South. Civil rights without robust enforcement were not civil rights at all. Nixon would continue to promise a middle course on civil rights, and his administration would even make some progress on desegregation. But the political game had changed—Nixon had sent a broad signal about what side he would take in a struggle between African Americans and segregationist Southerners. Nixon had tried throughout 1968 to reposition his campaign as a "respectable" alternative between two extreme positions. What happened that fall was subtle and telling. The "in-between" position, also the default position or the moderate position, was merged with what was ultimately a conservative position—on the side of white Southerners. There was no true middle course. As a result, Nixon's electoral efforts became indelibly linked with the idea of a "Southern strategy" to appeal to disaffected Democrats and civil rights opponents in the South.[31]

The racial themes of the 1968 election clarified that Humphrey, a multi-decade champion of civil rights within the party, was the candidate of civil rights, and Nixon responded by changing his strategy from his approach in 1960, when he tried to court Black votes.[32] New fissures were emerging between old and young, between traditional and new constituencies, and, most centrally for 1968, between pro- and antiwar factions. These new areas of contention built on some of the old fault lines, but the distinction between the two parties on race was much clearer than in the past. The result for the electoral dynamics in 1968 were divisions both inside the Democratic Party and between the parties.

On the Republican side, Nixon's embrace of populism had the eventual effect of changing the meaning of conservatism. In 1968, conservative media figures, who were not always impressed with Nixon's conservatism, recoiled from George Wallace's populism because they saw it as being at odds with conservatism.[33] Populist rhetoric not only constructed a "people" unified by (implied) whiteness—described as the "forgotten Americans"—but also relied on a sense of instilled victimhood at the hands of a corrupt elite.[34] Despite the qualms of conservative movement leaders, Nixon leaned on these themes in his 1968 campaign. Populist appeals surrounding race were especially prominent in Nixon's Charlotte speech, in which he suggested that the South ought not to be a "whipping boy" and suggested that federal enforcement of the laws was the strong picking on the weak (localities).[35] These populist formulations altered the foundations of conservatism, merging commitment to racial hierarchy with both a veneration of the ordinary and a sense of victimhood and anti-elitism.[36] This sense of victimhood did more than shift the meaning of conservative ideology. It also was a key element of Nixon's paranoid and aggressive behavior toward political opponents, which ultimately led to his near-impeachment and resignation.

For all three of the backlash presidents explored in this book, populism played a key role and helps to answer questions about the mechanisms connecting racial transformation to the politics of impeachment. Populism offers two advantages. First, it provides the necessary ideological flexibility to presidential candidates seeking to manipulate the changing informal rules of the political game. Andrew Johnson's early populism emphasized the needs of Southerners and former Confederates. For Nixon, populism was the rhetorical glue binding the victimhood of the Southern strategy with the respectability he sought to establish when appealing to other groups. And as we shall see in chapter 7, populism gave Donald Trump a way to maneuver around Republican divisions and provide plausible deniability for his racialized campaign. In this sense, populism is not simply a backlash, *herrenvolk* response—it is an adaptation to a polity that is newly in flux.

Second, populism eliminates the role of legitimate opposition. As we shall see in the rest of this chapter, the populist impulses of Nixon's time played out differently than in the 1860s or the polarized twenty-first century owing to the partisan dynamics of the late 1960s. Nixon's rejection of legitimate opposition did not take the form of partisan rhetoric or overt manipulation of party patronage machines; instead, he attempted to use modern bureaucracy to punish enemies and eliminate domestic dissent. These actions emanated directly from backlash politics and formed the foundation of the Watergate scandal.

Nixon as President

In the racialized election of 1968, Nixon had carved out a political identity, and he had shaped the meaning of that identity. Taking this middle course involved both answering to Southern leaders and moving away from the most extreme anti–civil rights positions. As president, Nixon faced the same dilemmas as well as the challenges of actually implementing policy. In some ways, the challenges he faced were not new— after all, the last three presidents had struggled over school desegregation. But Nixon's tenure in the White House was new and reactive, and thus the politics of his actions—some being more liberal, some leaning more conservative, and others charting a middle course—were different from the politics of his predecessors.

Like the presidents considered in chapter 4, Nixon's civil rights legacy is the subject of some contestation. His personal racism has been documented through the diary of his chief of staff, H. R. Haldeman, as well as revealed in his bigoted comments as captured on some of the White House tapes. On a policy level, Nixon once again stands out somewhat from the more overt racial hostility of the agendas embraced by Andrew Johnson and Donald Trump. School desegregation continued under the Nixon administration, and he did not interpret the 1968 election as a broad rejection of the civil rights progress under Lyndon Johnson. Instead, Nixon's approach to civil rights was guided by several factors. The first links back to familiar themes: the political promise to retrench and contain, while also facing the impossibility of that goal. Nixon had run on law and order as a general theme, and he had promised Southern constituencies that he would slow civil rights advances.[37] Yet the foundation of Nixon's political support was shaken when he was also confronted with the impossibility of moving backward. Nixon's circumstances were also notable for their new and reactive nature: As Johnson's successor, Nixon was maneuvering in a changed political environment, with shifting party coalitions, policy constraints, and informal expectations.

Several examples illustrate the difference between Nixon's efforts, on the one hand, to thread a delicate needle on civil rights policy and, on the other hand, to rip apart Democratic constituencies. When it came to administration decisions about desegregating schools, he took the needle-threading approach. Presidential directions to the US Department of Health, Education, and Welfare (HEW) slowed the desegregation of schools for the first time in several years, ultimately causing the resignation of HEW Secretary Leon Panetta.[38] The decision to enforce the law, but minimally and only to the letter of the law, had the impact of alienating people across the board. This included both Southerners, who perceived Nixon as having promised a greater break from the new civil rights regime, and the NAACP, which saw Nixon as wanting to "turn back the clock" and "side with the enemies of little Black children."[39] Enforcement problems also plagued the administration's record on employment and civil rights and left it open to considerable criticism from within, as well as from congressional Democrats and civil rights leaders.[40]

An example of the wedge approach was the "Philadelphia Plan" to implement affirmative action in the construction industry.[41] As a political maneuver, the Philadelphia Plan attracted about as many supporters as the needle-threading tactic; ultimately, when it came to be seen as a liberal, pro-Black policy to enact job quotas, it hardly endeared Nixon to any members of his coalition.[42] Yet it did not especially broaden his political support base either. Some scholars, particularly Dean Kotlowski, have cited this as evidence of Nixon's principled approach to race, one rooted in conservative principles of economic mobility.[43] Others have suggested that Nixon was a "preemptive" leader in proposing the Philadelphia Plan—a president who rode a wave of civil rights unease to the White House but then faced an increasingly established civil rights regime that was politically difficult to oppose directly.[44] As with initiatives for Black business promotion, the plan was an effort to signal to African American voters that the administration would help with economic advancement, while sidestepping some of the thornier issues around discrimination and civil rights enforcement.[45] That this approach was also a useful way to drive a wedge between two crucial elements of the Democratic coalition did not go unnoticed by civil rights leaders, including Clarence Mitchell and Bayard Rustin, who questioned both the motives and impact of the Philadelphia Plan.[46] Within the conservative fold, it also remained unclear whether Nixon had achieved his objectives; as figures like Kevin Philips and Pat Buchanan urged more clarity of strategy and attentiveness to white working-class votes, Nixon eventually backed away from efforts to court Black support.[47]

The Johnson administration had also left Nixon an avenue to pursue racially conservative policies not by rejecting the immediate past but by continuing it. As Elizabeth Hinton notes, Nixon "appropriated the regressive aspects" of the complex policy legacy left by Johnson's Great Society programs. Nixon's decisions to focus on urban crime control reflected the beliefs about inherent criminality in poor and Black communities that had begun to take hold among policymakers.[48] The turn in the Nixon administration toward crime control policies simultaneously worked to conceal more overtly racist ideas, and to legitimate new lines of racialized thinking.[49] Block grants, as Hinton notes, also became a way to use the policy process that restored state control even as the civil rights bills of the 1960s increased federal control.[50]

The other policy area where Nixon repudiated the civil rights era by splitting the difference was in voting rights. It was possible, at least in theory, to draw narrow distinctions between support for voting rights, concern about federal overreach, and sympathy with Southern grievance at having been made the "whipping boy" for national problems.[51] Ultimately, Nixon backed away from a voting rights proposal that would have effectively eliminated preclearance and eased federal controls on the South. The trajectory of the 1970 renewal of the Voting Rights Act, which highlighted both the political constraints on racial conservatism and the growing alliance of conservative Republicans and conservative Southern Democrats, reflected the newly unstable political terrain.

Nixon's political appeals in the 1968 election relied on the merging of several kinds of threats: threats from antiwar protesters, from agitators for social change (especially the threat of "changing neighborhoods"), from militant Blacks, and from the New Left. In the abstract, these threats to the traditional social order made for effective politics. Translating responses to them into policy while maintaining a somewhat patchwork coalition proved more difficult. As Seth Blumenthal explains in *Children of the Silent Majority*, Nixon's appeals to "ordinary" Americans against a disruptive minority bumped up against the fact that people who defined themselves as part of the wholesome and patriotic silent majority also sometimes participated in countercultural activities like antiwar protesting on campus and marijuana use.[52] What was left once the contested terrain of ordinariness had been carved up was racism, leaving Nixon bound by the backlash dilemma: Anti-Black politics were well defined, if unpopular, and national majorities were increasingly uncomfortable with both overt racism and too much progress and social integration. As a result, Nixon's political strategy depended in part on an evolving and obfuscated definition of who the "enemy" was.

The 1972 Election

Unlike Andrew Johnson before him or Trump afterward, Richard Nixon was able to assemble a national majority coalition for reelection. The 1972 election, though distinct from many of the others covered in this book, is relevant for our purposes in two ways. First, the Watergate scandal had its origins in the election campaign, when the break-in at DNC headquarters occurred. Second, the 1972 election demonstrated the consolidation and continuation of many of the party changes evident in 1968. The Democratic coalition continued to splinter over social questions and remained bound up in the debates about the Vietnam War. The connection between antiwar protests and broader conceptualizations of social disorder both divided the two parties from each other and informed divisions within each one.[53]

The early shakiness of the elite Republican coalition reflects two important contextual factors: that Nixon was perceived as weaker politically than he really was, and that his relationship with his own party was shakier than the eventual election returns would suggest.[54] The 1972 campaign, while successful, in many ways highlighted Nixon's political isolation from his party—the eventual victory was one for himself, not for the party.[55]

Divisions within the Democratic Party in the 1972 contest are well documented. The party's new reliance on primaries to select a presidential nominee gave an advantage to Senator George McGovern (D-SD), whose candidacy did not appeal to some of the traditional constituencies and leaders within the party. Several aspects of McGovern's candidacy illustrated the unsettling of political foundations. One was the process that allowed for the nomination of a candidate who was not competitive against a president who had been fairly unpopular in the past year. The Democratic Party in general was casting about in the post–civil rights period to find a political identity. The "rights revolution" had empowered new groups to make demands of the party and push for further social change, and civil rights leaders were renegotiating their role in the party after the victories of the Johnson presidency. McGovern was painted as a radical, countercultural figure associated with the phrase "acid, amnesty, and abortion."[56] The 1972 campaign set the course for Democrats for decades to come, orienting the party around concerns about appearing too radical or too indebted to the "special" interests of Blacks, feminists, and other excluded groups making claims on the political process.

Reevaluating Watergate

Watergate is typically described as a scandal arising from Nixon's personal shortcomings or the overreach of the modern presidency. One of the big debates is whether Watergate was really about "the cover-up or the crime." But where is race in this narrative? How did the emerging politics of the culture war in the 1968 and 1972 elections shape the administration's missteps and the country's response?

Making the case that Watergate was connected to the politics of race appears at first glance to have little to do with the standard story. When we look a bit closer, however, aided by recent scholarship interrogating the broader politics of Watergate, we see that it shares some themes with the impeachments of Andrew Johnson and Donald Trump: the role of race in the construction of political "enemies," the abuse of presidential power, and the breach of norms and institutional boundaries. Each of these themes connects to the racial politics of the Johnson and Nixon administrations and to the impact of destabilizing racial politics on political institutions.

The story of Watergate as a media event, centered on televised hearings and the journalism of *Washington Post* reporters Bob Woodward and Carl Bernstein, highlights the cover-up narrative. "What did the president know, and when did he know it?," as asked by Senator Howard Baker (R-TN), became the defining question. The "smoking gun" tape revealing that Nixon had interfered with the investigation and manipulatively cited national security to impede investigation of Watergate tipped the partisan scales and led Senate Republicans to contact Nixon privately and encourage him to resign, lest he be removed from office through an impeachment conviction. This version of the story, to be sure, emphasizes presidential abuse of power.

But the official documents of impeachment, reported from the House Judiciary Committee, focus on Nixon's abuse of presidential power undermining the public trust in ways that were not limited to the Watergate cover-up. Of course, the articles of impeachment cover the central efforts by the president to impede the Watergate investigation. But they also stress more substantive abuses of power, including Nixon's efforts to use the Internal Revenue Service (IRS) to attack political opponents. In other words, this analysis joins a growing body of commentary on Watergate that pushes back on the narrative that the event was mostly about the cover-up rather than the crime of a "third-rate burglary." Instead, the analysis here considers the events leading up to Watergate in the context of larger questions about how presidents use the office and how they justify such actions. The Watergate story begins not with the burglary or the October 1973 "Saturday Night Massacre," but with the Huston Plan for domestic surveillance of numerous groups and the ways in which Nixon sought to use his position to silence and harm political opponents of all kinds.

The second, related big question lies between interpretations that emphasize presidential character and those that emphasize social context.[57] The first interpretation, more common in popular depictions of Watergate, highlights Nixon as a "power-hungry executive" whose paranoia and other character flaws drove the scandals that ended his presidency. Ruth Morgan, summarizing the scholarship on Watergate in a 1996 review article, notes the scholarly interest in Nixon's "dangerous personality." Historians, on the other hand, tend to view Watergate as a "social crisis, a flashpoint for enmities born of Vietnam, the civil rights movement, and Nixon's lifelong clash with liberals."[58] Scholars have also been interested in what Watergate says about the growth of presidential power, an institutional story distinct from the social context story.[59] The objective of this chapter is to bridge these perspectives and, by drawing parallels with Andrew Johnson and Donald Trump, highlight how the context of political instability informed the election and behavior of a lawless president.

Enemies

The second article of impeachment cites Nixon's use of the FBI and attempted use of the IRS "in violation of the constitutional rights of citizens" to engage in illegal or inappropriate surveillance of political opponents. Known more colloquially as Nixon's "enemies list," this violation of the public trust has been connected to Nixon's personal shortcomings—his paranoia, his inability to withstand political opposition, and his willingness to blur the boundaries of the executive branch and his own political apparatus. Another aspect to these charges warrants its own scrutiny—the connection to racial backlash and the 1968 campaign's brand of law-and-order politics.

Who, after all, were some of these enemies? They were not all leaders on race issues, of course. But groups such as the Black Panthers figured prominently in an early version of White House efforts to use surveillance against political groups on the left. The Huston Plan, named for a young ideologue who drafted the plan in 1970, became a flashpoint as the public narrative of Watergate developed. In the spring of 1973, as the Senate held hearings on Watergate, the Huston Plan surfaced as evidence of the president's knowledge and approval of such politically charged surveillance. The plan, crafted by conservative White House aides Tom Huston and Bill Sullivan, with Nixon's approval, proposed the "surveillance" of political enemies. The groups considered "enemies" included New Left student groups, the Black Power movement, Marxist-Leninist parties, and the Puerto Rican independence movement.[60] The linkage between the list submitted and the broader racial politics of the moment was evident: The targets were "wartime dissenters, political radicals, and Nixon administration critics."[61]

A *New York Times* report by Seymour Hersh in 1973 focused on the Black Panthers as a target of the plan (along with potential foreign spies and "antiwar radicals"). According to Hersh, "One official who worked on the report [detailing the domestic surveillance program] described the most serious issue facing the Nixon White House in mid-1970 as 'the black problem,'" referring specifically to the Black Panthers and other "radical" groups.[62]

To the extent that Watergate and Nixon's scandals originated with surveillance of political opponents and crossing boundaries with federal agencies, the racial politics of the era are implicated. Just as Nixon regarded many of these activists as enemies, some Black leaders expressed a similar regard for the president and called for his impeachment as the scandal unfolded.

In July 1973, shortly after the Senate heard testimony about Nixon's surveillance activities, the national convention of the NAACP considered a call for Nixon's impeachment. The call for impeachment even suggested that the findings of the Watergate hearings might warrant the invalidation of the 1972 election A vocal proponent of this charge was Representative Parren Mitchell (D-MD), a founding member of the Congressional Black Caucus (and brother of Clarence Mitchell). At that time, these claims were hardly considered part of the political mainstream, and the proposal was ultimately rejected, as expected, by the convention body.[63] The organization's leaders did use the occasion to criticize Nixon's record on race, including his law-and-order politics.[64] As we'll see in chapter 7 with Trump's impeachment, the concerns of Black legislators that the president's offenses might rise to the level of impeachment started out as marginal but eventually became much more mainstream.

A year later, African American legislators, including Mitchell himself, began to draw together the Watergate charges of Nixon's corruption and abuse of power with their concerns that he had failed to serve Black America. Several Black legislators on the House Judiciary Committee told an ABC interviewer in May 1974 that they were convinced Nixon had committed enough "gross abuses of power" to warrant impeachment. These abuses of power were tied to racial concerns: Representative Andrew Young (D-GA) linked Nixon's alleged corruption to the economic problems experienced by the Black community. Foreshadowing the allegations levied against Trump, Representative Charles Rangel (D-NY) said that "President Nixon has made bigotry, which at one time was something one was ashamed to talk about, a very popular thing because you were more in line and more in tune with the administration."[65] Representative Mitchell picked up on this line of argument in another formal call for the president's impeachment. In an address to a real estate brokers meeting in Ohio and in a subsequent press release, he called for Nixon's impeachment because of his neglect of the Black community and its economic needs (this also occurred in May 1974).[66] Though there was little response at the time to Mitchell's call for Nixon's impeachment, it preceded House impeachment efforts by only a few months and underscored the connection between the administration's conduct and its record on race. Mitchell's call also directly challenged Nixon's claim that he supported African Americans in the form of economic advancement.

The impeachment issue continued to evolve in 1974. The House Judiciary Committee, with Representative Barbara Jordan playing a key role, eventually drafted impeachment articles. Race was not Nixon's only criterion for considering a group an enemy, nor was it determinative for those who, in turn, considered him an enemy. But race was an ever-present influence on the question of whether the president had violated his oath of office.

Abuse of Power

Abuse of power is a recurring theme in presidential impeachment crises, and Watergate was no exception. The problem of abuse of power is present in both the "cover-up"—the administration's efforts to hide the Watergate burglary and its connection to the president—and the "crime." Populist appeals and ideas connect racial backlash politics to presidential lawlessness. Here, we see a connection between the political backdrop of the time and the illegal, norm-breaking decisions made in the White House.

Let us turn first to the cover-up. The first impeachment article against Nixon referred to the abuses of power in his effort to thwart investigation into the 1972 burglary.[67] Two important turning points in the Watergate story illustrate how Nixon abused presidential power to cover up what had happened. The first, chronologically, was the incident known as the "Saturday Night Massacre," in which Nixon ordered the Attorney General Elliot Richardson to fire Special Prosecutor Archibald Cox. According to historian Timothy Naftali, the firing of Cox—after the resignations of Richardson and Deputy Attorney General William Ruckelshaus—"pushed America across a psychological line," attracting not only public and media attention but also, as a result, drawing the attention of members of the House of Representatives.[68]

The second turning point event was the "smoking gun" tape, which revealed that Nixon tried to use the CIA to curb an FBI investigation into the burglary, invoking bogus national security concerns in order to end the inquiry.[69] This abuse of power drew directly on the midcentury Cold War presidency and the power it had been allowed to accrue, a topic revisited in the next section on norms. This revelation also pushed some of Nixon's remaining allies in the Senate to encourage his resignation. Importantly, Nixon's fatal missteps grew out of an institutional arrangement that had been created to expand executive power in the name of national security. "National security," "executive privilege," and "presidential prerogative" are all contested terms that create boundaries around presidential power and that lack clear legal and political definitions. Of course, it is impossible to know the counterfactual: Would Nixon have been elected absent the social upheaval that came with antiwar protests and racial unrest? Would Nixon have been less paranoid and prone to lawless behavior if he had been elected, say, in 1960? Would the response to the Watergate scandal have been different had institutional norms and practices not been loosened by the civil rights era and the new political possibilities it opened up?

We'll never know the answers to these questions. But Watergate illustrates that the presidential use of different institutional capacities of the executive branch, the political construction of limits on those capacities, and the willingness of other political actors—namely Congress—to enforce these limits are all connected to political context.

How was Nixon's abuse of presidential power—his consistent commitment to amassing power in the presidency and using it to dominate other institutions—linked to the racial politics at the time? In *The Wars of Watergate*, Stanley Kutler describes Nixon's overall attitude toward Congress and conceptualization of American government as "the magic of the president and the people" at work solving the nation's problems, without a role for other institutions.[70] Populism informs such anti-institutional, president-centric ideas, and Nixon's brand of populism, as is so often the case, rested on racialized appeals and concepts. His populist appeals fit into a larger framework of both infusing the power of the "real" American people—the silent majority—into the office of the presidency and allowing that power to be used as necessary to defend the people's interests. As Michael Koncewicz notes, "[Nixon] felt that his willingness to bend the rules was justified during a period of civil unrest that was caused by the Left."[71] This logic certainly underpinned the abuse of the power Nixon used against political enemies, and he applied a similar logic in the Watergate cover-up—that he was protecting the presidency and the "mandate" of 1972.[72] In other words, once the presidency has been identified as the mouthpiece of the true and rightful (in this case, white) people, it is much easier to justify the consolidation of that power. Nixon's individualistic approach to the presidency and his emphasis on the "silent majority"—which seemed to be speaking more loudly than ever after the 1972 landslide—set the stage for this kind of thinking.

Norms and Institutional Boundaries

Related to presidential abuse of power, of course, are norms and institutional boundaries—the informal rules and understandings that limit what institutional actors can do. These rules not only limit presidential behavior but also apply to how other actors and institutions operate. One of the central themes of this book is that political norms are deeply rooted in racial orders; the disruption of these orders opens up questions about what institutions can do and how contending sides of the race issue might use them in new ways. We see changing norms and institutional boundaries at work in Watergate, both in the way the administration violated them in its attempt to use the FBI for political purposes and in the institutional response of Congress.

The midcentury FBI had no shortage of surveillance operations that were motivated by suspicion of activists on the left, including civil rights groups deemed by the bureau to be radical or extreme. But the Nixon White House pushed past the boundaries of FBI Director J. Edgar Hoover and his successor, L. Patrick Gray. The failure of the 1970 Huston Plan illustrates how the politics of race and social disorder informed Nixon's overstepping of institutional boundaries.[73] Hoover's FBI had been spying on a wide range of leftist activists for years, but the Huston Plan struck him as legally dubious and at odds with the bureau's independence.[74] At the center of Nixon's 1968 presidential campaign had been his drive to monitor groups he viewed as threats to social order and to the silent majority, and it was this that ultimately soured his relationship with the FBI and led to Associate Director Mark Felt's role as the "Deep Throat" informant who helped break open the Watergate scandal. Historian Beverly Gage has explicitly tied the struggle between Nixon and the FBI to administrative independence and norms.[75] Despite the FBI's involvement in past surveillance programs, its leaders resisted Nixon's encroachment on the agency's independence. In other words, one of the events in the lead-up to Watergate drew together racialized politics, reaction to social movements, the perception of social disorder, and the blurring (and reestablishment) of institutional norms.

The other area in which norms come into play is the role of Congress in initiating impeachment. In 1973, there was no one alive who had experienced a presidential impeachment. Members of Congress—namely those in the House of Representatives—needed to establish what an impeachment would look like. This included decisions about procedure, such as having the articles initially handled by the Judiciary Committee, as they had been in 1868.[76] But they also needed to think about how to make the case for beginning the process to remove a president from office, especially after an election victory like Nixon's in 1972. A crucial element of the process was the presence of liberals in Congress who had no reason to give Nixon any room or to defer to the long-standing, if unspoken, norm against using the presidential impeachment provisions in the Constitution.[77] On the contrary, in the post–civil rights political order, these sorts of institutionalist imperatives seemed to have faded away, leaving instead a nagging sense that both Nixon's racialized vision of the silent majority and the political motivations of at least some of the Democratic majority could not be reconciled. The pluralism and politeness of the past had given way when race entered mainstream electoral politics.

Both Nixon's decision to push back against norms and institutional boundaries in his request of the FBI and the decision of liberal Democrats to begin pushing for impeachment highlight a core argument of this book. Presidential impeachment is not simply a response to wrongdoing in the White House. The kinds of offenses that result in impeachment—often characterized in the process as abuse of power— occur at the margins of institutional boundaries when presidents push too far in a context of loosened norms. Also behind congressional motivations to impeach are questions about what would be acceptable in a new political environment. To contemplate this step, members of Congress need to be reasonably confident that the usual normative prohibitions on opposing the president will at least be weakened. Both of these factors were linked to the broader politics of racial unrest and the disruption of politics as usual by the changes brought about during the Johnson administration. In particular, the splintering of civil rights activists into more radical groups pushing for even greater change was connected to one of the central dynamics driving each of these moments: While some pushed for a return to the racial hierarchies of the past, others clamored for further change.

Legitimacy Twentieth-Century Style

Explanations of presidential impeachment also touch on the idea of legitimacy. In a comprehensive study of presidential impeachments published in 2020, a group of scholars note the role of national strife, including racial struggles, and divided government in determining whether a scandal blossoms into a full-fledged impeachment crisis.[78] Skowronek writes about the impeachment crises faced by opposition-party presidents whose authenticity eludes their critics.[79] It is not difficult to see why racial politics is repeatedly at the center of these legitimacy struggles.

And it is not difficult to see why this was just as true for Nixon as for Andrew Johnson and Donald Trump. While Nixon was more conventionally qualified and more moderate in his backlash politics, he provoked a similar dilemma for his fiercest critics early on in the 1968 campaign. His stances on civil rights enforcement and law and order alongside his construction of an implicitly white silent majority could not be reconciled with other visions of American democracy.

The feeling was mutual. Nixon's own denial of legitimate opposition ran through the entire Watergate scandal, from the thwarted Huston Plan and IRS surveillance to the enemies list and ultimately the interference in the 1972 election. The thread connecting Nixon's behavior to both Andrew Johnson's in the 1860s and Donald Trump's in the twenty-first century is the difficulty of being "president of all the people" in the wake of racial transformation. Nixon perhaps tried harder, at least superficially, to fulfill this obligation than the other two presidents. This difference is likely due to the unique structure of the party system in the twentieth century. Yet this balancing act proved impossible even under these conditions. Nixon's efforts at a middle way faltered both throughout his first campaign and once he took office, and civil rights supporters, especially African American leaders, remained unconvinced of the president's commitments.

Under political conditions in which delicately splitting the difference was no longer an option, Nixon also sought to eliminate political dissent when he could. It is not a coincidence that Nixon and Trump were both caught interfering with the election process. Nixon's interference is typically depicted in terms of his personality and paranoia, and sometimes also in partisan terms. Some of his other actions were about altering the executive branch to orient it toward personal loyalty.[80] But ultimately each of these actions was to prevent the other side—the side now associated with the political interests of nonwhites—from attaining power.

In sum, major changes to the racial status quo result in the elimination of existing blueprints for seeking the presidency and then being president. Politicians who can navigate these politics have tended to be those who effectively employ populist appeals, both evading and recasting new questions around race. These commitments and orientations follow them into office. Nixon's populism led to serial abuse of presidential power and shaky respect for legitimate opposition in a combustible and broadly dissatisfied political environment.

Ultimately, though the House committee approved impeachment articles, Nixon never faced a Senate trial. He resigned on August 9, 1974—the first, and thus far last, president to do so.

Not every aspect of the Watergate scandal and subsequent impeachment proceedings lines up with the other two cases considered in this book. Nixon is not a backlash figure on the same level with Andrew Johnson and Donald Trump. Racial attitudes had not sorted along partisan lines while Nixon was president, though his campaigns played a role in setting those forces in motion. The eventual abandonment of Nixon by

Republican members of Congress, as well as voters, is often cited as evidence that Watergate was less partisan than other impeachment crises. Nevertheless, race, ideology, and party all shaped this process.

As the beginning of this chapter notes, Barbara Jordan, one of the first African Americans to represent the South in Congress since Reconstruction, became a key figure in the House proceedings. Initial support for impeaching Nixon fell largely along ideological lines, with liberal Democrats supporting it and moderates and conservatives in both parties expressing more reservations.[81] While a Southern conservative, Sam Ervin, was one of the president's most active critics in the Senate, Southern Democrats were among Nixon's early defenders on the House Judiciary Committee.[82] In other words, as this chapter and the previous one have outlined, the racial transformation of the Johnson years disrupted existing party coalitions and assumptions about how politics should operate. In this context, the Democratic coalition had begun not only to shift in a more liberal direction on civil rights but also to think more expansively about political power and who held it. These new constituencies were less likely to buy Nixon's political project and thus were more amenable to impeachment at the outset. Much attention has been devoted to how moderates and conservatives came to oppose Nixon and eventually encourage his resignation. However, the process would probably not have gotten to that point without an initial core of legislators whose reservations about Nixon drove them to question his fitness to hold the presidency.

After Watergate

The period between Nixon's 1974 resignation and Reagan's 1981 inauguration represented neither a backlash period nor a clear move into a new racial era. Both Gerald Ford and Jimmy Carter seemed to back away from the emergent racial polarization of the time. Ford avoided the kinds of backlash appeals that had propelled Nixon into office. Carter was a racial liberal from the South, like Lyndon Johnson, but his approach to race issues betrayed both a different time and a different overall orientation.

In the administrations of Ford and Carter, we see a recalibration toward a new set of post–civil rights era norms and expectations about what the racial status quo would be and how presidents would uphold it. In both cases, we see evidence of personal commitment to equality. There is also evidence of the political imperative to smooth over relations with Southerners and other civil rights conservatives. We also see new triangulation and compromise over a mix of familiar and emerging issues. Ford, like Nixon, opposed forced busing.[83] He also signed a 1975 bill reinstating the citizenship of Robert E. Lee in an effort to "placate" angry Southern legislators claiming persecution of their region.[84]

Jimmy Carter's presidency is sometimes seen as a bridge between eras, though there is some disagreement among these characterizations about where exactly it fits. In some approaches, Carter represents the end of the New Deal Democratic era; his feuds with more traditional Democratic politicians and constituencies, the proponents of this approach point out, highlight the coalition's weakness.[85] Through another lens, Carter looks more like the beginning of a new era: He was the first president to take advantage of the newly reformed primary system and come to higher office as a relatively inexperienced governor, a path to the presidency that would become far more common in subsequent years. The nomination of Carter, a Southern moderate, also foreshadowed later moves by the Democratic Party, namely, the introduction of Super Tuesday to court moderates and Southern voters and the 1992 nomination of Arkansas Governor Bill Clinton.

Through the lens of race and civil rights, Carter also appears to be a transition president: His administration offered a preview of some of the ideas and tropes that would come to define the next era but had yet to settle into a central set of assumptions. We see both the rejection of pre–civil rights era demonstrations of "old-fashioned racism" and a struggle to figure out what would come next. Carter was a racial liberal, and he supported the new civil rights regime. But he was criticized for lacking "fire in the belly" on the issue and put forward little in the way of his own civil rights program.[86]

In Carter's language and in his hesitance about the *University of California Regents v. Bakke* case, which considered the legality of affirmative action, we see the first hints of how colorblind ideology would define presidential politics across party lines. The disagreement about the case within the Carter White House would mirror the disagreement among core Democratic constituencies.[87]

It is not difficult to see some parallels to the administrations of Grant and Hayes. Like these leaders, Carter came from the party associated with the past racial disruption and the new approach to racial politics. He shared a broad ideology of racial progress. Yet, like his predecessors, Carter came up against structural barriers to pushing forward. His appointments to important federal posts, most notably the selection of Griffin Bell as attorney general, were perceived by activists for racial progress as betrayals.

One of the objections raised to Bell's appointment illustrated the dilemmas of the new post–civil rights era. Bell, along with Bert Lance, Carter's choice to head the Office of Management and Budget, had belonged to private clubs in the Atlanta area that were reputed to exclude Jews and African Americans, and with his nomination, questions were asked about whether this exclusion was formal or simply expressed through informal expectations. A representative of the club was quoted as saying, "Any member who would invite a Jew or a Black into his own home could invite a Jew or a Black to the club."[88] Determining the meaning of unacceptable prejudice in the social realm in the post–civil rights era posed a new challenge for the newly elected Southern president as he made his appointments from the ranks of his own "Georgia mafia."

Despite the kinds of associations they may have had in the past, both Lance and Bell would serve the Carter administration at high levels. The *Bakke* decision sowed discord, but civil rights leaders were ultimately happy with the Justice Department's defense of affirmative action, if not quotas. Carter's presidency demonstrated, in the words of Edward Kantowicz, that "it was far easier to champion a social revolution than to administer its consequences."[89] Carter's anti-quota stance and denunciation of "prejudice," combined with the absence of a more aggressive agenda, laid some of the groundwork for the colorblind ideology adopted by subsequent presidents.

The 1980 election also showcased the ambivalence of the period—and of the Carter presidency. By the end of his presidency, Carter had attracted criticism from significant civil rights actors and Black media.[90] Grounds for dissatisfaction included representation and the lack of a clear agenda for African Americans. Early signs of colorblind-era politics were evident under Carter, who also fell into the familiar presidential pattern of not disrupting the status quo on race. The president's stances on economic issues were also criticized, as was the performance of the economy overall.[91] This criticism created an opening for Reagan and the Republicans to appeal to Black voters on issues of economic opportunity; ultimately Reagan drew the support of several prominent leaders and, in the November presidential election, 14 percent of the Black electorate.[92] These appeals were designed not to emphasize race, but to "transcend" it.[93] The civil rights era was over, and the colorblind era had begun.

6

"The Content of Their Character"

RONALD REAGAN TO BARACK OBAMA

"OUR CONSTITUTION is colorblind, and neither knows nor tolerates classes among citizens." These words came from the dissent written by Justice John Marshall Harlan in the 1896 *Plessy v. Ferguson* case. Although intended to register his disagreement with racial segregation, Harlan's statement supplied the language that, nearly a century later, would become the backbone of racial conservatism. The concept of colorblindness, which would elevate individualism over strategies to deal with the legacy of racism, shaped the norms that liberals and conservatives alike followed in the period between 1980 and 2008. With Ronald Reagan's 1980 presidential campaign, the colorblind approach bloomed into the mainstream of politics, and it ended with the election of the nation's first Black president.

The legal hierarchies of slavery and Jim Crow no longer existed, and explicit appeals to racism fell increasingly out of bounds.[1] But politics remained racially polarized. Conservatives and liberals alike found it tricky or even impossible to address issues of racism. The success of Republican presidential candidates in the 1980s also made Democrats cautious about appearing too liberal or too wedded to the interests of nonwhite Americans.[2] As presidents in this period navigated this unsettled post–civil rights political terrain across rhetoric,

140

policy, and party politics, African Americans and other nonwhite Americans were often left by the wayside. As in previous eras, however, the balance of political power seemed unlikely to shift in favor of change. Until it did.

Initially hailed as the culmination of colorblind politics, Obama's 2008 election was the subject of articles like one on NPR that asked whether a generation of "color-blurred" voters might be emerging.[3] But this narrative that race could now be transcended with Obama's election was quickly transformed from an inspiring story into a bitter joke.

Instead, Obama's presence in office belied the colorblind fiction of whiteness as a neutral default, and white Americans were forced to contend with race in places and times they were not used to. Insinuations that Obama would use the office to favor nonwhites prompted backlash against often fictitious or distorted reports about the administration's policies.[4] A more complex problem was that merging the power of the presidency with the history of racism and marginalization upset norms about colorblind justice, equal opportunity, and racial innocence. The line between crucial political opposition and racist political attacks blurred even more, ultimately altering politics on both the left and the right.

In the years leading up to Obama's presidency, presidents across the political spectrum were constrained by pressures not to highlight race politics that frequently clashed with the reality of persistent race disparities and growing polarization. The dilemmas were different for Democrats and Republicans, but these pressures were present for both. Thus was the stage set for a highly combustible era of presidential politics, which would see three presidential impeachments.

Polarization alone is insufficient to explain the tumultuousness of this period. There have been other periods of intense polarization, such as the 1890s and the 1850s, that did not produce multiple impeachments. Some of the most polarized presidents of this time, George W. Bush and Barack Obama, never dealt with serious impeachment threats. Hostility between the parties is a necessary but not sufficient condition for impeachment. What we see instead is the emergence of presidential populism, the loosening of political norms, and a backdrop of political parties that are both polarized and internally divided by race.

What It Means to Be "Colorblind" and Why It Matters

While Justice Harlan intended for the "colorblind Constitution" to represent progress, recent commentators have been less positive about the idea. According to scholars who have studied the phenomenon, applying a "colorblind" lens to contemporary American society has a couple of major negative effects. One is that such a lens can downplay the role of racism, especially historical and structural racism, in explaining the life outcomes and experiences of Black, Latino, and other nonwhite Americans.[5] This thinking lends itself, in turn, to explanations for these disparities that rest on merit, hard work, or culture.[6]

Political scientists Candis Watts Smith and Christopher DeSante distill decades of scholarship into a few key tenets on "color-blind racial attitudes": treating race as an "invisible characteristic" and a "taboo topic"—implying that any discussion of race is "impolite" and potentially revealing of racial prejudice—and treating racism as an individual and interpersonal issue.[7]

Some analysts, like Desmond King and Rogers Smith, identify colorblindness predominantly with conservative politics: "The modern conservative coalition built around Ronald Reagan took as one of its unifying themes, the importance of public policies that reinforce and reward individual good character and penalize individual bad character, from the ideology of the colorblind racial policy alliance and its call to judge people not on the color of their skin but on the content of their character."[8] Scholars working in this area explicitly identify the policy manifestations of these ideas. A recurring issue is affirmative action, which helped to shape conservative race politics in the Reagan era.

The "policy alliance" King and Smith identify, however, also includes some conservative and moderate Democrats. And other scholars have pointed out that these ideas inform liberal politics as well, such as ideas about meritocracy and racial innocence.[9] In his study of race and education in California, sociologist Daniel HoSang observed white Americans in liberal communities arguing that because they did not cause the problems or disparities affecting nonwhite school districts, they could not "be compelled to participate in their improvement."[10]

As the colorblind ideology took hold, the political risks of bringing up race in presidential politics, especially in structural or historical terms, became significant. Statements or policies that threatened white racial innocence, carried substantial backlash risk. Political and interpersonal norms made it increasingly difficult to bring up racial topics, and some considered it "impolite" to do so or to dredge up the ills of the past.[11] Overt racism carried significant political risk as well.[12]

In sum, racial politics became a new kind of minefield for politicians. The policy stakes and dynamics were quite different from the 1840s or the 1950s, but the possibilities for violating norms about race in presidential speech or politics were everywhere. These risks were not unique to presidents and presidential candidates, of course. But the imperative to represent the entire nation, combined with the focus on the public presidency in this period, created distinct political pressures.

These pressures were different for Democratic and Republican presidents. For Republicans heard competing calls to become more inclusive and to maintain the support of racially conservative whites.[13] Many in the party wanted to avoid being branded as a racially reactive party, but racial fears and backlash remained a rich source of electoral support. This situation gave Republican presidents a strong incentive to speak cautiously about race, but also to reinforce the taboo against talking about racism, especially historical or structural racism, in order to provide cover for dog-whistle language and make space for navigating their own dilemma.

For Democrats, the challenges mirrored some of the familiar coalition problems of the past. Getting elected, especially in the Reagan era, required appealing to both moderate and even conservative whites, while also mobilizing African American voters. Despite the importance of Black voters for Democratic success, the party had to avoid carving out an identity as a "racially liberal" party or appearing to prioritize Black interests.[14] As a result, Democratic political messages have sometimes relied, though less commonly than Republican messages, on the implied racial cues in appeals on crime or welfare.[15]

These political incentives created unsustainable contradictions for presidents of both parties when it came to race issues. How this contradiction would collapse under its own weight was less straightforward, and less predictable, than in the previous two eras. In this era, the dual pressures to elide the role of race and to expand political representation to new groups culminated in the historic rise of Barack Obama to the presidency. The racial politics of Obama's presidency were different, but in the decades it took to get there race issues remained charged and polarizing, creating a combustible political environment once again.

Ronald Reagan and the New Politics of Racial Conservatism

Ronald Reagan kicked off his third presidential campaign with a speech in Philadelphia, Mississippi, at the Neshoba County Fair. The county fair, an institution dating back to 1889, was much loved by the local community.[16] But that community bore a stain on its reputation: In 1964, three civil rights workers were killed there. While fairgoers enjoyed "black-eyed peas, grits, country ham, fried chicken, iced tea and sippin' whiskey," Reagan introduced the big ideas of his campaign to a Southern audience.[17] He spoke of his frustration, and the nation's, with decades of Democratic dominance, especially the incumbent Carter administration's mishandling of the economy. The scourge of welfare was one of the problems he highlighted, connecting his plans for the future with his experience as governor of California.

And then he put his governing philosophy into words that were deceptively simple and connected to more than a century of racial history in the South:

"I believe in states' rights."

Although he never mentioned race, civil rights, or the deeper history of the Civil War, some heard the dog whistle in that remark. Andrew Young, who had been both a civil rights leader and a member of the Carter administration, called the speech "chilling" and insisted, "Surely Black political memories are not that short."[18]

Reagan's vision of America, of conservatism, and of public policy defined the post–civil rights-era relationship between race and the presidency. In that era, overt racism and legal discrimination were out of bounds.[19] But pathways to egalitarianism that ran through government action, especially any suggestion of differential treatment, were treated as suspect. This kind of thinking was especially prevalent among conservatives, and in a period when conservatives often set the terms of debate, liberals often found themselves responding to these unwritten rules.

The upshot for presidential politics was that race was everywhere, but its presence remained largely unspoken. The 1980 campaign was crucial in forging this path—in Reagan, the conservative movement had finally found a candidate they trusted to push their agenda forward. And though the movement outwardly defined itself in terms of cultural issues—abortion, gender, church and state—conservatives' agenda was filled with issues that had serious implications for race. Crime, law and order, and busing were all concepts that carried over from the 1960s and 1970s. These issues also fit together into a new anti-government conservative philosophy. The implication that "crime" was associated with Black Americans encouraged whites' belief that they needed guns for self-protection, and welfare—also presumed to have a Black face—could be logically opposed by lowering taxes. Some conservative campaign materials also stated opposition to "reverse discrimination" against whites.[20] Objections to "quotas" in hiring or college admissions also played a role in Reagan's campaign.[21]

Combined with Reagan's past opposition to the Civil Rights Act and the Voting Rights Act, these kinds of statements were enough to label the Reagan campaign racist and regressive. Leadership Conference on Civil Rights leader Clarence Mitchell called Reagan a "sophisticated racist." Such assessments drew on a wide range of the Republican candidate's issue stances—from his rejection of affirmative action to his statements about crime and welfare to the campaign's Southern strategy moves like the Neshoba County Fair speech.[22] Jimmy Carter at one point drew attention to his opponent's statements and actions on civil rights, bringing up the "states' rights" issue at Ebenezer Baptist Church in Atlanta.[23] The response foreshadowed how colorblind presidential politics would operate for the next several decades: Carter was questioned by a reporter about "running a mean campaign."[24] Because the racial meaning conveyed in Reagan's language and issue positions required some interpretation, the act of addressing a racially coded statement was itself a norm violation. Making such a claim was portrayed as introducing race into the conversation and leveling a serious accusation that rested on that very interpretation.

The racial dynamics of the campaign were further complicated to some extent by the many issues that drove the 1980 election, central among them the state of the economy and the shortcomings of the Carter presidency. In the beginning of October, Reagan had not received public support from a major Black figure, but that changed when he won an endorsement from civil rights leader Ralph Abernathy, with Hosea Williams soon following and Charles Evers (mayor of Fayette, Mississippi and brother of Medgar Evers) "call[ing] on Blacks to vote against Carter."[25] These leaders, including Abernathy, who had campaigned for Reagan, pointed out how poorly Black Americans had fared under Carter and cited a lack of results from the administration in terms of improvements in their daily lives.

Ultimately, widespread dissatisfaction with Carter helped Reagan defeat the incumbent president by ten percentage points. The response to this victory revealed that not all civil rights leaders felt as Abernathy, Williams, and Evers did. In the weeks following Reagan's election, the Black press featured stories that expressed concern about Reagan's stances on states' rights, his support for anti-busing measures, and his inclusion of African Americans in top decisions.[26] An editorial in the *Philadelphia Tribune* described Reagan's plans to scale back national efforts in the areas of affirmative action, busing, and criminal justice reform.[27]

Urban League President Vernon Jordan told the press that he would wait to see how the new president-elect acted in office and contrasted Reagan with Senators Jesse Helms (R-NC) and Strom Thurmond (R-SC), whose anti–civil rights records and remarks left little room for ambiguity. Jordan said that he would wait to see if Reagan's promises to address Black well-being from a conservative perspective would bring results. Meanwhile, he stressed the contradiction of modern racism: "I do not worry about the Klan mentality that's dressed up in white sheets and marching around. I really worry about the Klan mentality in this country that I cannot see, a mentality I know is there, that is operating in three-piece suits and nice dresses."[28]

Reagan in Office: Rhetoric and Policy

During the campaign and throughout his presidency, Reagan became angry when accused of racism.[29] He saw himself as "colorblind" and free of racial prejudice and took pride in stories about his family's rejection of bigotry.[30] But once Reagan took office, the contradictions of color-blind politics, especially as they informed the conservative movement, became apparent. Reagan ran on the promise of rolling back the power and reach of the federal government. Whether he meant to or not, this meant attacking—sometimes directly—laws that were deeply connected to Black political, economic, and social progress.

Reagan first introduced the story of the "welfare queen" during the 1976 campaign, when he referred to a specific individual who had set up "eighty aliases" in order to fund a luxury lifestyle on the taxpayers' dime.[31] Two things about this image are particularly significant. First, the welfare queen became a stand-in for all welfare recipients, presented as the rule rather than the exception.[32] Second, the image was unmistakably rooted in race and gender and, as political theorist Ange-Marie Hancock as documented, connected to long-standing and harmful stereotypes of African American women, specifically those depicting them as irresponsible single mothers.[33] This image fed into a broad range of justifications for the kinds of program cuts that were the backbone of the new conservative agenda: By depicting recipients of public assistance as morally lax, lazy, and—crucially— predominantly nonwhite, the Reagan administration could explain such cuts as promoting personal responsibility and protecting the taxpayers.[34] Reagan translated these ideas into policy reality, including cuts to public housing and job training and changes to welfare regulations that "left welfare recipients much worse off than they had been."[35]

One area where Reagan's "colorblind" vision was stated up front was affirmative action. He made real inroads in the reframing of the issue by talking about "quotas" and implying that quotas elevated unqualified people (minorities) at the expense of hardworking whites. Despite these implications, according to one political science study, "the Reagan administration was careful to present its racial policies as the fulfillment, not the rejection, of the principles of the modern civil rights movement."[36]

As the head of the executive branch, Reagan was responsible for the enforcement of civil rights laws through the Justice Department and for appointing people to carry out the laws. Reagan selected William Bradford Reynolds, a known opponent of affirmative action, to head the Civil Rights Division of the Department of Justice. A vocal critic of "quotas" and a strong spokesperson for the colorblind approach, Reynolds cited the need to focus on recent progress rather than past injustices and declared that each person in the country was a "minority of one."[37]

The Reagan Justice Department put these views into action, shifting away from the established approach to antidiscrimination policy. A major element of this shift was a "change of focus from group rights to individual rights."[38] This shift had implications for the Justice Department's approach to affirmative action lawsuits. According to legal scholar Drew Days, "the Reagan administration also opposed voluntary efforts to achieve greater desegregation [in schools] and job opportunities for minorities" by supporting efforts to reverse legal cases that allowed businesses to adopt their own plans for diversifying their workforces; the DOJ labeled some of these plans "quotas" and implied that they put white applicants at a disadvantage.[39] In a similar vein, Reagan's Equal Employment Opportunity Commission, under the direction of eventual Supreme Court Justice Clarence Thomas, "abandoned" lawsuits aimed at policies that had disparate racial impacts in order to focus solely on those of demonstrated individual discrimination.[40] Thus, the Reagan administration's overall approach was to deemphasize federal remedies for discrimination in hiring and in schools and to treat discrimination as a matter of personal prejudice between individuals rather than a systemic issue to be addressed through policy.

Treating racism as an individual failing and promoting the prospect of "reverse discrimination" undermined the legitimacy of affirmative action and other policies designed to aid minorities. It also constrained how political leaders could talk about race in public without facing charges of reverse discrimination or race-baiting.

Colorblind ideology does cut both ways, however. Staffing and lawsuits in the Justice Department were one thing. But Reagan carefully sought to avoid the appearance of blocking racial progress when it came to legislation. When the Voting Rights Act came up for renewal in 1982, the administration supported several provisions that would have weakened the act, but Reagan eventually signed the bill and even touted it as a show of the administration's commitment to voting rights.[41]

A similar dynamic accompanied the passage of a bill establishing a federal holiday in honor of Martin Luther King Jr. In one sense, Reagan's signing of the bill cut against attempts to cast him as a racial reactionary.[42] But a full accounting of Reagan's history with the holiday tells a somewhat different story. In 1982, Reagan was asked at a press conference whether he had taken a stand on the proposal to make a federal holiday honoring King. Reagan responded:

> No, I haven't taken a stand one way or the other. And I certainly can understand why the black community would like to do that. I know that from some of the past—I just have to confess with all that's been going on, I haven't been able to dig as deeply as I want to into it.
>
> But one of the problems from those who have preceded me in this office with regard to that is the discovery of how many—we're quite a mix in this country—how many other people there are with—people who just as sincerely want them also. We could have an awful lot of holidays if we start down that road.[43]

These words were typical of Reagan's approach to the holiday early on in the debate. They insinuated that King was a figure for only the Black community rather than for the nation as a whole.[44] In addition to showcasing Reagan's reluctance to sign on to anything seen as overtly for the benefit of Black Americans, the path of the legislation also revealed division in the Republican Party.[45] Senator Bob Dole (R-KS) had guided the bill through the Senate and announced upon its passage, "I'm proud of my party today. We're in the mainstream."[46] But his GOP Senate colleague Jesse Helms had initially filibustered the bill. Faced with this party rift, Reagan sought to placate both sides by promising to sign the legislation, but also acting to "protect his right flank" by not criticizing efforts on the right to block the legislation and paint King as a Communist.[47] Indeed, Reagan himself had expressed reservations that the image of King was based on "image, not reality," in a letter to former New Hampshire Governor Meldrim Thomson.[48] Reagan had also commented that the country would "find out in thirty-five years" whether King had Communist sympathies (upon the unsealing of FBI files).[49]

After the bill passed in Congress and headed to the president's desk, the lobbying group Conservative Caucus presented the president with 43,700 signatures on a petition asking him to veto it.[50] In this case, the president saw too much political disadvantage in vetoing a popular bipartisan bill. Instead, in his remarks upon signing the legislation, he adapted King's vision in service of the colorblind ideology that the administration had used, and would continue to use, to dismantle support for civil rights: "Dr. King had awakened something strong and true, a sense that true justice must be colorblind, and that among white and black Americans, as he put it, 'Their destiny is tied up with our destiny, and their freedom is inextricably bound to our freedom; we cannot walk alone.'"[51] Reagan would draw this linkage in later statements to justify his opposition to affirmative action and "quotas," also using the King legacy to depict racism as a problem of the past.[52]

Nearly two decades after the passage of the Civil Rights Act, the nation was still contending with the meaning and implications of those changes. And when these conflicts surfaced in a public way—for instance, in debate over legislation—the president was still charting a compromise course. As ever, "compromise" often meant protecting and appeasing racial conservatives. Reagan pursued conservative approaches to school desegregation, affirmative action, and other civil rights issues through administrative action. But to avoid alienating moderate voters, the president had to soften his stances in public on questions like the King holiday and the Voting Rights Act renewal. Nevertheless, Reagan was able to cloak these conservative aims in moderate language that adapted the rhetoric of colorblindness to claim the legacy of the civil rights movement. This trick would prove to be a delicate and easily disturbed compromise, but it would constrain the political options of his successors when it came to talking about and acting on race questions.

George H. W. Bush and the Limits of Conservative Color Blindness

George Bush served only one term in the White House. But during his four years, several events forced him to confront race issues directly and made colorblind avoidance of those issues difficult.[53] These included the retirement of the first African American Supreme Court justice, Thurgood Marshall, the passage of civil rights legislation in 1991, and the beating of a Black motorist, Rodney King, in Los Angeles by police officers and the controversial aftermath of this incident.[54]

Bush's 1988 campaign is infamous for the "Willie Horton" ad. Now used as a textbook example of a campaign spot that played directly to white fears about Black crime through dog-whistle language and visual imagery, this ad was part of a successful strategy to depict the Democratic candidate, Massachusetts Governor Michael Dukakis, as a weak, soft-on-crime liberal.[55]

But matters proved more complicated once Bush actually became president. Sure, the forty-first president could sing from the conservative hymnal, talking about "dependency" on state programs or achieving a colorblind society. However, presidents—especially those serving under divided party government—cannot always control their political circumstances.

The Democratically controlled Congress passed a civil rights bill intended to address the standards for employment discrimination. This legislation was a direct response to the *Wards Cove Packing Co. v. Antonio* Supreme Court decision, which made it more difficult for employees and job applicants to sue for discrimination. In 1990, Congress passed a bill addressing this question and making it easier to establish discrimination, as well as heightening the penalties. Bush vetoed the bill on the basis that it would "lead to quotas" by making employers who did not use them vulnerable to discrimination charges.[56]

Even though he was stoking the anger that surrounded the language of quotas and reverse discrimination, Bush eventually signed a later version of the bill. His signature was accompanied by a controversy over the possibility of executive action limiting affirmative action.[57] This sequence of events showed the political bind of Bush's position. His own political past showed a mix of views, from opposition to the 1964 Civil Rights Act during a congressional race in Texas to a moderate stance on many other issues.[58] As president, he used patrician language about dependency when he talked about government assistance programs and poverty. But Bush's approval of the 1991 legislation also reflected the political pressure not to veto two successive civil rights bills and to show his commitment to equality while also tending to the concerns of racially conservative whites.

As has been so often the case when presidents tried to split the difference on race, Bush ultimately pleased neither side. Some Democrats refused to come to the signing ceremony in the Rose Garden because of affirmative action disputes, while Bush's association with the legislation left him vulnerable to attacks from the far right. Avowed white supremacist David Duke used the president's "waffling" as a talking point in a short-lived primary challenge. Populist nativist Pat Buchanan also drew on the "quota bill" in a more wounding primary bid against the incumbent president.

Rodney King

In the spring of 1991, a video was released showing the brutal beating of motorist Rodney King by Los Angeles police officers. Like many Americans at the time, Bush expressed shock and disgust at the video, despite his strong political support from police departments.[59] A year later, when a jury acquitted the police officers charged with the violence against King, sections of Los Angeles exploded into serious unrest, with substantial property destruction, theft, and violence. Much of the violence was directed at the Korean community in the area. The stunned response to the "not guilty" verdict for a crime caught on tape—a beating that had lasted fifteen minutes—gave way to pleas for "law and order" to return.

In his address to the nation in May 1992, Bush decried the violence while also highlighting the horror of what had happened to King. Bush fell into familiar patterns for presidents addressing race—cautious calls for order and equality, without examining too closely the relationship between the two. White House press secretary Marlin Fitzwater suggested that the unrest could be traced to the failed programs of the Great Society.[60] Political journalists expressed frustration and disappointment with the president's response. Jack Germond and Jules Witcover suggested that Bush might be inclined to run a law-and-order campaign and use to his advantage the "race card that has been handed to him by the rioters."[61] Mary McGrory took the president to task for the absence of "outrage and resolve" in his response to the crisis.[62]

In other words, Bush had trouble meeting the colorblindness standard set by Reagan. The retirement of Thurgood Marshall, the Rodney King incident, and the passage of civil rights legislation by a Democratic Congress all required that Bush acknowledge the long-standing role of race in American political life. Moreover, he had little choice but to accommodate more liberal perspectives in order to avoid looking hostile to equality and civil rights. When it came to maintaining the racial order and preserving its politics, Bush at times was barely able to hang on.

The 1992 campaign simmered with racial themes. Starting in the primaries, Bush attracted considerable populist ire. Pat Buchanan was direct and unsubtle in his critique of Bush's signing of the 1991 "quota bill."[63] Taken straight out of the backlash playbook, Buchanan's primary ads accused Bush of depriving whites—white children, in particular—of equal opportunity in the future because of the 1991 bill.[64] Buchanan challenged Bush from the right—the cultural right—in a campaign that never had much shot of winning the nomination but was successful enough to alarm the Bush camp.[65]

Buchanan's bid also foreshadowed the more centrist campaign of H. Ross Perot, which also channeled the general impulse toward "protest voting." These protest votes are often linked to the economic conditions at the time, but the cultural and racial dimensions are difficult to disentangle. Buchanan didn't bother with dog whistles but explicitly linked the declining prospects of white Americans to the cultural laxity of Bush-style Republicanism. Perot's third-party candidacy was arguably only indirectly related to backlash dynamics within the Republican fold, but his presentation of "protest" politics drew on a number of implicitly racialized ideas. Perot's brand of populism highlighted the anger of "ordinary" "middle" Americans and took aim at both "divisiveness" in day-to-day politics and government excess, both ideas that had been associated with the demands of nonwhite Americans. Perot also drew criticism for a speech at an NAACP gathering for using the phrase "you people" in reference to his Black audience and for his heavy emphasis on crime in the speech.[66] In November, Perot won only 7 percent of the Black vote to Bush's 10 percent, and he performed more poorly with Hispanics as well. In other words, the protest politics of the right and the center were implicated in a sort of backlash-lite—the sense that "ordinary" white voters were losing out to minoritized "special interests" that had captured the government and rendered it dysfunctional. These dynamics ultimately helped Bill Clinton win the presidency.

A Democrat in the Colorblind Era: Bill Clinton

Clinton's campaign as a "new kind of Democrat" would not have been possible without the politics of colorblindness that came before. The "New Democrat" label drew an implicit contrast between Clinton and past liberal losers like Walter Mondale and Michael Dukakis. But the contrast was also with a direction for the Democratic Party embodied in figures like civil rights leader Jesse Jackson, seen (probably correctly) as antithetical to the party's aims of attracting more moderate voters and distancing itself from claims that Democrats were captured by "special" (read: minority) interests.[67]

These appeals had policy implications. Among them were Clinton's promise to "end welfare as we know it" and his plans for addressing the "reverse racism" he talked about at a Rainbow-PUSH coalition event, in a direct rebuke to Jesse Jackson.[68] Another policy implication was that, after becoming president, Clinton had to maintain a coalition that at once depended on Black votes and on appeasing moderate white voters.[69]

During the campaign, Clinton had "courted endorsements from police associations and unions [and] touted his support for the death penalty."[70] But the contradictions in Clinton's relationship with race and politics were soon apparent. At different points during the campaign, Clinton had shown a comfort and familiarity with Southern African American culture and speech that was rarely seen in white politicians at the national level.[71] The new president immediately began appointing a diverse cabinet, though not without struggle. One of the highest-profile struggles was Clinton's nomination of Lani Guinier for attorney general. After selecting her, Clinton distanced himself from some of her more controversial legal writing about race and civil rights, including "her general views on the need to increase the political power of blacks and other minority groups."[72] Faced with the prospect of a difficult confirmation battle, and citing his own disagreement with some of her views, Clinton withdrew the nomination.

Clinton's policy agenda also reflected his New Democrat political identity. Along with some congressional Democrats who were determined to reclaim the crime issue, Clinton made it an early priority; he helped to craft a wide-ranging bill that incorporated liberal priorities, like crime prevention programs, alongside provisions to lengthen sentences and expand the list of federal crimes eligible for the death penalty.[73] When legislative negotiations required it, Clinton accepted a compromise that made the bill more punitive and cut funding for the prevention programs.[74] While African American lawmakers and voters had expressed concern about crime, there is ample evidence that this was not the bill they were looking for. The harsh death penalty measures drew criticism from the House Congressional Black Caucus chair, Kweisi Mfume.[75] Despite the common perception that there was serious Black support for the anti-crime measures, the potential for discriminatory impact did not go unnoticed or unremarked.[76]

The other signature policy of the first term was welfare reform. Clinton signed the 1996 Personal Responsibility and Work Opportunity Reconciliation Act (PRWORA) after long negotiations with Congress. The political situation appeared precarious: The 1994 midterm elections had ended five decades of Democratic House majorities, delivering Republican control of both chambers. The president vetoed two Republican welfare bills, but his more risk-averse advisers urged him to work with Congress rather than veto reform a third time.[77] In this sense, Clinton's promises to "end welfare as we know it" and his reluctant cooperation with Republicans, who had a much more austere vision of what this would look like, reflected the political constraints of the time. Clinton was operating in the Reagan era.[78] In other words, he was navigating a public conversation about welfare that was shaped by race and in a political context in which rhetoric about American values and about deservingness and work informed media portrayals and public attitudes.[79] The cover of *The New Republic* featured an editorial urging the president to "Sign the Welfare Bill Now," accompanied by a photograph of a Black woman feeding a child, a cigarette dangling from her mouth. The message was clear.

Clinton tried to adapt this message in two ways that were reminiscent of past presidential efforts at racial maintenance. He argued that reform would improve the lives of welfare recipients by enabling them to gain a sense of pride and independence from hard work.[80] And in a move harkening back to the compromises of the early nineteenth century, Clinton expressed hopes that signing a reform bill would alter the tone of further debates about welfare, suggesting that it would "neutralize the polarizing effect of two-party partisan politics on this issue."[81] This may have been true in a narrow and literal sense. Later studies have shown, however, that media coverage and corresponding public attitudes were still influenced by race.[82] And while welfare may have faded from the public agenda, questions about race, poverty, and deservingness became neither less pressing nor less divisive over time.

Clinton's policies fit fairly well into the established pattern of presidential politics: maintaining the racial status quo and favoring the needs and demands of moderate white voters. But the Clinton case has an important wrinkle: Clinton, too, was impeached.

Some elements of the Clinton story are common to the other impeachments. From the beginning, Clinton's detractors sought out scandal. Special prosecutors investigated the real estate deals of Bill and Hillary Clinton, as well as accusations from a former Arkansas state employee, Paula Jones, who alleged that Clinton had harassed and propositioned her when he was governor of the state.[83] Through Clinton's first term and 1996 reelection, few of these allegations seemed to turn up much evidence, but the controversies followed him and were a drag on his presidency. Clinton, owing in part to the populist dynamics of the 1992 election, was also a president without a majority—twice over. And he had the hybrid political identity of the other impeached leaders, posing a special threat to Republicans by co-opting their policy agenda. Multiple scholars who have studied the Clinton impeachment suggest that this threat provided enough incentive to congressional Republicans.

But was an incentive enough? The cases of Andrew Johnson and Richard Nixon suggest that members of Congress face significant political barriers to thinking about impeachment. The politics of racial backlash and resulting presidential lawlessness help to overcome these barriers. The other side of the equation is the loosening of political norms at a time of major national upheaval. Again, the politics of the 1990s are a bit ambivalent on this point. There were no crises on the level of the Civil War or the Vietnam War and no social changes to match the civil rights revolution.

What had changed was the configuration of power. Just as Clinton was the first Democrat in the White House since Reagan had won in 1980, House Speaker Newt Gingrich led the first Republican House majority since 1955. Gingrich and his political allies came to power with a new approach that stressed national over local issues, engaged conservative media, and generally took a more combative tone. Norms and informal practices were shifting on Capitol Hill, and pushing at the boundaries of what the relationship between the branches could look like was part of that shift.

In the course of the Paula Jones investigation, Clinton answered a question under oath about his relationship with a White House intern, Monica Lewinsky. As revealed later, he lied under oath by denying that he had had a sexual relationship with the young woman. This lie became the basis for the House to pursue impeachment charges.

In September 1998, amid the fervor over the first full presidential impeachment process in memory (Clinton vowed not to resign) and the salacious details included in the special prosecutor's report, acclaimed writer Toni Morrison wrote an essay about Clinton in *The New Yorker* in which she penned the now-famous line about Clinton being the "first

Black president." This was a reference not to Clinton's well-documented comfort with and appreciation for Southern Black culture, but rather to his treatment by the news media and political opponents:

> Clinton displays almost every trope of blackness: single-parent household, born poor, working-class, saxophone-playing, McDonald's-and-junk-food-loving boy from Arkansas. And when virtually all the African-American Clinton appointees began, one by one, to disappear, when the President's body, his privacy, his unpoliced sexuality became the focus of the persecution, when he was metaphorically seized and body-searched, who could gainsay these black men who knew whereof they spoke? The message was clear: "No matter how smart you are, how hard you work, how much coin you earn for us, we will put you in your place or put you out of the place you have somehow, albeit with our permission, achieved."[84]

As Morrison's comments and others like them imply, Clinton's presidency did suggest a challenge to traditional notions of who wields presidential power. Clinton represented a different class background. He elevated women and people of color to high-level positions. And early in his first term Clinton tried to address the issue of allowing gay men and lesbians to serve openly in the military, only to be rebuked by conservatives.

In 1998, his conservative congressional opponents tested their limits. Like past impeachments, issues were muddled between the legal issues at hand—specifically, perjury—and questions about Clinton's behavior and moral character. But the Clinton impeachment also differed from the Andrew Johnson and Richard Nixon situations in a few important ways. Although it addressed presidential abuse of power, the charges put forward by the House Judiciary Committee were largely connected to Clinton's conduct rather than, as constitutional scholar Keith Whittington notes, larger constitutional issues about the executive branch. In contrast with the previous (and later) impeachments, Clinton did not stand accused of interfering with elections or undermining his political opponents.

Whatever the real substance of the proceedings—perjury or a White House affair—it did not resonate with the electorate. Clinton's approval rating soared, and the Republican Party's loss of seats in the 1998 midterms was widely understood as a public rejection of the impeachment.

Clinton was acquitted on February 12, 1999, with five Republicans as well as all Senate Democrats voting in his favor.[85] But the impeachment process had consumed a year of Clinton's final term. If he had intended for his presidency to puncture the ceiling of the power that those of a certain class, race, and gender held on to so tightly, the impeachment derailed that goal. And it left some voters interested in a president with a firmer moral orientation, one who would not quibble about what "the meaning of 'is' is" and who was less inclined to challenge the flow of power.

George W. Bush—Compassionate Conservatism

If Reagan and the first Bush left questions about how conservatism would address race in the post–civil rights era, George W. Bush offered "compassionate conservatism" as a partial answer. As a political movement, compassionate conservatism reflected some intent to address the problems with race and conservatism.[86]

In the 2000 election and in the early administration, however, civil rights hardly registered as a priority. Bush spoke outwardly about diversity while continuing to act with the Reagan administration's hostility toward affirmative action.[87] Early on, the administration's signature policy on civil rights was its education reform, known as "No Child Left Behind." Addressing the NAACP during the 2000 campaign, Bush promised to fight what he called "the soft bigotry of low expectations" by pursuing widespread educational standards. The faith-based initiatives effort also reached out to African American religious organizations and targeted them for funding.[88]

But crisis after crisis pushed the Bush administration to address race issues from many angles, and not just in ways that they had anticipated or planned for. In the wake of the terrorist attacks of September 11, 2001, the "War on Terror" revealed the difficulty of framing patriotism and nationality in twenty-first-century America. Then, in 2005, Hurricane Katrina once again turned the nation's attention to the starkness of the white/Black divide while also highlighting the challenges of talking about it. Bush and his surrogates navigated these divides in different ways, some of which were more successful than others. Ultimately, their decisions reinforced the norms of colorblindness, while showing the limitations of those norms as a means of dealing with the problems of twenty-first-century America.

The War on Terror

The 9/11 attacks changed the course of George W. Bush's presidency, pushing anti-terror policy to the front of his agenda and making him a war president. But Bush also influenced the politics of 9/11, effectively framing the meaning of the events and thus the nation's response.

In the days following the attacks, Bush spoke about how "the terrorists" hated American freedoms and the American way of life. This identity-based explanation for what had happened crowded out other narratives and closed off avenues for dissent.[89] Yet, at the same time, Bush cautiously tried not to tie terrorism to all Muslims, particularly American Muslims. Six days after 9/11, Bush spoke at a mosque, affirming that "the face of terror is not the true faith of Islam."[90] Writing for *Slate* in 2020, Aymann Ismail asserted that Bush's efforts, even though his rhetoric was accompanied by policies that harmed Muslims, demonstrated that the White House wanted to tamp down anti-Muslim backlash. "But that little bit of affirmation that we weren't the enemy, even if it was superficial, protected me from feeling entirely cast out as an American," writes Ismail.[91]

But Bush's attempts to curb Islamophobia were met with mixed success, perhaps in part because of the tension with his own rhetoric about how the terrorists "hate our freedoms." Bush's "good and evil" approach to the War on Terror, exemplified in language like the reference to the "axis of evil" in his 2002 State of the Union address, undercut claims to inclusiveness. "You're either with us or against us" became a defining phrase of the War on Terror, and the president vowed to "make no distinction" between terrorists and those who abetted their crimes—leaving the nation to wonder what other kinds of distinctions could also be blurred. And for all of their talk about separating terrorism from the peaceful religion of Islam, the Bush administration oversaw a program that required men over the age of sixteen from twenty-five (most majority-Muslim) countries to register with the government.[92]

Prejudice against Muslims and Arabs fit easily into an era of colorblind race politics. Pointing to "cultural differences" and fear of radicalization, anyone pushing Islamophobia could deny that they were engaging in real racism.[93] The 9/11 era also connected fears and prejudices with newly powerful frames about national security, terrorism, and the "homeland," creating fertile ground for later politicians to exploit these linkages.

The role of identity in American political polarization would start to make an appearance in 2004 as commentators talked about "culture wars." It would not be until 2016 that the implications of stoking white identity would become a front-and-center matter of public discussion. But the ways in which this language could be used to fuse national and partisan identity can be traced to Bush's post-9/11 language.

Hurricane Katrina

About a year after Bush's 2004 reelection, a devastating storm on the Gulf Coast of Louisiana would do lasting damage to the region—and to Bush's reputation. Some New Orleans residents went without food or water for days, and many had to scrambled onto roofs or into attics to escape the rising water.[94]

In interviews, the director of the Federal Emergency Management Agency (FEMA), Michael Brown, seemed disconnected from the desperation of the evacuees in the Louisiana Superdome, telling journalists he had not learned of them until September 1—several days after media had begun reporting on the plight of the people of New Orleans. President Bush himself flew over the region in Air Force One on his way back to the White House after a vacation at his ranch in Crawford, Texas. The image of the president looking out the plane window at the devastation on the ground came to symbolize the administration's lack of investment in addressing the crisis.

It wasn't long before some observers began to link the administration's slow and seemingly disorganized response to the fact that the New

Orleans residents most affected were poor and Black. Scholars debated whether the issue was race or class. Or did a fuller explanation require attention to the ways in which these were historically linked in New Orleans, dating back to the slave trade in the port city?[95]

Perhaps no one put this as bluntly as hip-hop artist Kanye West, who remarked to actor Mike Myers during a telethon to raise money for victims, "George Bush doesn't care about Black people." Myers stared back in silence. This remark was a serious transgression of colorblind norms. West's comments were removed from the West Coast feed of the fundraiser, and the network hosts hastily distanced themselves from the musician's remarks.[96]

Despite this reaction, the impact of race in the response to Katrina was difficult to deny. Media stories were criticized for depicting Black individuals and families as "looting" and white people as "finding" food.[97] Almost immediately, polls showed a wide gap between white and Black evaluations of the government response.[98] A study by four political scientists found significant differences in the emotional responses of Americans, with Black Americans reporting higher instances of depression and anger in response to Katrina than white Americans.[99] Polls also showed that Black Americans were more likely than whites to think that the government response would have been faster if the victims of the disaster had been predominantly white, and more likely to link the tragedy to broader problems of racial inequity.[100]

In the face of plentiful evidence of racial disparities, the country lacked a shared framework to talk about it. Bush's addresses showed the contradictions: In one speech, he insisted that "the storm did not discriminate" and neither would aid workers rescuing victims. But a few days later, he addressed the linkages between the effects of the hurricane and the city's structural poverty, rooted in racial discrimination.[101] Responses to discussions of race in the Hurricane Katrina context often highlighted the prevalence of ideas about meritocracy (hardworking people could have avoided the poverty that made them so vulnerable to the storm) and the colorblind view (natural disasters have nothing to do with race).[102] Kanye West's transgression against the norm of not accusing someone of racism became a distraction from the human costs of the hurricane.

When race came into the public conversation during the Bush years, it tended to reveal the contradictions of the unwritten rules of the post–civil rights era. Race continued to play a defining role in American political life, from partisan voting patterns to the War on Terror to the ever-present effects of historical inequality. Yet public conversation remained stymied by colorblindness norms that made it difficult to name problems without swift backlash.

Obama and the End of Colorblind Presidential Politics

In March 2008, the Democratic primary had become competitive between New York Senator and former First Lady Hillary Clinton, the assumed favorite and establishment front-runner, and Barack Obama, an ambitious new senator from Illinois. With the nomination of either candidate representing a historic first for the party and the country—either the first woman or the first African American would receive the nomination for president—the country found itself without a script. By that March, stumbles around race and the Obama candidacy had become common. Early in the primary campaign, then-Senator Joe Biden referred to Obama as "the first mainstream African-American who is articulate and bright and clean and a nice-looking guy."[103] And Bill Clinton had come under fire for comparing Obama's victories in South Carolina to those of Jesse Jackson in the 1980s, putatively suggesting that both could succeed with Black voters but not in the nation at large.[104]

The cracks in colorblind racial politics were beginning to show in a new way the lines blurred between typical campaign rough-and-tumble and the use of a dog whistle. What was a legitimate critique of a candidate seeking the highest office in the land, and what was a racist attack? It is not that the distinction was so difficult for those who had been closely observing race and politics. But in a context in which calling someone a racist constituted a serious norm violation—maybe a violation more serious than actually saying something racist—dealing with such comments about Obama opened up a new element of primary-season conflict.

In April 2008, as the primary contest between Obama and Clinton remained unsettled, Obama's past attendance at a Black church in Chicago came under scrutiny. A pair of ABC journalists broke the story that Reverend Jeremiah Wright, the pastor of the church the Obamas had attended for years and the officiant at their wedding ceremony, delivered an incendiary sermon about American complicity after the September 11, 2001, attacks. These revelations opened up candidate Obama to charges that he had sat passively while "un-American" and "unpatriotic" comments were made in a house of worship. Even worse, Wright's comments were found to be in direct violation of colorblind norms, and he was saddled with the accusation of being "racist" against whites.[105]

Obama's initial response was to downplay and distance, in the hope that lack of attention would make the controversy go away. But the public remained preoccupied by Wright's remarks, potentially because of the media's "sensational" treatment, including the original ABC broadcast.[106] The situation was a direct threat to Obama's efforts to embrace a message of racial unity. When nearly twice as many white Americans as Black reported in a Pew poll that they were "offended by Wright's sermons," one of Obama's central campaign messages—that Americans shared values and priorities across racial and other divides—was challenged.[107]

When it became clear that the controversy would not go away on its own, Obama decided to deliver a speech addressing the issue of race and Jeremiah Wright directly. What is most notable about this address and the response to it is how much it flouted the norms of colorblindness by being direct about American racial history and contemporary racial divisions, while affirming many of the ideas that informed colorblind ideology.

Obama delivered the "More Perfect Union" speech in Philadelphia before a backdrop of American flags.[108] In it, he broke with his usual caution about bringing up race, mentioning it more than he had in any other address.[109] In one of the speech's most iconic lines, he noted:

I am married to a black American who carries within her the blood of slaves and slaveowners—an inheritance we pass on to our two precious daughters. I have brothers, sisters, nieces, nephews, uncles and cousins of every race and every hue, scattered across three continents, and for as long as I live, I will never forget that in no other country on Earth is my story even possible.[110]

With this line and numerous others like it, Obama simultaneously challenged colorblind norms and affirmed their aspirations.

The unsettling effects of this departure were evident in the response from commentators across the ideological spectrum. The presidential hopeful had "spoken to the nation like adults" about race, said *The Daily Show*'s Jon Stewart.[111] Even the positive reactions to the speech—and there were many—revealed how much the moment and the presidential candidate differed from what had come before.

But the speech also showed that even as Obama disrupted the existing racial order, he was making efforts to affirm it. Analysis by political scientists with expertise on race and politics explains how he did this.[112] By presenting the conversations "in the barbershop or the beauty shop" in parallel with white racism, Obama created an equivalence between the two contexts, flattening out "structural inequalities that maintain black exclusion and subordination," in the words of political scientists Valeria Sinclair-Chapman and Melanye Price. As they observe, Obama's speech gave "equal weight to Black demands for the full privileges of citizenship and white resentment toward those very demands."[113]

Obama delivered his first major speech about race—not wholly on his own terms but in response to a controversy that would not go away—before it was clear that he would secure the Democratic nomination, much less become president. As it happened, it offered a powerful preview of what was to come: Obama's efforts to transcend race would inevitably foreground it, and such efforts would be met with anger.

Ultimately, Obama did secure the Democratic nomination over opponent Hillary Clinton. The same racial questions—whether Obama would favor nonwhites, whether his true identity was something other than what he presented, and whether he was truly an American—resurfaced throughout the general election. Obama's Republican opponent, Senator John McCain of Arizona, was not especially given to racial populism, but he chose a running mate who was. On the campaign trail,

Alaska Governor Sarah Palin enthralled Republican audiences with her warmth toward "real America," her race-tinged allegations that Obama "palled around with terrorists," and her symbolic embodiment of the thoroughly white archetype of Western, frontier womanhood.[114] These invocations of whiteness followed the Reagan-era colorblindness script, using coded language and rejecting urbanism over visions of suburban and rural America. But they had a twenty-first-century, post-9/11 edge as well and took on a different significance when employed against the first African American presidential nominee.

In the end, Palin came to be seen as an unprepared liability, and McCain was unable to escape the baggage of his party, which was divided by infighting over how to respond to the financial crisis and whom to blame for the unpopular Iraq War. Obama won easily, capturing the Electoral College votes of states where a Democratic presidential candidate had not been victorious in decades, like Indiana and North Carolina. The Illinois Democrat was the first Northern liberal to be elected since Kennedy, and his victory seemed like a turning point for the country.

One such turning point was the emergence of a "postracial America" narrative. *New York Times* television critic Alessandra Stanley offered a preview of the debates to come: "It was labeled by almost all as a postracial election, but African Americans had the floor."[115] An editorial in the *Richmond Times-Dispatch* cited the "hope for a colorblind society" but also pointed out the apparent contradictions in the racial gaps in voting patterns: Most white voters over thirty chose McCain, and younger, more diverse generations supported Obama. Nevertheless, the article maintained, "there are good reasons to believe that the vast majority of people voted for McCain for reasons other than race."[116]

Different interpretations of the postracial concept abounded. In the *Dallas Morning News*, one writer observed that this election would not be the end of Americans observing racial differences. But "that's no longer a liability. It's a plus. A big plus."[117] An editorial in the *Chicago Daily Herald* commented not on the racial tenor of the nation but on the president himself, observing that Obama's inaugural address made only a few mentions of race and connected its themes not to the civil rights movement or Lincoln but rather primarily to George Washington and the full sweep of American history "without annotation or mental reservation."[118] By cultivating a "racially transcendent" image and maintaining that he was president of the entire country, not just Black America, Obama was consistently trying to contain the disruptive impacts of his leadership, as other racially disruptive presidents had done.

Claims about the emergence of a "postracial" America highlighted how the Obama presidency exposed the tensions and contradictions of colorblind politics. These claims also revealed the nation's uncertainty about how to navigate the merging of presidential power with the country's racial history. One thing was clear: No one could talk about presidential politics anymore without somehow reckoning with race. And not everyone was happy about it.

Obama in Office

Obama periodically made a point of saying, "I'm not the president of Black America. I'm the president of all of America."[119] And a substantial number of voters seemed to take him at his word. Once Obama became the face of power and the face of the nation, however, acting as the president of all of America became more complicated. The early agenda in 2009 was crowded with emergency measures to blunt the impacts of the 2008 recession, including an economic stimulus package and measures to prop up failing industries. After this initial flurry, Obama got to work on his signature legislation, and the legislative aim of every Democratic president since Harry Truman: health-care legislation. The legislation that eventually became the Affordable Care Act exemplified Obama's approach to being president of Black America—it was legislation intended to benefit Americans of all races, with the additional benefit of evening out racial disparities in health-care access.[120]

Obama's 2009 efforts to "go public" in support of the bill led to some of the defining racial moments of his early presidency. A press conference in July 2009 focused on the health-care bill turned to another topic when Lynn Sweet of the *Chicago Sun Times* asked the president about an incident the previous week in Cambridge, Massachusetts. Harvard professor Henry Louis Gates reportedly forgot his keys, broke into his own home, and was arrested on his porch after neighbors called the police. Not for the last time, Obama's habit of using casual language mixed awkwardly with his status as president. Recounting his understanding of the situation, he remarked, "The Cambridge Police acted stupidly in arresting somebody when there was already proof that they were in their own home."[121] Then he linked Gates's arrest to the history of "unfair treatment" of Blacks and Latinos by police.

Writing for *Slate* years later, Jamelle Bouie identified the 2009 press conference as the turning point for Obama with white Americans. The history that Obama invoked was relevant, Bouie wrote, "but Obama was supposed to be beyond race. By evoking past discrimination, he disturbed that fantasy. Immediately, because of his comments, the arrest of Gates went from minor kerfuffle to an issue of national discussion."[122] When the arresting officer, James Crowley, met with Gates and the president at the White House for a "beer summit," Obama's point about systemic issues was undercut and the gesture reinforced the idea that racism is a conflict among individuals rather than a feature of political structures. Moreover, Obama never enjoyed majority approval among white Americans again.[123] He might not have sought to be the president of Black America, but after July 2009, at least some Americans started to perceive him that way.

A few months later, Obama addressed a joint session of Congress about the health-care bill. When the president stated that the plan would not cover "illegal immigrants," a Republican congressman from Illinois, Joe Wilson, yelled, "You lie!"[124] The incident didn't amount to very much—congressional leaders of both parties rebuked Wilson for his behavior—but it did foreshadow some recurring themes in Obama's presidency. It showcased the contempt that he would face from some Republican lawmakers and others on the right, as well as the misinformation that would spread about the Affordable Care Act. Notably, the particular myth Wilson had in mind was that the legislation would benefit outsiders—presumably nonwhite undocumented immigrants—at the expense of white Americans.

The idea that Obama represented a foreign threat in the White House, allocating resources to undeserving minorities, was a motivating idea behind the Tea Party movement.[125] Formed initially to protest the so-called bailouts for people who could no longer pay their mortgages, the Tea Party framed the Obama presidency as one of illegitimate handouts and an unacceptable break with American constitutional tradition. They mobilized anger about government spending and claimed at different points to be focused on policy rather than race. Yet surveys and interviews repeatedly showed that these attitudes were not so easily disentangled from race.[126] It is also difficult to deny that the Tea Party was formed in direct response to the Obama presidency. There was a persistent accusation among its adherents that Obama was somehow inauthentic—that he was not a natural-born citizen, or that he was a Muslim instead of a Christian, as he claimed.

Tea Party leaders and followers, as well as other detractors, also expressed concern that Obama would favor African Americans (and sometimes other minority groups) over the needs of white Americans. A *New York Times* poll from April 2010 showed that Tea Party followers were more than twice as likely as other respondents to say that the Obama administration favored Black Americans over white Americans.[127] In qualitative studies, Tea Party supporters expressed sentiments about Obama being an "affirmative action" president who got his job solely because of his race and who, like other nonwhites, had been held to a lower standard.[128]

Decades of delegitimizing affirmative action and race-consciousness helped Obama opponents develop a series of resonant criticisms rooted in the colorblind idea that any discussion or acknowledgment of race was illegitimate and consciousness of race was evidence of reverse racism or relaxed standards. Thinking about Obama's presidency as a disruption of these colorblind assumptions helps us understand how movements like the Tea Party didn't just undermine Obama's legitimacy—they also challenged many of the assumptions driving politics more generally.

As the president and his allies worked to promote the Affordable Care Act, the duel fires of outrage over the president's "otherness" and the specter of government overreach continued to burn. The anger expressed at town hall meetings throughout the country signaled a shift away from politics as usual, even from the polarized politics of the Bush years.[129]

Scholars and journalists have now extensively documented the reception of Obama's presidency in racial terms and the impact on how race shaped American political attitudes. Perhaps the most extensive study has been Michael Tesler's analysis of the "spillover" of racial attitudes into Americans' policy views, especially on health care.[130] If we compare the relationship of race attitudes to policy opinions before and after Obama took office, we see that relationship becoming much stronger, suggesting that this was a major turning point in modern politics.

But what was the exact nature of that change? Obama was elected twice with a national popular vote majority, and he won support in states, like Iowa, with very small minority populations. He did not win the majority of the white vote.[131] It should be noted, however, that no Democratic presidential candidate has done so since the 1960s.[132]

By merging the power of the presidency with the idea of the "other," Obama's presence in the White House activated not only anti-Black racism but also other forms of xenophobia and prejudice. His Kenyan father, his Muslim-sounding name, his Black family—this background was, as many would point out, quite different from the background of every past president. Despite Obama's careful efforts not to upset the racial status quo, from calling out Black behavior and culture in his speeches to highlighting his biracial heritage, the fact remained that to think or talk about the forty-fourth president was to think or talk about race.

One such impact was to connect partisanship with anti-Muslim sentiment. Anti-Islam attitudes first emerged as associated with opposition to Obama in the 2008 election, including the primary. But later research has found that these effects lasted beyond the 2008 election, and even beyond the 2010 midterms. During the latter, a proposed Islamic mosque and cultural center in New York City near the former World Trade Center site became a campaign issue. What is more, feelings about Muslims and the Islamic faith were not simply connected to evaluations of Obama; they also proved to be important in determining votes in congressional races during the Obama years.[133] After decades of burying race in coded language, insisting on individual explanations for social problems, and denying the lasting impact of the country's racial history, rising Islamophobia upended political scripts for Republicans and at least some Democrats.

Race also crept into the conversations surrounding Obama's signature policy issue. After months of debate and legislative maneuvering, the Affordable Care Act passed along party lines and was signed into law on March 23, 2010. Obama had scored a major policy victory, achieving what past Democratic presidents—most recently Bill Clinton—had been unable to do. But he never fully gained control of the political story of the law. Although parts of the bill were often rated highly in polls, the bill itself, especially when tagged with the moniker "Obamacare," was much less popular. Racist myths proliferated about who the bill would benefit and what it would do.[134]

The Tea Party helped to fuel landslide Republican victories in the 2010 midterms, decreasing the Democrats' Senate majority and altering control of the House. Substantial Republican gains at the state level further affected the tenor of national politics and stymied the implementation of the health-care law. They also delivered to Obama an opposition party in Congress that was determined to undermine and oppose him at every opportunity—blocking legislation and nominations, threatening not to raise the debt ceiling in 2011, and shutting down the government in October 2013.

Despite the fierce opposition that Obama inspired on the right, his cautious approach also sometimes disappointed activists on the left. After running on a campaign promising change, Obama appeared to possess neither the will nor the tools to alter the status quo. As American studies scholar Keeanga-Yamahtta Taylor writes, "By any measure . . . African Americans under Obama are experiencing the same indifference and active discrimination; in some cases, these have become worse. Black unemployment has remained in the double digits throughout the Obama presidency. Even Black college graduates are more than twice as likely to be unemployed as white college graduates."[135]

While Obama was president, several high-profile shootings of young, unarmed Black men served as the catalyst for the organization of the Movement for Black Lives. The emergence of this movement highlighted the complexity of criticisms of Obama from the left, which decried the persistence of anti-Black violence alongside other political, economic, and institutional problems. Social movement scholar Elizabeth Jordan Davies explains the contradictions of this movement through the idea of "alienated activism"—the suggestion that Black Lives Matter activists sought institutional change and levied serious criticism of mainstream politics, while also sometimes operating within the party politics framework of the moment, forging some connections with the Democratic Party. As this period unfolded, its impact was twofold: First, the increasing social movement pressure on the Democratic Party to approach race differently ultimately moved it—if unevenly—away from its cautious stance. And second, the arrival of a significant movement that voiced its objections to conventional methods of doing politics created energy for less frequently pursued tactics like impeachment.

Protests against anti-Black violence once again highlighted the distinct role of the first Black president. In one sense, Obama could offer perspective that no past president could. After the murder of Trayvon Martin, a seventeen-year-old walking in his Florida neighborhood, Obama remarked that if he had a son, "he'd look like Trayvon." The president also said that he saw himself in the face of a young Black teenager, and he connected this personal resonance with the systemic issues facing African Americans, especially young men.

But these comments also brought backlash. By foregrounding race, the president had violated any pretense of living in a colorblind society, and critics accused the president of "race-baiting."[136] Critics pointed out that Obama's hypothetical sons would also have been born into "tremendous privilege," and that it was inappropriate for the president to make a local legal matter into a personal one.[137] The man who was eventually acquitted of Martin's murder, citing self-defense, also spoke out against Obama's remarks, claiming, "I'm also my parents' child, and my life matters, too."[138]

Obama had merged his race and all the history that it evoked with the immense symbolic power of the presidency. Presidential politics were permanently changed, and the race questions that had often bubbled under the surface of public debate had officially come to a boil. In the frequent moments when a Black president made race impossible to ignore, outrage from some corners was quick to follow.

In June 2015, a white supremacist named Dylann Roof opened fire in a Black church in Charleston, South Carolina. Among the nine people slain was Pastor Clementa Pinckney, whose eulogy Obama would deliver. Following these racist murders, the president took a leading role in a memorial service unmistakably rooted in African American tradition, and he spoke of grace and the tradition of civil rights activism in the Black church. The president could have treated the shooting as a single, tragic incident, but instead he connected it to history, placing Roof's actions in the context of slavery, and to public purpose, urging the American people to reflect on systemic racism and work to remedy it.[139] To the surprise of nearly everyone watching, Obama broke into song during the eulogy, leading the congregation in singing "Amazing Grace." Any pretense of a postracial presence was long gone. On the eve of an ugly and racially divisive presidential campaign to determine his successor, the nation saw a Black president in a Black church, raising his voice in response to violence and tragedy.

7

"Hostile Takeover"

THE TWO IMPEACHMENTS
OF DONALD TRUMP

AS THE election returns came in on the evening of November 8, 2016, it became clear that the nation was in for a big surprise. The polls had consistently favored Democratic candidate Hillary Clinton, if narrowly. On Tuesday evening, however, early returns cast this prediction into doubt. By midnight it was all but over: Trump, a businessman with no elected experience, had won the presidency. Clinton won the popular vote, but Trump victories in Michigan, Wisconsin, and Pennsylvania were enough to propel him to an unexpected victory in the Electoral College. And he had won it with a campaign that broke all the unwritten rules about what candidates could say—about women, about immigrants and racial minorities, and even about Senator John McCain's time in a prisoner-of-war camp in Vietnam.

Trump's constant and wide-ranging norm violations led to strong reactions to the election result. A recurring theme among these reactions was the role of race in the election. On the night of the election, *New York Times* data journalist Nate Cohn posted on the social media site Twitter that predictions had not counted on the possibility that white voters would act like a racial voting bloc, yet that was exactly what had happened.[1] Many analysts agreed that race was part of the story, though they disagreed on exactly how it had shaped the vote.

In a more comedic and pointed analysis, *Saturday Night Live*'s Cecily Strong proclaimed in a sketch about election night, "I think America is racist." Her statement was received by knowing glances and eventually peals of laughter from Black comedians Chris Rock and Dave Chappelle.[2] The sketch hammered home two critical ideas: White liberals might have been shocked by Trump's appeal, but their Black counterparts were not surprised, and relatedly, Americans know that race drives US politics but often lack the precise language to describe it.

Gender also made the race story more complicated. The surprising defeat of the first woman to run for president on a major party ticket, especially after controversial statements and the discovery of a tape on which Trump bragged about committing sexual assault, lent itself to interpretations that put the campaign in stark gender terms. But these interpretations—featuring tearful women who had worn Hillary Clinton's signature pantsuit or dressed in suffragist white to the polls on election day—were swiftly criticized as "white feminism" that neglected a broader range of women's experiences. "White women voted for Trump" became a common refrain.[3]

These divisions emerged immediately in the planning of the Women's March for the day after Trump's inauguration. While some marched enthusiastically in pink "pussy hats," others decried the event's lack of inclusion.[4] By the end of the day on January 21, 2017, two things were clear. First, Trump's election had exposed the many social fault lines in American politics, but the legacy of the colorblind era had left Americans fumbling to find the words to talk about them. And second, with record numbers of Americans turning out to march against a president who had failed to win the popular vote and yet called himself the voice of the true people, the foundations of his presidency were shaken before he even moved into the White House.

Trump's Path to the Presidency

The Nomination

Donald Trump had been a household name for years by the time he sought the Republican nomination in 2015. He had flirted with presidential bids before, but they never went very far. Two factors propelled him to the nomination in 2016: his ability to harness and use the backlash against the Obama presidency, and the Republican Party's difficulty in coordinating its response to the same. Obama's presidency offered a unique opportunity to capitalize on racial backlash themes and turn white fear into donations and votes—but it also undermined the central conceit of that strategy.

Since the early 1980s, racially coded language had stood in for more overt appeals.[5] With the first African American president in the White House—the mixed-race son of a Kenyan Muslim—racial fears were a newly fertile terrain for ambitious politicians. Some elected Republicans chose to ride the wave of this backlash without engaging it directly.

But other Republicans, especially those on what were once the fringes of the party, embraced this approach more fully. In 2011, Trump attached himself to the "birther" movement, spreading the false claim that Obama had not been born in the United States and thus was not eligible to serve as president. At the time, Trump was also floating the idea of a presidential bid. As the *New York Times* reported several years later, "The more Mr. Trump questioned the legitimacy of Mr. Obama's presidency, the better he performed in the early polls of the 2012 Republican field, springing from fifth place to a virtual tie for first."[6] But Trump ultimately chose not to run in that cycle, and Obama defeated Mitt Romney for reelection.

However, Trump's promotion of a racist conspiracy theory set the stage for his later candidacy. By the end of Obama's second term, more material for a backlash had accumulated. In addition to the usual second-term frustrations, Obama had also attracted criticisms that were specifically related to the accusation that he favored immigrants and people of color over white Americans.[7] A few months prior to the 2012 election, Obama had issued an executive order authorizing Deferred

Action for Childhood Arrivals (DACA), which provided some relief for undocumented immigrants who had been brought to the United States as children. And in 2014, the Black Lives Matter movement emerged, forcing Obama to take a position on explosive questions about race and policing.

The growth of the Tea Party movement created a space for candidates who would take a hard-line stance on immigration and oppose the "others" that Obama represented.[8] Yet at the presidential level, the candidates still reflected a party consensus from a very different time and ideological persuasion. Jeb Bush, whose family name and traditional résumé made him appear a likely front-runner, tried to position himself as the "diversity" candidate, the one with a more favorable view of immigration.[9] Marco Rubio, a son of Cuban immigrants and a Florida senator also seen as an up-and-coming presidential hopeful, stated his support for a path to citizenship for undocumented immigrants.[10] But other Republican elected officials and candidates aligned themselves with the anti-immigration wing of the party.[11]

The increasingly ugly and abstracted debate about immigration captured elements associated with other racialized issues, such as crime and terrorism, as well as ethnonationalist concerns about language and culture. These issues—race, culture, and immigration—distinguished Trump supporters from other Republican primary voters. As John Sides, Michael Tesler, and Lynn Vavreck observe in their study of the 2016 election, "Trump's views on racial issues like affirmative action and crime did not necessarily put him at odds with other Republicans. But his views on immigration did."[12] Nevertheless, a wide swath of racial attitudes have been connected to support for Trump over other 2016 primary candidates, such as views on racial inequality and immigration and feelings toward Muslims and African Americans.[13] Another study found that white voters who felt strongly about their racial identity— meaning that identity was important and politically mobilizing to them—preferred Trump over the nine other top GOP candidates.[14]

Trump also ran explicitly against the "system" and the Republican Party, even as he sought that party's nomination. Research on political speeches from the primary season showed that Trump stood out among all the candidates for "anti-establishment" language that blamed elites and outsiders and was "simple and collectivist"—he used short sentences and words and frequently referred to "we" and "our."[15] His appeals also fit into historical patterns of right-wing populism. In the words of political scientist Joe Lowndes, "Trumpism links anxious racial standing to economic precarity, masculine worth, and political abandonment."[16]

Trump's insurgent campaign defeated the party's supposed rising stars—Senator Marco Rubio and Wisconsin Governor Scott Walker. (The latter dropped out before any voting began.) Trump defeated experienced politicians like Governor John Kasich of Ohio and former Governor Jeb Bush of Florida. As he won over primary voters despite the objection of party leaders, commentators characterized his nomination as a "hostile takeover" of the party.

But this characterization obscures the usefulness of Trump's "outsider" stance for these leaders. For a party that was divided over immigration during the Bush years and then had to scramble to address the backlash to the first Black president, Trump embodied a crucial compromise: His candidacy allowed party leaders to distance themselves from the bluntest expressions of backlash sentiments, while still cultivating the electoral benefit they brought to the party. Trump had great potential as a safety valve to release the worst of the anger and allow the party to move on.

Instead of collapsing in the primaries and allowing a more traditional nominee to advance, Trump instead showed considerable strength early and often as he paved a path to the GOP nomination. In this sense, Trump's nomination was a product of the kinds of dilemmas that hit the opposition party—and the more racially conservative party—after a disruption in the order.

The 2016 Republican National Convention was like none the nation had ever seen. Sure, there had been divisive conventions before, including the 1964 Republican convention, at which the unease with nominee Barry Goldwater was readily evident.[17] Many elected Republican officials were not in attendance in Cleveland, including John Kasich. Arizona Senator Jeff Flake, who would continue to clash with Trump until retiring from Congress in 2018, claimed to be "mowing his lawn."[18]

The convention itself presented a mix of standard speakers—politicians, hopefuls, and party officials—and unusual choices, such as 1980s TV star Scott Baio, Milwaukee County Sheriff David Clarke, and parents whose children had been murdered by undocumented immigrants. Absent some of the party's elder statespersons and up-and-coming stars, the convention was instead focused on the particular politics of the nominee. The combination conveyed the dual nature of an unusual convention that was superficially engaged in an entertainment-focused politics while also playing a deadly serious game of demonizing "others" and glorifying state violence.

The refrain of the convention, "Lock her up!"—a reference to Trump's Democratic opponent, Hillary Clinton—played directly to critics' concerns that the party had taken an authoritarian turn. In addition to inflammatory claims about immigrants and crime, the convention also took issue directly with Black Lives Matter protesters. These arguments came directly from Black conservatives at the convention touting the "Blue Lives Matter" and "All Lives Matter" slogans and praising the acquittal of a Maryland police officer accused of murdering a Black man.[19] After riding racial animus and anxiety to the nomination, Trump and his surrogates used the convention to continue to stoke the flames.

Populism in the Democratic Party in 2016

The Democratic Party also had a populist moment in the aftermath of Obama. Populism on the left has repeatedly proven to be very different from the George Wallace–style populism that Nixon harnessed or the brand that Trump embraced. Nevertheless, its emergence in the 2016 primary contest highlighted some crucial divisions within the party.

A left critique of the Obama presidency took aim at both the specific policies of his administration and at the modern Democratic Party as an institution. Obama had not done enough to address the economic inequality between Black and white Americans, these criticisms maintained, and his response to the 2008 financial crash was typical of a tepid Democratic Party captured by powerful financial interests. The Black Lives Matter movement had also formed, notably, during the tenure of a Black president. Both developments were traceable to a growing sense that the party was not living up to its stated commitment to poor citizens and citizens of color.

The Democratic presidential candidates in 2015 struggled with this issue. Both Martin O'Malley and Hillary Clinton were criticized for saying "all lives matter" in response to activist demands. For Clinton, this was an early stumble in a campaign that would often be caught in a difficult position with regard to "identity" issues. In some ways, such as showcasing a wide range of social groups in her 2015 announcement video, Clinton took a progressive approach to these questions. Her position as Obama's successor—free of the constraints he faced as the nation's first Black president—allowed her to talk on the campaign trail about systemic racism.[20] But Clinton faced struggles over her past statements and positions, particularly a comment she made about "super-predators" in the 1990s in connection with a crime bill championed by her husband, former President Bill Clinton. In February 2016, Clinton was confronted publicly by an activist about her words twenty years before: "No conscience, no empathy, we can talk about why they ended up that way, but first we have to bring them to heel."[21] Clinton apologized when confronted, but continued to be burdened by the baggage from her identification with the racist language and ideas around crime that were prevalent in both parties in the 1990s.

Clinton's mixed racial record created an opportunity for another candidate to step in, though Vermont Senator Bernie Sanders would find this role an uncomfortable fit. Some well-known Black progressive thinkers lent their support to Sanders. Michelle Alexander and Ta-Nehisi Coates, authors of popular works on structural racism in the United States, endorsed Sanders, as did the lively and controversial public intellectual Cornel West.[22] But Sanders remained a relative unknown among Black Democratic primary voters. The Congressional Black Caucus Political Action Committee endorsed Clinton, with civil rights hero John Lewis stating that he had "never seen" Sanders while organizing for civil rights in the 1960s—a direct refutation of Sanders's claims to have been active in the movement.[23]

The Democratic presidential candidates exemplified the challenges facing the party on race issues after Obama. The chosen successor of the first African American president was well known in Black political circles, but she carried the baggage of the party's turn to the center in the 1990s. The choice of progressive activists was a relative unknown to Black voters, and his critique of establishment politics revealed the fraught nexus of outsider claims, race, and the political parties. While racial inequality persisted in American life, Black politicians had become a crucial pillar of Democratic Party politics.[24] As a presidential candidate, Sanders sought to position himself to the left of Clinton on race issues, but as an insurgent candidate, he was implicitly (and sometimes explicitly) critical of both Obama and a party establishment partially defined by figures like Representative Lewis, the Democratic National Committee's Donna Brazile, and Representative James Clyburn (D-SC). Sanders's brand of leftism also lent itself to later complaints that the party's emphasis on "identity" should be replaced by greater attention to economic issues.[25] These divisions looked different from past party dilemmas after racially disruptive presidencies, but when it came to moving forward after Obama, the Democratic Party, as in the past, lacked a clear road map.

The General Election

The puzzle of the 2016 election was that it broke with precedent and norms in many ways—the first woman was nominated by a major party, as was a reality TV star with no history of military or public service. However, after a campaign that was often unconventional and shocking, the voting results looked much like what political scientists' prediction models had suggested: A close race ended with a slight edge in the popular vote for Hillary Clinton.[26] The shifts that did occur reflected the long-term trend in partisan politics toward racial polarization, which, as we saw in chapter 6, dated back at least to the Reagan years.

Yet the blunt treatment of race and identity in the campaign resolved an old paradox. In the years leading up to Obama's presidency, the influence of race was everywhere and yet often remained unspoken. When

Obama's entry into presidential politics made this untenable, these divisions surfaced—racism, anxiety, and prejudice among some Americans, alongside dismay and anger at the lack of racial progress among others. The 2016 campaign did not resolve all of these contradictions, but it brought these topics into the mainstream of the political conversation and offered politicians new opportunities to "say the quiet part out loud." Resolving contradictions in racial attitudes, however, was not the same thing as resolving or addressing the underlying issues. Far from it, in fact.

Trump's campaign tactic of whipping up anti-immigrant attitudes continued through the general election. The rallies that became the mainstay events of his campaign were an especially apt and chilling venue for these tactics. While campaigning for the nomination, Trump had called for a "total and complete shutdown of Muslims entering the US," and he continued to call for such a policy after he became the official GOP candidate. Trump's language connected immigration and national security and suggested that Muslims did not share American values or "love our country."[27] Applying the national security frame to Muslims was a throwback to Bush administration ideas and also bled into a more disturbing nationalist framework. As a result, anti-Muslim sentiment, from stereotyping to dehumanization, was associated with support for Trump and his proposed restrictionist policies.[28] As rhetoric scholar Jennifer Mercieca explains, "Trump portrayed the nation as inherently pure and illegal immigrants as a dangerous infestation."[29] The idea of the border wall reinforced the sense of immigration as not a policy or humanitarian issue but a foreign invasion.

Election Night

Going into election night 2016, Trump was expected to lose. Despite close polls, many election-watchers assumed that Trump's lack of experience and lack of conventional "ground game" would drag him down.[30] Inflammatory statements that seemed to "insult every possible group" didn't seem like they would enhance Trump's chances at the ballot box.[31]

In anticipation of a Clinton triumph, women posted photos of themselves on social media going to the polls in pantsuits, a gesture meant to honor Clinton's signature outfit. So many came to Susan B. Anthony's grave, which was covered with their "I Voted" stickers, that the cemetery extended visiting hours on election day.[32]

And Hillary Clinton did win the popular vote by three million votes, marking the 2016 election with the largest discrepancy between the popular and Electoral College results in American history. Past Electoral College reversals, as in 1876, 1888, and 2000, had been the product of razor-thin margins, electoral confusion, or both. The 2016 election featured neither.

What had happened was that a handful states presumed to be safely in the Clinton column had instead been won by Trump: Wisconsin, Michigan, and Pennsylvania. Narrow victories in those states propelled Trump to a solid victory in the Electoral College. In addition to those states, Trump won handily—and expectedly—in Ohio, once considered a crucial swing state, and he came within two percentage points of Clinton's vote share in Minnesota.

Trump's surprising success in these Midwestern and Rust Belt states prompted a particular set of explanations for the election. Amid numerous accounts of the result examining, for instance, campaign choices, Hillary Clinton's shortcomings, and Russian interference, those that emphasized identity and the political transformation of the "white working class" held a special place in the debate about why Trump won the presidency.[33]

The White Working Class

Trump's populism can be broken down into three facets: complaints about the political establishment; departure from traditional Republican policy positions in favor of, for example, more protectionist stances on trade; and the claims that some Americans—namely, the much-storied "white working class"—were being left behind. As with Andrew Johnson and Richard Nixon, Trump's populism, once he took office, connected racial backlash and lawless, norm-flouting presidential behavior.

While Trump's overtly racist statements undercut his legitimacy, some of the larger narratives advanced by academics and journalists emphasized other aspects of his appeal. In the wake of the surprising election result, J. D. Vance's *Hillbilly Elegy*, a book about his Ohio upbringing with his Kentucky-born parents, gained popularity, as did sociologist Arlie Russell Hochschild's *Strangers in Their Own Land*.[34] Hochschild's claims about Trump voters amounted to an argument that they were not racist per se, but instead resented others whom they perceived to have "cut in line" and received special treatment while they themselves were unable to get ahead.[35] As political scientist Laura Bucci wrote in a review of the academic literature on the white working class, "The perception that others are succeeding while people like you are not is pervasive."[36]

These claims, especially Hochschild's, echoed Richard Nixon's "silent majority" rhetoric, stripping backlash of its racial content and arguing instead for a nostalgia for a time when a particular set of rules determined merit and justice. They also amplified an economic narrative, suggesting that part of Trump's success in 2016 was owed not to attitudes about race, immigration, or identity but to the sense of "economic anxiety" in areas of the country that had been ravaged by globalization, poverty, and drugs. A plethora of social science studies challenged this narrative, however, and found instead consistent support for the race, immigration, and identity explanation.[37] In other words, people were talking about race and about whiteness. The colorblind era in presidential politics was definitively over, and whiteness was no longer an unspoken default. But the mythology surrounding the "white working class" vote for Trump sometimes served to undermine the race story and replace it with an economic story, emphasizing those perspectives over the stories of other Americans.

The Trump Presidency

Setting the Tone

Donald Trump was inaugurated as the forty-fifth president of the United States on an overcast and unseasonably mild day in Washington, DC. His speech made it clear, once again, that this would not be a standard presidency and that a dark, far-right populism would motivate its main political claims. The address mixed Nixon-esque themes of "forgotten Americans" with stark images of an America divided between the establishment and the people: "Their victories," he proclaimed, "have not been your victories." These populist messages were, crucially, combined with nationalist ones: The president promised to make all decisions according to the principle of "American first" and to end "American carnage." Painting a grim and violent picture of the status quo, the new president invited the audience to blame their political adversaries for the country's problems and to reject and resent anything deemed foreign or different.[38]

In the hours after inauguration, several key features of the Trump presidency began to take shape. One was the new president's determination to repudiate and compete with his predecessor, Barack Obama. Immediately, Trump began insisting that his inauguration crowds had been larger than Obama's, a fact clearly refuted by photographs of the events. Only hours after being sworn in, he signed an executive order allowing agencies to "ease the economic burden" of the Affordable Care Act, Obama's signature legislation.

A week after taking office, Trump also fulfilled one of his campaign promises: He signed an executive order banning entry into the United States of travelers from seven predominantly Muslim countries. In more ways than one, Trump soon learned that campaigning and governing are not the same. First, the order created chaos as well as controversy. The White House had not consulted with the relevant cabinet departments about the legality and logistics of the policy, and the provision banning entry was so vague as to be unclear about whether US residents arriving from those countries would be allowed to enter.[39]

It was also unclear whether the order truly was a "Muslim ban." The American Civil Liberties Union and other advocates went to work immediately to challenge the executive order in court on religious freedom grounds. Trump's past statements left the administration very vulnerable to such challenges. Critics pointed to a 2015 campaign statement calling for a "complete shutdown of Muslims entering the United States until our country's representatives can figure out what is going on."[40] Trump revised the travel ban two times before it took effect in late 2017, having survived later legal challenges. Defenders argued that the excluded countries represented only a fraction of the world's Muslim population; nevertheless,

Trump could not help making more incendiary statements on social media. In June he tweeted that the Justice Department was issuing a "watered down version" of the ban, in a concession to political correctness, instead of the "extreme vetting" that the president had advocated. Advisers like Stephen Miller, a well-known ally of far-right causes, also clarified the intent and meaning behind the policy.[41]

The early lessons were clear: The new administration would orient itself toward its supporters rather than aim at building a broader coalition. It would use the tools of the executive branch, rhetorical and legal, to those ends. It would not be especially concerned about norms or even legal boundaries. And the statements about race in the campaign—about the true, "forgotten" Americans, about the state of the inner cities, about Muslims and immigrants—were not mere election rhetoric. They were real promises about how Trump would govern.

Early Impeachment Talk

As with both Andrew Johnson and Richard Nixon, Trump drew an immediate set of detractors who saw him as unfit for the presidency. Over time, new revelations and events intensified these concerns. At the same time, others in the opposition party were cautious about the possible political fallout from going near the topic of impeachment.

The first round of discussion of Trump's possible impeachment was sparked by revelations about Russian interference in the 2016 election. In the weeks and months following the 2016 election, journalists uncovered Russian efforts to sway the election in Trump's favor. Possible interference included misinformation campaigns on social media, opposition research efforts, and hacking into Democratic National Committee emails. The big question moving forward was whether the Trump campaign had worked with the Russians, possibly violating campaign finance and other laws.[42]

In early May, Trump fired FBI Director James Comey, just as the bureau was beginning investigations into the campaign collusion issue. Based on Trump's firing of someone charged with investigating him, the "Saturday Night Massacre" comparisons began immediately, with commentators questioning whether the firing constituted an egregious abuse of power that would eventually spell the president's downfall.[43]

Early on in these discussions, the blend of legal and political concerns was evident. The extensive focus on lies told by Trump and his associates about their contacts with Russia was reminiscent of the debates during the Watergate scandal over "the cover-up versus the crime." Trump's decision to fire Comey was also in this gray area. Presidents enjoy wide latitude to select executive branch personnel, but the proximity to an investigation fueled an existing line of criticism among Trump opponents and sat poorly with the American public. In June, one poll found that an overwhelming majority responded that Trump had fired Comey "to protect himself" (61 percent) rather than for the good of the country (27 percent).[44] Another poll showed that more Americans disapproved than approved of Comey's firing, though nearly one-third reported not knowing enough to form an opinion.[45]

Journalists started asking if the Russia story would be the unraveling of the Trump presidency. The Watergate frame was powerful. But in 2017 as much as in 1973, the steps for holding the president accountable were anything but automatic. The process was guided instead by the often slow and highly risk-averse politics of Congress. Despite the consistent hum of talk about impeachment as more Russia revelations came to light, congressional attitudes toward impeachment remained cautious.

A steady public uneasiness about Trump's presidency echoed Andrew Johnson as well as Richard Nixon. Not only was this president willing to break laws and norms and to use executive power for his own ends rather than the good of the country, but, as with Nixon, the wrongdoing taking shape was beginning to look like disregard for institutions and obsessive disdain for political opponents. And recalling the Andrew Johnson administration, Trump's misuse of the presidency was also done in the pursuit of turning back racial progress.

Charlottesville

A turning point in Trump's presidency came in the middle of August 2017. The "Unite the Right" rally in Charlottesville, Virginia, drew a group of violent neo-Nazis to the area and ultimately resulted in the death of a local activist, Heather Heyer, who had come to protest the far-right rally. This disturbing event signaled the growing presence of white nationalism and the threat that it posed to peace and democracy. But it was the president's reaction that reverberated through politics, enraging critics and altering the political debate. Trump's most famous reaction was to state in a press conference that there were "good people on both sides" of the clash between protesters. This statement was repeated frequently by Trump's political opponents and formed the basis of Joe Biden's ad announcing his candidacy in 2019.

But in his comments Trump did not simply suggest that the far right deserved some sympathy. He also empathized with the rally's racist motivation: to protest the removal of Confederate statues (specifically, Robert E. Lee) by the left in an attempt to "rewrite history." Rhetoric scholar Samuel Perry describes Trump's comments as "mournful"—not for the activist who lost her life, but for a way of life in which the dominance of whiteness and masculinity was unquestioned.[46] In other words, when it was time to renounce white supremacy, Trump fumbled (especially off-script). When it was time to take sides on the issue of removing Confederate statues, Trump's loyalties were clear.

Charlottesville focused national attention on exactly what had changed in American politics. The unspoken connections between race and politics were now stated explicitly and were increasingly difficult to obscure or dodge. For the many politicians who had built their careers sidestepping the issue—conservatives relying on dog whistles, liberals engaging in more subtle forms of racial distancing—this was a profoundly uncomfortable and destabilizing position.[47] The incident also pinned down Trump's place in this evolving landscape: To many observers, Charlottesville removed all doubt that he sided with white supremacists. Other Republicans did not want to be forced to triangulate between a conservative position on Confederate monuments and related cultural issues while also rejecting neo-Nazism.[48] For Democrats, the president's missteps offered an opportunity but also opened up difficult questions about how to respond.

Suggestions that Trump's statements and actions on race might warrant impeachment had been floated prior to the Charlottesville violence. Representative Joaquin Castro (D-TX) had suggested the possibility that the "travel ban" was impeachable.[49] Representative Maxine Waters (D-CA) had made remarks in April 2017 that paralleled descriptions of Andrew Johnson: "He's not working in the best interests of the American people. His motives and his actions are contemptible."[50] Waters pointed to Trump's efforts to "delegitimize" the first African American president as evidence for her claims about his intent and lack of fitness to serve as president. Notably, Waters "walked back" her calls for impeachment, though her criticisms remained spirited. By late summer 2017, the idea that Trump's racial views could constitute an impeachable offense had become a recurring, if controversial, point among Trump's fiercest critics in the House of Representatives.

For legislators who harbored suspicions of Trump's far-right sympathies, his Charlottesville response was an anchoring event. When Representative Steve Cohen (D-TN) announced his intent to file articles of impeachment against Trump, he described the events in August as reminiscent of Nazi Germany.[51] A few weeks later, the Congressional Black Caucus met to discuss racism in the federal government, citing numerous Trump administration policies and statements. Caucus chairman Cedric Richmond (D-LA) also suggested that the group had discussed impeachment.[52]

Trump's Charlottesville remarks both clarified and muddled the role of race in debates about presidential legitimacy. The events offered a concrete set of complaints, complete with vivid images of white supremacist violence and the president's oft-repeated line about "fine people on both sides." For those already inclined to believe such a story, Trump's reaction proved that he was not concerned with representing the entire country and that, when pressed, he would stand with white supremacists, even in the face of violence and extremism.

The arguments about Trump and race added new dimensions to the persistent dull roar of impeachment discussion. Questions about whether racism and white supremacy were impeachable offenses were added to the debate about Russia, the Comey firing, and other problems more in line with the "abuse of power" reasoning that had long dominated impeachment politics. The possible causes for impeachment spanned a wide array of faults and factors, some with more overt racial implications—just as impeachment politics had unfolded with Johnson and Nixon. The broadening impeachment discussion was also met with concerns about the political risks. Prominent Democrats had spent the summer advising caution and fighting the possibility that they would be perceived as trying to nullify the 2016 election or remove the president over policy and philosophical disagreements rather than his concrete actions.[53]

By late 2017, the impeachment conversation was conducted at the intersection of these two problems. Past impeachments had not clarified what met the standard for "high crimes and misdemeanors," though they had established some common themes. The essence of the Johnson and Nixon impeachments had been a critical mass of congresspersons becoming convinced that the president was using the office for his own political goals rather than to protect and defend the interests of the nation. But now, while Democratic leaders disavowed, understandably, the role of politics in the process, politics—especially racial politics— were inseparable from what makes a president impeachable: a persistent pattern of undermining the public interest.

The 2018 Midterms

As the 2018 midterms approached, the shift in the congressional terrain became more apparent. Early in the year, Republicans had attempted to frame the midterms as a referendum on impeachment, hoping for an outcome similar to the 1998 Clinton impeachment.[54] Republican members of Congress as well as administration surrogates used the threat of impeachment to charge their opponents with having no agenda. Impeachment talk, whether coming from legislators, members of the White House team, or the president himself, helped to unify the party around a sense of being persecuted by the other side.[55] Republicans were not the only people who saw the issue this way. Moderate Democrats, along with the party's leadership, backed away from impeachment in favor of other priorities, especially those that corresponded with local pressures from members facing tough reelections, like Senator Joe Manchin (D-WV). The impeachment question was less unifying, however, for Democrats, whose base was "clamoring both for aggressive investigations and movement to remove Trump from office before 2020."[56] Earlier in the year, a poll suggested a wide gap between Democrats and public opinion in general: 71 percent of Democrats supported impeachment, but only 38 percent of the general public had warmed to the idea.[57]

The 2018 midterm elections also showed that a post-Obama era had opened up new possibilities. Several progressive candidates defeated long-term incumbents in Democratic primaries. Among them, four women of color with progressive politics and an anti-establishment bent who formed what came to be known as "the Squad" in the House of Representatives emerged as important foils for Trump. A new group of officeholders elected in 2018 included more members of minority religions and nonwhite and LGBTQ individuals than ever before. Many had also forged their political careers in an explicitly anti-Trump mold.[58]

As the new class of legislators took their seats, the tension within the Democratic Party over the impeachment issue continued to roil. Rashida Tlaib celebrated her election to Congress by yelling, "We're going to impeach this motherfucker!" mere hours before being sworn in.[59] The new congresswoman's enthusiasm for the constitutional procedure underscored a sense among Republicans that fighting Trump for the sake of it was a central political goal for Democrats, especially some of those in this new and diverse class. Tlaib fit into many of the ideological and demographic categories associated with the emerging anti-Trump politics. In contrast, much of the Democratic leadership—an older, whiter, and less politically confrontational group—hewed to long-standing fears about impeachment. Their concerns were not without merit. Public opinion continued to be tepid, Clinton memories loomed, and a clear evidentiary path still remained elusive.

In other words, in a highly partisan and racialized political environment, the old impeachment dilemma was packaged in a new and more politically combustible way. Under backlash presidencies, the opposition has been divided between those who simply doubt the president's legitimacy and those who feel more bound by norms against impeachment talk. As with Andrew Johnson and Richard Nixon, legislators in the former category saw race questions as part of the problem with the legitimacy of Trump's presidency. While in past impeachment cases the role of race in questions around presidential legitimacy may have been subtle or implied, in the Trump case it was stated more clearly by some Democrats. Others, however, saw impeachment as reserved for presidents who had more clearly violated the rules of the political process.

Trump's Race Record

Trump called his agenda "America First," but as president he was constantly trying to police the boundaries of who was an American. In the months and even years following Hurricane Maria in Puerto Rico, the forty-fifth president of the United States continually spoke about the island territory as if he did not understand that it was part of the country he led.[60] In 2018, the president riled his base by picking a fight with NFL players who had chosen to kneel during the national anthem in protest against police brutality. He had previously called Colin Kaepernick, the NFL player most famous for taking a public stand on the issue, a "son of a bitch."[61] When referring to the other NFL players, Trump suggested that maybe they "shouldn't be in the country." He complained to advisers about too much immigration to the United States from "shithole countries"—the racial subtext of which was not difficult to decode by then.

In 2019, he said that the four congresswomen known as the "Squad" should go back to "their countries." All four women of color were US citizens at the time, and all but one were US-born. The facts in this situation did not deter the political response. Referring to Congresswoman Ihlan Omar, angry crowds chanted, "Send her back!" at a July 2019 rally, thus tying together the persecution of people of color, women, and immigrants.[62]

In these examples, we also see how the racial themes of Trump's presidency, conveyed through the president's consistent and thinly coded racism, shaped the same characteristics that ended in his two impeachments. In parallel with both Andrew Johnson and Richard Nixon, we observe in Trump a pettiness and an inability to tolerate political dissent. In his inaccurate declarations about who and what was part of the United States, we see an unwillingness to abide by the norms and rules set by others in society. Trump's remarks not only showcased his attitudes toward nonwhites and about the boundaries of what makes a true American but also underscored the politically reckless behavior that led Congress to initiate impeachment proceedings against him not once, but twice.

The Mueller Report and the Ukraine Impeachment

While congressional leaders shied away from impeachment talk during and after the midterms, the events of the fall of 2019 changed all that. Politics in 2019, starting with a monthlong government shutdown over budget negotiations, had not done much to smooth the relationship between the two parties. The main sticking point in these negotiations was the president's promised border wall, which he conceived of as a means of keeping immigrants from Mexico out of the country. The border wall issue demonstrated how questions of race and identity drove Democratic opposition to the Trump agenda. The president's State of the Union address was delayed when Speaker of the House Nancy Pelosi (D-CA) rescinded her invitation to him during the government shutdown. Trump eventually delivered the address, a week later than originally planned, but the exchange illustrated the tone between the parties at that point in time.

Nevertheless, Pelosi remained a voice for caution on impeachment, preferring to assemble a larger and ideally bipartisan coalition. Others looked to the release of Special Counsel Robert Mueller's report on the investigation of Russian interference in the 2016 election for the kind of concrete evidence needed to prove their intuition that the president was unfit for his office.[63]

The special counsel's findings, released in a redacted version that spring, did little to clear up the major questions of the day. Instead, the report was just ambiguous enough to be susceptible to political spin from all sides, and ambivalent enough in its conclusions to frustrate the administration's strongest critics. Mueller's report and his subsequent congressional testimony over the summer avoided offering ammunition to either side of the partisan debate. The report instead suggested that the Russian government had sought to interfere with the 2016 campaign and that the Trump campaign had not objected to its assistance. Yet the actions of Trump and his associates fell short of collusion or of criminal standards for campaign misconduct.[64] The report also adhered to a standard established during the Nixon administration that sitting presidents should not be indicted. Although the report made it clear that the special counsel's decision not to pursue criminal charges was based on this standard and not on an absence of evidence, Trump claimed that the report cleared him of all wrongdoing.

With the Mueller report concluding so inconclusively, Democrats' impeachment dreams were temporarily dashed. However, the events of that fall would change all that.

The Ukraine case was important on its own, but it is impossible to remove it from its context: Throughout Trump's time in office, his critics had looked for reasons to undercut his legitimacy in office. These legitimacy issues stemmed directly from Trump's use of racial backlash politics to build a political following: his comments about immigration, his attacks on nonwhite legislators and citizens, and his intolerance for competing perspectives or Democratic opposition. The pervasive sense that Trump did not belong in office and was incapable of carrying out his constitutional mandate to represent the nation as a whole was not without reason. But this perspective lent itself to the kind of scandal-shopping that unfolded with Andrew Johnson and Richard Nixon (and Bill Clinton, to a degree). The hope was to find a specific offense that sounded plausibly like an article of impeachment and could bring together a sufficient coalition in Congress to support an impeachment. Finding an offense that was concrete and serious enough to help members of Congress overcome the political barriers to impeachment was key in each presidential impeachment case.

In September 2019, congressional Democrats found their concrete offense. On July 25, shortly after Mueller testified in Congress about his report's findings, Trump had a phone call with Ukrainian president Volodymyr Zelenskyy. During this call, the US president threatened to withhold congressionally authorized financial assistance to Ukraine unless the Ukrainian government agreed to investigate the business dealings of Hunter Biden, the son of Trump's top rival for the 2020 election. The Ukraine phone call provided that offense for House Democrats in 2019. In addition to the abuse of power and the illegality, it was also revealed that various White House officials had gone to great lengths to conceal the record of this call.[65] The Ukraine story also changed how House Speaker Nancy Pelosi, previously cautious on the impeachment question, thought about moving forward with an inquiry. And the national security implications of withholding aid from Ukraine for political reasons spurred the "national security freshmen"—a moderate and risk-averse group of Democrats elected from swing and right-leaning districts in 2018—to open up to the possibility of impeachment.[66]

Testimony before the House of Representatives highlighted some of the recurring Trump themes, including the questionable competence of his circle of loyalists and his willingness to put his own political fortunes ahead of the national interest and the needs of figures like Alexander Vindman, a Purple Heart veteran and member of the National Security Council who testified against the president.[67]

Nothing about the impeachment process in 2019 was explicitly linked to racial backlash, despite previous and repeated suggestions that Trump's words and deeds in that area might be worthy of impeachment. But race themes are never far from election issues, especially where election interference is concerned. Russian involvement in the 2016 race had been aimed at discouraging Black voters and taking advantage of racial divisions.[68] The accusations leading to impeachment centered on Trump's effort to derail former Vice President Joe Biden, the candidate most favored to beat him in 2020 and the one preferred by Black Democratic voters. Biden was also the candidate who had taken on Trump's connection with white supremacy directly in his campaign announcement.[69]

When the impeachment went to the Senate, the most familiar Trump-era theme of all dominated the process: the closing of partisan ranks. The Republican-controlled Senate voted against hearing witnesses at the trial, shortening the process.

The two articles, abuse of power and obstruction of Congress, echoed past impeachment themes. And like past impeachments, the formal charges against Trump seemed to get at the main issues only indirectly. As with the boredom that met charges that Andrew Johnson had violated the Tenure of Office Act, or the endless rumination about "the cover-up or the crime" surrounding Watergate, Democrats second-guessed the Ukraine impeachment. Representative Jamie Raskin (D-MD) began to wonder, inspired by middling public support for impeachment, if the party should have gone for something less legally clear-cut but with more public resonance.[70] The legalistic nature of the impeachment process directs would-be impeachers toward specific infractions, but the politics driving these efforts are usually linked to larger patterns and problems.

The final vote on February 5, 2020, returned a not-guilty verdict, as expected. Mitt Romney became the first senator in US history to cast a conviction vote for a president of his own party: He voted "guilty" on the first article, abuse of power. Romney's own explanation for his vote cited a recurring theme in racialized impeachments: election interference. In his remarks on his historic vote for conviction, Romney emphasized the larger implications of the phone call that Trump had described as "perfect": "Corrupting an election to keep oneself in office is perhaps the most abusive and destructive violation of one's oath of office that I can imagine."[71]

These moments of anger, populism, and instability have produced presidents who are unusually willing to break laws and norms and to risk their entire political fortunes by refusing to accept the typical give-and-take of the election process. It was accusations of election interference—based on collusion with Russia—that primed the first impeachment of Trump. And it was the prospect of Trump's interference in the 2020 elections that finally tipped the scales in Congress toward pursuing impeachment in 2019. But as with past impeachment trials, neither article of impeachment was able to clear the necessary two-thirds threshold by garnering sixty-seven votes for conviction in the Senate.

The Crises of 2020

When Trump's impeachment trial ended in February, the crises of 2020 were just getting started. The Centers for Disease Control and Prevention (CDC) had learned at the end of 2019 that an "unidentified pneumonia outbreak" had occurred in China and connected to a "wet market" in

Wuhan.[72] By the end of January, numerous cases had been identified worldwide, including on cruise ships bound for US ports.[73]

As the world slowly realized the scope of the coming crisis, the Trump team debated internally about what to do. Trump was especially resistant to measures that might harm the economy, foreshadowing the partisan conflict over closing businesses, schools, and churches in order to stop the spread of the virus. In addition to increasingly bitter partisan conflict over measures to contain the virus, now identified as COVID-19, the chaos inflicted on American society by the pandemic had distinct racial dimensions. For example, the much more profound effect of the virus on communities of color was linked to structural factors, such as the greater likelihood that members of these communities worked in "essential" and public-facing jobs, such as retail, delivery, and health care.[74]

Because of its origins in China, the pandemic also opened up an opportunity for xenophobic slurs, demagoguery, and violence. While engaged in a back-and-forth in March with Chinese President Xi Jinping, Trump tweeted about "the Chinese virus," and in several other statements he used that phrase or the phrase "China virus."[75] When confronted with the racial implications of these statements—already circulating and offering pretext for increased hate crimes—Trump tried to walk back his statements and speak out in support of Asian Americans. On March 24, the president tweeted, "It is very important that we totally protect our Asian American community in the United States, and all around the world."[76] But in the context of Trump's past statements and overall political agenda—and his continued use of objectionable phrases like "Kung flu" at rallies—the racial impact of such speech was not easily escapable.[77]

By late spring, the pandemic had already killed thousands of Americans, sickened countless others, and upended many aspects of daily life. Against this tense backdrop, Trump became more vulnerable to many of the central criticisms that had persisted throughout his presidency. He was driven by loyalty, which took the form of partisanship in the American political landscape. His administration lacked competence, stability, and expertise. And much like Andrew Johnson and Richard

Nixon, Trump found that any claims he made to being "president of all the people" were increasingly difficult to prove.

The summer of 2020 only heightened the pressure. On May 25, a police officer in Minneapolis, Minnesota, arrested a Black man, George Floyd, in a gas station parking lot, then held his knee on the man's neck for eight minutes, killing him. Floyd's murder sparked protests across the nation as Americans in cities, suburbs, and small rural towns became outraged at racial injustice, police violence, and widespread social inequality. Towns and cities adopted curfews as the unrest turned into property destruction and occasionally worse violence.[78]

The protest activity created another moment in which the racial scripts of the recent past would not suffice. Long-serving Democrats and Republicans were accustomed to blurring their positions on the most divisive or unsettling racial issues and sticking to platitudes about equality and colorblindness. Obama's presidency had challenged that response, and Trump's had embodied the subsequent unraveling of the unsteady consensus. But now, nearly four years into Trump's administration, another moment had arrived that made race salient and forced politicians to stake out a position.

Trump responded to the protests by returning to familiar territory: condemning the protesters and advocating strong executive action. Specifically, he spoke with advisers about the possibility of deploying ten thousand troops in the streets of Washington, DC. Defense Secretary Mark Esper, Joint Chiefs of Staff Chairman Mark Milley, and Attorney General William Barr pushed back against this idea. Countering speechwriter Stephen Miller, who urged the president to take strong and decisive action against the "riots," Milley, Barr, and Esper warned against blurring the lines between military and civil authority, raising the chances of loss of life, and overplaying the federal government's hand.[79]

Trump, however, was determined to make his chosen statement in the moment. While law enforcement used tear gas to disperse protesters across the street, he announced from the Rose Garden that he was the "president of law and order."[80] After the area had been cleared, Trump posed for a photo outside of Saint John's Church in Lafayette Square, a move that was roundly criticized for its heavy-handed treatment of protesters and attempt to redirect attention to the president in a moment of national mourning and crisis.

The year of catastrophe and conflict set the stage for the 2020 election to be heavily inflected by racial themes. Some of the summer protests culminated in a controversial slogan, "Defund the Police." Questions circulated about whether the nation was undergoing a "racial reckoning," with new attention to issues of structural and historical inequity.

Amid these questions, Democratic presidential candidate Joe Biden chose Senator Kamala Harris (D-CA) as his running mate. With both Indian and Jamaican-American heritage, Harris became the first woman of color to run for vice president on a major party ticket. Race had already affected the Democratic contest to take on Trump: Biden had captured the support of Black voters in order to clinch the nomination, despite a historically diverse candidate field. In her own presidential bid, Harris had confronted the former vice president on the issue of busing in the first debate.[81] But her candidacy had failed to take off among nonwhite Democratic primary voters—or among anyone else—and the refrain "Kamala is a cop," a criticism of her decisions as a prosecutor in California, defined her among progressive activists.[82] But her nomination to the second slot on the ticket was well received among Democrats in the electorate, and the Biden-Harris ticket established itself as the political opposite of everything that Trump stood for.

The Trump campaign continued to make appeals for minority votes, highlighting the administration's criminal justice reform legislation and bizarrely holding a naturalization ceremony for new American citizens during the Republican National Convention. These efforts may have paid off, as polls suggested that Trump improved his performance with Hispanic voters, and maybe even with African Americans.[83]

But the Trump brand never shed its ties to white supremacy. During the first debate with Joe Biden, Trump was asked to disavow militias and white supremacist groups. In the words of historian Kathleen Belew, the president "attempted to misdirect attention to leftist violence before saying, 'Proud Boys, stand back and stand by.'" Despite Trump's later statements that he had meant "stand down" and his not especially credible claims that he did not know who the Proud Boys were, his statement was widely perceived as a "call to arms" for such groups.[84]

If the 2016 election reshuffled the electorate along identity lines, the 2020 election largely reinforced those patterns. In what political scientists John Sides, Chris Tausanovich, and Lynn Vavreck describe as the "Trumpification" of racial attitudes, questions about race and identity became all the more closely tied to partisan identity. An election held in an extraordinary year yielded very stable results: Many voters chose the same party in 2020 that they had in 2016.[85]

Winning just over 51 percent of the popular vote, Biden fell short of some expectations but nevertheless could claim not only a popular majority but the same Electoral College vote margin that Trump had garnered in 2016. Because of the high volume of mail-in ballots during a pandemic, combined with the prohibition in some states on counting votes before Election Day, the result was not called by the Associated Press until the Saturday after votes had been cast. That night, the new president-elect addressed the nation and spoke not only about restoring democracy but specifically about racism and about the rights of transgender Americans.

As a deeply contested campaign came to a close, the most rancorous season of the 2020 election had just begun. Trump refused to accept the result, riling supporters about the prospect of voter fraud.

In addition to the more than sixty lawsuits filed in the competitive states that tipped the election for Biden—Pennsylvania, Wisconsin, Michigan, Georgia, and Arizona—the press obtained a recording of a phone call between Trump and the Republican secretary of state in Georgia, Brad Raffensperger.[86] The president pleaded with Raffensperger to find 11,780 votes for him.[87] Despite his lack of success in court—nearly every lawsuit alleging voter fraud was dismissed, sometimes by very conservative judges, some of whom Trump himself had appointed to the bench—the Trump inner circle continued to press their baseless election claims. The accusations of fraud were concentrated on cities with large African American populations—Atlanta, Detroit, Milwaukee, and Philadelphia.

On January 6, Congress met to certify the Electoral College votes. According to the rules set by the Electoral Count Act of 1887, members of Congress could object to the certification of a state's votes. Any such objection had to be signed by both a senator and a member of the House, then approved by a majority in both chambers to be sustained. This process had not always been fully tranquil. For example, in 2001, members of the House, without the requisite counterparts in the Senate, objected to the "fraudulent" result in Florida owing to the disenfranchisement of voters there.[88] Vice President Al Gore, gaveling in his own defeat, continued with the day's business of certifying George W. Bush's victory. Notably, recent interruptions of the electoral vote counting process had been linked to race as legislators highlighted disenfranchisement and other voting challenges in states like Florida and Ohio. Some of these objections were presented, pointedly, by Black legislators.

The situation was different in 2021. Speaking at a rally that morning, the sitting president encouraged his supporters—who had traveled from around the country to support this cause—to march to the Capitol. Recalling Andrew Johnson's 1866 warning that "the substance of your government may be taken from you and the shadows remain to you," Trump told supporters, "And if you don't fight like hell, you're not going to have a country anymore."[89] As Congress did its work, legislators took the floor to speak for or against the election lies being circulated by Trump.

We know a lot more about what happened on January 6, 2021, in retrospect than most of the country knew at the time. The work of the Select Committee to Investigate the January 6th Attack on the United States Capitol in 2022 revealed new perspectives from within the White House as well as the experience of those in Congress that day. These hearings uncovered what many knew instinctively at the time: That many in the president's inner circle had told him that he had lost and should abandon his doomed fight to stay in office. That he had encouraged the mob in various ways. That for 187 minutes the president of the United States did nothing while insurrectionists brought chaos to the Capitol, threatening lawmakers, injuring police officers, and flying the Confederate flag in the halls of Congress.

That afternoon, Trump finally addressed the protesters, telling them, "Go home," then adding, "We love you. You're very special."

The Capitol was secured, and that night Congress returned to finish certifying the vote. An objection was raised against Pennsylvania's votes, and 138 House Republicans—a majority of the party caucus—voted to sustain it.

A nation already battered by the events of the past year was left reeling. There was talk of invoking the Twenty-Fifth Amendment, which provides for the president's removal if he is unable to discharge the duties of office. But this option was quickly abandoned. The possibilities for the president to push back were too many and too unpredictable, and it was unclear that a majority of the cabinet could be convinced to approve such an action. Some members of the administration, including Education Secretary Betsy DeVos, resigned in protest of the insurrection. After some back and forth over the Twenty-Fifth Amendment option, House Democrats began drafting impeachment articles.

A week later, the House passed a single impeachment article, inciting an insurrection, with ten Republicans joining the Democrats voting in favor. The Senate would not reconvene until after Biden's inauguration, making Trump the first president whose impeachment trial would take place after he had left office. Since removal was not an issue, the main consideration at stake was whether Trump would be ineligible to run for office again.

In the end, seven Republican senators joined Democrats to vote for Trump's conviction—not enough for conviction, but enough to challenge the idea that the impeachment was purely about partisanship. Some of the Republicans who voted against convicting Trump insisted that their objections were rooted in the unconstitutionality of impeaching a president who had already left office. Senate Minority Leader Mitch McConnell immediately gave a speech that, in lambasting Trump's role in the January 6 insurrection, was reminiscent of comments about Andrew Johnson's shortcomings after his 1868 acquittal.[90] It was just as evident that impeachment was a contested and ambiguous process that consistently fell short of imposing accountability. At least for the time being, Trump had evaded the consequences of his actions.

Though it was unsuccessful in convicting Trump or barring him from future office, the second impeachment tied race and presidential lawlessness together in lasting ways. A study published in 2024 established the connection between support for the insurrection and racial attitudes, arguing that the George Floyd protests had primed a sense of "racial threat" among some white Americans.[91] More than a year after these proceedings had concluded, the January 6th Select Committee met to go over Trump's role in the insurrection in a series of televised testimonies. The chairman of the committee, Representative Bennie Thompson (D-MS), highlighted the role of race when he introduced himself as a representative from a region where his own father was denied the right to vote under Jim Crow laws.[92] The hearings also prominently featured the experiences of Ruby Freeman and Shaye Moss, two Black women who worked as election officials in Georgia. They recounted the accusations from the Trump campaign that they had passed a flash drive between them "like heroin or cocaine," as well as the racist threats they received as Trump made them the face of his false Georgia election claims.

Trump's exploitation of the political environment after the upending of racial politics fit into a recurring historical pattern. Like Andrew Johnson, he escaped conviction in the impeachment process despite the widespread sentiment that he was unfit and had crossed important boundaries. Richard Nixon resigned the presidency, in the name of national unity, and avoided further consequences. Yet the distinct features of Trump's backlash presidency are difficult to deny: What came before him was not a civil war, a series of constitutional amendments, a second founding, or landmark legislation. It was simply a Black president. And even compared to Johnson and Nixon, Donald Trump's disregard for political practices, for laws, and for the election process was profound.

Joe Biden's Racial Presidency

On April 25, 2019, Joe Biden announced his candidacy for president. A highly diverse field of women, people of color, and the first openly gay major party candidate, South Bend Mayor Pete Buttigieg, had already joined the race. Biden's role as an older, white man with strong name recognition due to his service as vice president was soon clear. The keyword of the nomination race soon became "electability," a term often tied to the electorate's perceived anxieties about candidates who diverged from past molds. After Hillary Clinton's surprise defeat in 2016, Democrats were nervous about the electoral vulnerability of women, people of color, and anyone who might be perceived as stressing "identity politics."[93]

But Biden kicked off his campaign by reminding voters of one of the most racially tense and regressive moments of the Trump presidency: the Charlottesville, Virginia, "Unite the Right" rally and the president's response to it. The argument was clear: that with a president who represented a break with a nation that had historically fought for its ideals, this election would be a struggle for the "soul of the nation"—for its very identity. Biden's announcement signaled the potential start of a new presidential era—one in which the norms of colorblindness had been completely abandoned in favor of a keener sense of the role of race in the nation's history, and one in which the next president would have to pursue a reset in the wake of Trump's lawless populism.

Unlike Jimmy Carter, Ulysses S. Grant, and Rutherford B. Hayes, Biden's appointments to the executive branch and the Supreme Court—and his selection of a Black and Asian American woman to serve as his vice president—affirmed rather than refuted racial progress. Part of the story was a changed Democratic Party. After Trump, white Democrats demonstrated more progressive racial attitudes and emphasized the concerns of marginalized groups.[94] As a result, they were more receptive to the kinds of claims made during the 2020 Black Lives Matter protests, and Biden's party coalition was very different from Bill Clinton's in the 1990s. The party was better able to sidestep the long-standing strategy of "silence and evasion" in favor of more action-oriented calls.[95]

Political scientist Robert Smith notes that growing protest movements, alongside a changing Democratic coalition, made Biden uniquely responsive among modern presidents to Black interests. Yet Smith questions the long-term potential of the politics that made this possible.[96] Over the course of the Biden presidency, the racial political landscape became not only polarized but also fragmented, with different institutions moving in disparate directions. Opponents of racially targeted policies largely succeeded in challenging these programs in court. Biden pursued an economically liberal agenda in line with modern Democratic priorities, many of which were successfully signed into law. However, progressive critics registered dissatisfaction with the administration's inability to persuade recalcitrant lawmakers on voting rights.

Immigration also trapped the administration between critics across the ideological spectrum. Conservative narratives about immigration policy featuring "chaos at the border" resonated with voters and propelled Democratic legislators to adopt stances in favor of stronger security measures. But immigration advocates registered deep dissatisfaction with the administration as well. Vice President Harris earned the ire of critics on the left by saying, "Do not come," to potential migrants from Guatemala.[97] As the 2024 election approached, Biden issued an executive order to limit asylum access, drawing dissent from progressive Democrats.[98]

Shifting voting patterns also spurred talk of racial "depolarization," with African American and Latino men shifting toward the GOP in the 2020 election. Questions arose about whether movements to "defund the police" truly reflected the needs and wishes of Black communities.[99] In response to these shifting tides, Biden insisted in his 2022 State of the Union address that the right solution was to "fund the police." Perhaps the racial dynamics of the 2016 election had given way to something as new, muddled, and ambivalent as in past eras.

But at the state level, partisan differences remained as strong as ever. Republican-controlled state governments enacted bans on "diversity, equity and inclusion"—shortened as DEI in state programs. These bans sometimes include laws prohibiting educators from teaching "divisive concepts." Governor Ron DeSantis announced that Florida was "where woke goes to die," and he helped usher in a right-wing takeover of the state's acclaimed public liberal arts college, the New College of Florida.

Biden, Carter, and Grant

Some common threads tie Biden to past presidents who came after racial transformation, periods of disruption, and impeachment crises. Like Grant and Carter, Biden sometimes had difficulty figuring out how his presidency would fit into the politics that came before. These struggles came from personal politics as well as from the barriers posed by the system. Because of a changing Democratic Party, Biden was able to continue with some of the Obama administration's priorities and to carry the revolution further, referencing structural racism, enacting federal protections for transgender rights, and making a diverse array of appointments.

However, Biden's choices for federal office set him apart from Grant and Carter. He also faced significant political obstacles, including a party divided over whether more radical positions on race issues might harm its election chances. And as in the past, the Biden era saw remnants of racial backlash animating policy at the state level, highlighting one more way that federalism has been used to establish and preserve racial hierarchy.

The similarities between Biden and his similarly situated predecessors show how much the same structural factors limit what presidents in this position can do. But the differences showcase how much politics can change, and how much depends on the political choices of leaders in these aftermath periods.

8

Conclusion

THE CHOICES WE FACE: RETHINKING PRESIDENTIAL IMPEACHMENT

THE US CONSTITUTION says precious little about presidential impeachment, and the original document says even less about race. But the political system it created has bound these two features of American politics together.

We've long known that presidential impeachment crises happen when the larger political environment is under strain. The political chaos that results from challenging racial hierarchy also paves the path to impeachment. By studying the cases of Andrew Johnson, Richard Nixon, and Donald Trump, we see that populism is the connective thread. Populist leaders are able to seize on the forces of racial backlash to deliver a potent political message that unites the most regressive and riles those who are merely unsettled by a changing environment. Populism provides language to tell those who oppose racial progress that they are the "true people." It also has no room for political opposition and offers leaders a license to claim they represent the people as they flout laws and undermine their opponents. This is where presidents have gotten into trouble, ultimately courting impeachment.

Viewing populism through a race lens allows for a more fine-grained analysis of the connection between crisis politics and impeachment. It also helps to resolve some questions about impeachment by demonstrating that the individual actions of presidents certainly matter, but so does their context. The recurring politics of racial backlash help to explain how populist figures, prone to undermining institutions and rejecting the idea of the opposition, end up in the presidency at these moments.

Impeachment is about the behavior not only of presidents but also of Congress, which must overcome uncertainty and fear of political risk in order to put forward impeachment articles. Majority parties tread with caution, hampered by a lack of clear precedent for what makes an impeachable offense. Notably, however, each impeachment crisis has originated in a tension between representatives who pushed for impeachment early on and those who favored a more guarded approach. The former sensed something wrong with the president's leadership from the beginning, and such impressions have been consistently connected to race. But other members of Congress—often those in formal leadership positions—have proven more circumspect. The more measured approach to impeachment has been to consider political repercussions and to wait until grounds for more concrete and legalistic charges surface.

The Johnson, Nixon, and Trump impeachments have some common features at the intersection of legal and political considerations. As expected, all three were concerned with the boundaries of presidential power. All of them touched on election interference as well. Andrew Johnson was accused of meddling in the 1866 midterms by denouncing congressional Republicans. The impeachment articles that prompted Richard Nixon's resignation stemmed largely from his cover-up of the break-in at Democratic headquarters in 1972. And both of Trump's impeachments were over election issues—urging a foreign government to investigate Joe Biden in 2020, and when that did not work, encouraging an angry mob to storm the Capitol and interrupt the count of Electoral College votes. Furthermore, no impeachment process has resulted in the removal of a president. Nixon resigned, and the others were acquitted by the Senate.

Instead, presidential politics at these junctures enters a transitional period as each party negotiates what the next era of racial politics will look like. In these moments, the same political features—federalism, fragmented parties, and the pivotal influence of racially conservative voters—have helped to establish a "new normal" that retains many features of the old.

For the twenty-first-century "new normal," the road map of the past proves instructive. After the Civil War and then again after the civil rights era, the nation settled into a new racial order that substantially backed away from the most revolutionary commitments of the brief transformative period. Both parties have contributed to this development in the past. After the pattern has repeated for a third time with the Trump impeachments, the political system appears poised to repeat some elements of the past, but some crucial differences remain. Historically, the racially transformative party has retreated from its radical wing, bowing to electoral pressures to moderate its positions and accommodate more racially conservative forces. The racially conservative party—the Democrats in the 1870s and the Republicans in the 1970s—has in turn leaned into backlash positions, pursuing them at the state and sometimes national level.

After Trump left office in 2021, each party showed signs of settling into these familiar patterns. As chapter 7 notes, the Democratic Party led by Joe Biden and Kamala Harris has hardly been the party of the coalition's most progressive activists. And racial reaction politics is still readily evident within the Republican Party. However, two potentially countervailing political circumstances may guide the parties to a different kind of future.

The first is racial polarization, which built up in the United States for decades and still defines the party coalitions. As Desmond King and Rogers Smith note in *America's New Racial Battle Lines*, the racially liberal coalition has moved to the left, with more elements favoring solutions that directly address past racial harms and depart significantly from the status quo, such as abolitionism and reparations.[1] Similarly, King and Smith note that the conservative coalition has moved rightward. This political reality has produced presidential candidates who represent very different racial perspectives than in the past: Trump's consistent appeals to a racialized Christian nationalist vision of the nation are heard alongside an increasingly liberal and diverse set of Democratic voices.

The second change in American politics is the emergence of an increasingly diverse nation, including a more racially diverse political class. Although Trump's GOP seems to have abandoned the idea of minority outreach that was promoted during the Obama era, the party has nevertheless made some overtures toward racial diversity and appeals to nonwhites. The possible fissures in the coalition are evident in these developments.

Another crucial feature of this latest era of racial politics is a decisive move beyond a politics dominated by Black and white as racial categories evolve to reflect a changing populace.[2] Immigration and the politics of the US border have become central to national debates. And as ever, questions about gender and sexuality are intertwined with race in ways that create opportunities for populist politicians.

The racial politics of each period studied in this book—before the Civil War, before civil rights, and before Obama—were created by an environment in which the most divisive and explosive issues could be pushed off the political agenda. As the next stage unfolds, this seems a less likely scenario. Partisan polarization and never-ending media cycles ensure that these challenging issues will remain front and center for the politically engaged.

The lesson of the past is that these transitional periods are filled with choices. With coalitions in flux, presidents make decisions about what kinds of statements, appointments, and policies are politically feasible. When faced with the political consequences of pursuing further racial change, they have tended to pull back on these efforts. The months and years after backlash presidencies have often been associated with preservation, rebuilding, and restoring the national fabric of democracy. In this context, the more racially liberal party has tended to be pulled away from bold moves and has reverted instead to more risk-averse ways of doing politics. But in the twenty-first century, Americans determined to protect democracy can affirm that protecting democracy includes achieving racial justice.

In each iteration, racially transformative presidents have linked their actions to the nation's founding documents and promise. Each has gone back to the Declaration of Independence and its assertion that "all men are created equal" as not only a moral truth but the purpose of the nation.[3] Lincoln spoke and wrote about the importance of the Declaration, connecting the nation's "new birth of freedom" with its past. In advocating for the Voting Rights Act, Lyndon Johnson also drew on the Declaration's commitment that "all men are created equal." Barack Obama revisited these commitments in a 2015 speech commemorating the voting rights marches.

It is not a new observation that a deep tension exists between this purpose and the practices of the United States. What I hope I have done in this book is to highlight how these contradictions have informed presidential politics. Each time power has shifted as a result of direct confrontations with that simple proposition of equality, politics have been profoundly destabilized. These stories of "backlash" presidents demonstrate the depth and nature of the disruption that occurs when presidents use their power to bring political reality a bit closer to these ideals. As a result, US racial hierarchies continue to be rebuilt into the compromises and norms that make politics possible. Grappling with what this fundamental American problem means in institutional terms seems like the first step toward finding solutions that are deep and durable.

As in the past, both parties entered the post-impeachment period with internal tensions over what politics would look like in the future. Changing party coalitions heighten both the risks and the rewards of presidential action on difficult racial issues. And the range of issues that qualify has expanded—as has the pool of plausible presidential candidates. History is an imperfect guide to what might happen next with regard to race and the presidency. But both transformative and backlash presidents remind us of what is possible.

We Are Going Back

The 2024 election offered a preview of what the next era for race and the presidency might look like. As in past eras, the new seems poised to continue some of the problems of what came before. The period bookended by Reagan and Obama was characterized by racial polarization but constrained by norms of colorblindness and a lack of shared language to discuss disparities and conflicts. This tension was evident throughout the 2024 contest, from the unusual nomination process through Trump's November victory.

While Trump sailed easily to the GOP nomination for a third time, his main critic and rival was former South Carolina governor and UN ambassador Nikki Haley. Haley, the daughter of immigrants from India, adapted the colorblindness message for a new era by making a campaign talking point around the idea that "America is not a racist country."[1] After her presidential bid was over, Haley announced that she would support Trump. Other primary opponents who ultimately praised and endorsed Trump included Tim Scott, the first Black Southern senator since Reconstruction, and Vivek Ramaswamy, who, like Haley, is of South Asian descent.

Both Scott and Ramaswamy were considered vice presidential hopefuls, though it's unclear just how seriously they were taken by the campaign. Nevertheless, Trump went in a very different direction, selecting Ohio Senator J. D. Vance as his running mate. Vance's contributions to American politics had been somewhat inconsistent leading up to his 2024 selection for the Trump ticket. In 2016, he emerged as a prominent

Trump critic and offered his memoir, *Hillbilly Elegy*, as a critique of white working-class America and an explanation of the Trump phenomenon. However, eight years later, Vance embraced the nativism of the Trump movement with seeming alacrity, repeating lies about Haitian immigrants in Ohio eating pets. Vance ultimately acknowledged that the story was false.[2] When confronted with the fact that the immigrants in question were in the country legally, Vance responded that he considered them illegal anyway because he disagreed with the Biden administration's extension of temporary protected status to this group.[3] Vance's statements, and the resulting outrage from immigration advocates, would seem to portend a long period of partisan disagreement over basic facts and legal structures surrounding race and immigration.

On July 21, 2024, the previous election's electable candidate, Joe Biden, announced that he would suspend his campaign. His vice president, Kamala Harris, quickly garnered endorsements from all corners of the Democratic coalition. Harris's unexpected 2024 presidential candidacy demonstrated the impact of Obama on the party and the interest in candidates in the Obama mold. Such candidates would be outside the historical boundaries of presidential demographics but squarely within the usual ideological range, highly educated and credentialed, and decidedly nonradical.

Harris's cautious politics, sometimes derided on the left, did not do much to curb racist attacks. Some Republicans wasted little time in calling Harris a "DEI candidate," using race and gender to undercut the qualifications of the former senator and sitting vice president. These attacks from figures like *Fox News* commentator Jesse Watters and some Republican congressmen drew rebukes from the party's formal leaders.[4] Trump accused Harris of playing the "race card."[5]

Throughout the campaign, Harris drew praise for letting her race—and gender—speak for itself. As Jessica Bennett wrote of Harris in the *New York Times*, "Other people can talk about history; she'll be too busy making it." Yet the piece also noted the ways in which the Harris campaign evoked race and gender in other, unspoken ways. Harris held her first campaign event in West Allis, Wisconsin, just outside Milwaukee, one of the cities whose votes Trump had questioned in 2020. She spoke about abortion rights and voting rights but made no direct reference to her race or gender. Her historic status as a Black and Asian woman presidential candidate was clear enough to all observers. The aspirations of historically marginalized groups, as well as a message about abortion rights, were captured by one of her campaign slogans: "We're not going back."[6]

The visual and musical cues her campaign chose told a more subtle and historically connected story. The campaign chose "freedom" as its central message, accompanied by the song of the same name by Beyoncé. Modern campaign issues—gun violence, abortion rights, health care—dominated the campaign ad's text. But the subtext of a Black artist singing about freedom as the backdrop for a historic candidacy evoked the long history of struggles against slavery, oppression, and inequality.[7]

This implicit acknowledgment emerged in conversations about her candidacy, especially those about potential running mates. The possible running mates on the lists that circulated were nearly all white—Michigan Governor Gretchen Whitmer, Senator Mark Kelly (D-AZ), and the eventual nominee, Minnesota Governor Tim Walz. Commenting on a *Washington Post* podcast, political reporter Aaron Blake remarked of these candidates, "They all code more conservative than her."[8]

A changing American political landscape offered the Trump campaign the opportunity to capitalize on grievance politics—over race, immigration, and gender issues. A prominent advertisement featured Harris talking about support for "taxpayer-funded sex changes for prisoners" and maintained that "Harris is for they/them. Trump is for you," stoking fear and stereotypes about transgender Americans. Trump's closing rally in Madison Square Garden was described by the *New York Times* as "a carnival of grievances, misogyny, and racism."[9]

These strategies appeared to work. Unlike in 2016, Trump won both the popular vote and the Electoral College, staging one of the most remarkable political comebacks in US history. But Trump's victory and support coalition can be read several ways: Further gains with Black and Latino voters were evident, and likely concentrated among men. White voters remained the foundation of the Republican electoral base, and analysis revealed that race attitudes among Hispanic and Latino voters have driven partisanship, just as they have for whites.[10]

At first glance, the election of an impeached past president seems rather jarring, and perhaps out of step with past iterations of the pattern I've laid out in the previous chapters. Trump's extensive legal troubles, some of which were related to his efforts to subvert the 2020 election result, make this all the more startling an epilogue to the tumultuous events of 2021. But the past also shows that the disgrace of impeachment does not last for long. Andrew Johnson died a US senator. Richard Nixon, though never fully rehabilitated, remained a figure in Republican politics and enjoyed, before and after his death, some efforts to highlight other aspects of his presidency beyond Watergate. Upon his death in 1994, then-President Bill Clinton issued a proclamation that showcased Nixon's accomplishments and referred only to "defeats that would have ended most political careers."[11] Trump's polarizing politics seem unlikely to be received this way. But, perhaps fittingly, even the long-term political impact of impeachment has repeatedly proven to be ambiguous. And the major themes of racial backlash that Johnson and Nixon embraced were woven into the politics that came after them.

Trump's second inaugural address laid bare the ways in which the next era of the racial presidency would carry on themes from the Reagan years, while incorporating the sharp edges introduced during Obama's tenure. Sandwiched between promises to "begin the process of returning millions and millions of criminal aliens" to their countries of origin and declarations that the US government would recognize only two genders, male and female, Trump declared that "we will forge a society that is colorblind and merit-based."[12]

As in the past, racial politics have both faded from their heightened status in the 2016 election and settled into new contradictions. But the impact of the Obama years and the initial Trump backlash are also evident. It is hard to imagine Kamala Harris's ascendance to the vice presidency and to the Democratic nomination without Obama's presidency and its message that presidential politics can include a wider range of Americans—at least in theory.

A notable feature of racially transformative presidents is that their legacies in this area remain distinct. If subsequent Democratic presidents have talked about emulating LBJ's accomplishments, they focused on the major social legislation of the Great Society, not the civil rights revolution. Lincoln's Republican successors never came close to establishing the national and constitutional principles that he did—even as the task of enforcing Reconstruction policies could have used just as much care and creativity.

It is difficult, though not impossible, to imagine Obama's impact being similarly limited. His election opened up new possibilities for the kinds of Americans who could expect to perhaps serve as president. Two of the contenders to carry this legacy, Hillary Clinton and Kamala Harris, narrowly missed the opportunity. With Trump's return to office in 2025, it is likely that Biden's legacy will be subsumed into Obama's story, and that Biden will be seen as a figure who would not have become president without serving as Obama's vice president. The state of American politics at the start of a second Trump term suggests that race will remain on the public agenda, colorblindness claims notwithstanding, and that it will remain contentious. Democratic presidential hopefuls are unlikely to be limited to straight white men. The next president who falls outside these categories will have the Obama precedent to draw on, and thus be less poised to play a truly transformative role. But that story remains to be written.

January 20, 2025

NOTES

1. Introduction: Race and Presidential Impeachment

1. "Photos: *Black Enterprise* Exclusive Interview with President Barack Obama," *Black Enterprise*, April 13, 2012, https://www.blackenterprise.com/inside-black-enterprise-exclusive-oval -office-interview-with-president-barack-obama/ (accessed October 11, 2023).

2. "Rush Limbaugh: 'Obama's America—White Kids Get Beat Up with the Black Kids Cheering,'" *HuffPost*, November 16, 2009, https://www.huffpost.com/entry/rush-limbaugh -obamas-amer_n_288371 (accessed January 21, 2024).

3. Michael D. Shear, "Gingrich: President Exhibits 'Kenyan, Anticolonial Behavior,'" *New York Times*, September 13, 2010, https://archive.nytimes.com/thecaucus.blogs.nytimes.com /2010/09/13/gingrich-president-exhibits-kenyan-anti-colonial-behavior/.

4. "On Views of Race and Inequality, Blacks and Whites Are Worlds Apart," Pew Research Center, June 27, 2016, https://www.pewresearch.org/social-trends/2016/06/27/on-views-of -race-and-inequality-blacks-and-whites-are-worlds-apart/.

5. Josh Clinton and Carrie Roush, "Poll: Persistent Partisan Divide over 'Birther' Question," *NBC News*, August 10, 2016, https://www.nbcnews.com/politics/2016-election/poll-persistent -partisan-divide-over-birther-question-n627446.

6. Keeanga-Yamahtta Taylor, *From #BlackLivesMatter to Black Liberation* (Haymarket Books, 2016).

7. Michael Tesler, "Views About Race Mattered More in Electing Trump than in Electing Obama," *Washington Post*, November 22, 2016, https://www.washingtonpost.com/news /monkey-cage/wp/2016/11/22/peoples-views-about-race-mattered-more-in-electing-trump -than-in-electing-obama/ (accessed August 23, 2022).

8. Ta-Nehisi Coates, "The First White President," *The Atlantic*, October 2017.

9. Hakeem Jefferson and Victor Ray, "White Backlash Is a Type of Racial Reckoning, Too," *FiveThirtyEight* (blog), January 6, 2022, https://fivethirtyeight.com/features/white-backlash-is -a-type-of-racial-reckoning-too/.

10. Brenda Wineapple, *The Impeachers: The Trial of Andrew Johnson and the Dream of a Just Nation* (Random House, 2020).

11. Russell L. Riley, *The Presidency and the Politics of Racial Inequality: Nation-Keeping from 1831 to 1965* (Columbia University Press, 1999), 11.

12. Megan Ming Francis, *Civil Rights and the Making of the Modern American State* (Cambridge University Press, 2014).

13. Lilliana Mason, *Uncivil Agreement: How Politics Became Our Identity* (University of Chicago Press, 2018); Hans Noel, *Political Ideologies and Political Parties in America* (Cambridge University Press, 2014); Edward G. Carmines and James A. Stimson, *Issue Evolution: Race and the Transformation of American Politics* (Princeton University Press, 1990).

14. Andrew Busch, *Ronald Reagan and the Politics of Freedom* (Rowman & Littlefield, 2001).

15. Eduardo Bonilla-Silva, *Racism Without Racists: Color-Blind Racism and the Persistence of Racial Inequality in America* (Rowman & Littlefield, 2017).

16. The question of whether impeachment is primarily political or legal remains a point of contention in the scholarly literature, with some political scientists contending that impeachment is mostly about politics (Jody C. Baumgartner and Naoko Kada, *Checking Executive Power: Presidential Impeachment in Comparative Perspective* (Bloomsbury Publishing USA, 2003). Legal scholars have pointed out the importance of legal regimes in shaping those politics (John Ohnesorge, "Comparing Impeachment Regimes," *Duke Journal of Comparative and International Law* 31, no. 2 (2021): 259–300. Analyses that draw comparisons across different instances of US presidential impeachment engage with legal and informal rule violations, but invariably also take into account the political environment, including the balance of power in Congress and the broader political environment. See, for example, Lawrence J. Trautman, "Presidential Impeachment: A Contemporary Analysis," *University of Dayton Law Review* 44 (2019): 529; Frank O. Bowman III, *High Crimes and Misdemeanors: A History of Impeachment for the Age of Trump* (Cambridge University Press, 2023).

17. Jeffrey Tulis, "Impeachment in the Constitutional Order," in Joseph M. Bessette and Jeffrey K. Tulis, eds., *The Constitutional Presidency* (Johns Hopkins University Press, 2009).

18. Tulis, "Impeachment in the Constitutional Order," 236.

19. Keith E. Whittington, *The Impeachment Power: The Law, Politics, and Purpose of an Extraordinary Constitutional Tool* (Princeton University Press, 2024), 83.

20. Stephen Skowronek, *Presidential Leadership in Political Time: Reprise and Reappraisal,* 3rd ed. (University Press of Kansas, 2020).

21. Daniel P. Franklin, Stanley M. Caress, Robert M. Sanders, and Cole D. Taratoot, *The Politics of Presidential Impeachment* (State University of New York Press, 2020).

22. Anna Grzymala-Busse, "How Populists Rule: The Consequences for Democratic Governance," *Polity* 51, no. 4 (October 2019): 707–17, https://doi.org/10.1086/705570.

23. See, for example, descriptions of populism as connected to "authoritarian strongman" leadership. Cas Mudde and Cristobal Rovira Kaltwasser, *Populism: A Very Short Introduction* (Oxford University Press, 2017), 63.

24. Eric Foner, *A Short History of Reconstruction*, updated ed. (HarperCollins, 2015), 84–85.

25. Ashley Jardina, *White Identity Politics* (Cambridge University Press, 2019), 19.

26. Steven Levitsky and Daniel Ziblatt, *How Democracies Die* (Broadway Books, 2018).

27. Others have made this argument, including Corey Robin in "Democracy Is Norm Erosion," *Jacobin*, January 29, 2018, https://jacobin.com/2018/01/democracy-trump-authoritarianism-levitsky-zillblatt-norms (accessed January 21, 2024).

28. Desmond S. King and Rogers M. Smith, "Racial Orders in American Political Development," *American Political Science Review* 99, no. 1 (February 2005): 75–92, 75, https://doi.org/10.1017/S0003055405051506.

29. King and Smith, "Racial Orders in American Political Development," 79.

30. Stephen Skowronek, *The Politics Presidents Make: Leadership from John Adams to Bill Clinton*, rev. ed. (Harvard University Press, 1997).

31. Skowronek, *Presidential Leadership in Political Time*.

32. Boris Heersink and Jeffery A. Jenkins, *Republican Party Politics and the American South, 1865–1968* (Cambridge University Press, 2020); Edward O. Frantz, *The Door of Hope: Republican Presidents and the First Southern Strategy, 1877–1933* (University Press of Florida, 2011).

33. Skowronek, *Presidential Leadership in Political Time*.

34. Skowronek, *The Politics Presidents Make*, 44.

35. Joseph E. Lowndes, *From the New Deal to the New Right: Race and the Southern Origins of Modern Conservatism* (Yale University Press, 2008).

36. Vesla M. Weaver, "Frontlash: Race and the Development of Punitive Crime Policy," *Studies in American Political Development* 21, no. 2 (2007): 230–65, 237, https://doi.org/10.1017/S0898588X07000211.

37. Foner, *A Short History of Reconstruction*.

2. A New Birth of Freedom: George Washington to Abraham Lincoln

1. Abraham Lincoln, *Collected Works of Abraham Lincoln*, vol. 3, *August 21, 1858 to March 4, 1860* (Rutgers University Press, 1953).

2. Brian R. Dirck, *Abraham Lincoln and White America* (University Press of Kansas, 2015), 71.

3. Ibram X. Kendi, *Stamped from the Beginning: The Definitive History of Racist Ideas in America* (PublicAffairs, 2016).

4. Frederick Douglass, "Oration in Memory of Abraham Lincoln," April 14, 1876, University of Rochester Frederick Douglass Project, https://rbscp.lib.rochester.edu/4402.

5. Julia Azari, "Presidential Ratings Are Flawed. Which Makes It Hard to Assess Trump," *FiveThirtyEight*, March 5, 2018, https://fivethirtyeight.com/features/presidential-ratings-are-flawed-which-makes-it-hard-to-assess-trump/; Alvin B. Tillery Jr. and Hanes Walton Jr., "Presidential Greatness in the Black Press: Ranking the Modern Presidents on Civil Rights Policy and Race Relations, 1900–2016," *Politics, Groups, and Identities* 7, no. 1 (January 2, 2019): 71–88, https://doi.org/10.1080/21565503.2017.1318760.

6. Gautham Rao, "US Presidents and Slavery," n.d., University of Virginia Miller Center, https://millercenter.org/us-presidents-and-slavery.

7. Daniel Walker Howe, *The Political Culture of the American Whigs* (University of Chicago Press, 1979).

8. Daniel W. Crofts, *Lincoln and the Politics of Slavery: The Other Thirteenth Amendment and the Struggle to Save the Union* (University of North Carolina Press, 2016), 34.

9. Annette Gordon-Reed, *The Hemingses of Monticello: An American Family* (W. W. Norton & Co., 2009).

10. Erica Armstrong Dunbar, *Never Caught: The Washingtons' Relentless Pursuit of Their Runaway Slave, Ona Judge* (Simon & Schuster, 2017).

11. Alexis Coe, *You Never Forget Your First: A Biography of George Washington* (Penguin, 2020).

12. Paul Finkelman, *Slavery and the Founders: Race and Liberty in the Age of Jefferson* (M. E. Sharpe, 1996), 23; David Waldstreicher, *Slavery's Constitution: From Revolution to Ratification* (Farrar, Straus and Giroux, 2010), 92.

13. Waldstreicher, *Slavery's Constitution*, 98–99.

14. Robert Pierce Forbes, *The Missouri Compromise and Its Aftermath: Slavery and the Meaning of America* (University of North Carolina Press, 2009), 27.

15. Michael J. McManus, "President James Monroe's Domestic Policies, 1817–1825: 'To Advance the Best Interests of Our Union,'" in Stuart Leibiger, ed., *A Companion to James Madison and James Monroe* (John Wiley & Sons, 2012), 438–55.

16. Robert Pierce Forbes, *The Missouri Compromise and Its Aftermath: Slavery and the Meaning of America* (University of North Carolina Press, 2009), 79.

17. McManus, "President James Monroe's Domestic Policies," 451; Forbes, *The Missouri Compromise and Its Aftermath*.

18. Forbes, *The Missouri Compromise and Its Aftermath*, 58.

19. McManus, "President James Monroe's Domestic Policies," 451.

20. Critically, Jackson's commitment to national unity and strength, often portrayed by modern presidency scholars as his main redeeming quality, derived from his ideas about Native American policy, specifically Indian removal from homelands in the Southeastern United States. Stephen J. Rockwell, *Indian Affairs and the Administrative State in the Nineteenth Century* (Cambridge University Press, 2010).

21. Christopher Brian Booker, *The Black Presidential Nightmare: African-Americans and Presidents, 1789–2016* (Xlibris, 2017), 100; Richard Young and Jeffrey Meiser, "Race and the Dual State in the Early American Republic," in Joseph E. Lowndes, Julie Novkov, and Dorian T. Warren, eds., *Race and American Political Development* (Routledge, 2012), 46.

22. Kenneth O'Reilly, *Nixon's Piano: Presidents and Racial Politics from Washington to Clinton* (Free Press, 1995), 31.

23. In Jackson's famous "bank war," funds were taken from the Second Bank of the United States and deposited in state banks. Part of the argument against the Second Bank of the United States was its concentration of economic power in a federal institution. Richard J. Ellis and Stephen Kirk, "Presidential Mandates in the Nineteenth Century: Conceptual Change and Institutional Development," *Studies in American Political Development* 9, no. 1 (Spring 1995): 117–86, https://doi.org/10.1017/S0898588X00001188. But another one of Jackson's more forceful moves as president, asserting the power of the federal government in the nullification crisis of 1832, suggests that his belief in state autonomy had limits. Marc Karnis Landy and Sidney M. Milkis, *Presidential Greatness* (University Press of Kansas, 2000).

24. O'Reilly, *Nixon's Piano*.

25. Russell L. Riley, *The Presidency and the Politics of Racial Inequality: Nation-Keeping from 1831 to 1965* (Columbia University Press, 1999), 44.

26. Riley, *The Presidency and the Politics of Racial Inequality*, 45.

27. Riley, *The Presidency and the Politics of Racial Inequality*, 47.

28. Andrew Jackson, "Seventh Annual Message," December 8, 1835, The American Presidency Project, https://www.presidency.ucsb.edu/documents/seventh-annual-message-2 (accessed January 7, 2025).

29. Van Buren's leadership among his colleagues in trying to "curb Northern colleagues' antislavery zeal" started well before he became president. Sean Wilentz, "Jeffersonian Democracy and the Origins of Political Antislavery in the United States: The Missouri Crisis Revisited," *Journal of the Historical Society* 4, no. 3 (September 2004): 375–401, 392, https://doi.org/10.1111/j.1529-921X.2004.00105.x.

30. Van Buren had owned one slave, who escaped to freedom before Van Buren's rise as a national political figure. Donald B. Cole, *Martin van Buren and the American Political System* (Princeton University Press, 2014), 110.

31. William G. Shade, "'The Most Delicate and Exciting Topics': Martin Van Buren, Slavery, and the Election of 1836," *Journal of the Early Republic* 18, no. 3 (1998): 459–84, 469, https://doi.org/10.2307/3124674.

32. Shade, "'The Most Delicate and Exciting Topics,'" 471.

33. Martin Van Buren, "Inaugural Address|," March 4, 1837, University of Virginia, Miller Center, https://millercenter.org/the-presidency/presidential-speeches/march-4-1837-inaugural-address.

34. Jeffery A. Jenkins, "The Gag Rule, Congressional Politics, and the Growth of Anti-Slavery Popular Politics," paper presented at the annual meeting of the Midwest Political Science Association, Chicago, April 7–10, 2005.

35. O'Reilly, *Nixon's Piano*, 35.

36. Tyler's Southern sympathies are well illustrated by his position on the nullification question and Jackson's "Force Bill." He objected to Jackson's treatment of a Southern state and joined the party that had formed to oppose Jackson's wielding of presidential power. William Freehling, "John Tyler: Life Before the Presidency," n.d., University of Virginia, Miller Center, https://millercenter.org/president/tyler/life-before-the-presidency. Yet Tyler eventually had his differences with the Whig Party as well.

37. Riley, *The Presidency and the Politics of Racial Inequality*, 60.

38. Walter R. Borneman, *Polk: The Man Who Transformed the Presidency and America* (Random House, 2009).

39. Borneman, *Polk*, 106.

40. Robert W. Merry, *A Country of Vast Designs: James K. Polk, the Mexican War and the Conquest of the American Continent* (Simon & Schuster, 2010), 6; Stephen Skowronek, *The Politics Presidents Make: Leadership from John Adams to Bill Clinton*, rev. ed. (Harvard University Press, 1997).

41. James K. Polk, "War Message to Congress," May 11, 1846, University of Virginia, Miller Center, https://millercenter.org/the-presidency/presidential-speeches/may-11-1846-war-message-congress.

42. Skowronek, *The Politics Presidents Make*.

43. Crofts, *Lincoln and the Politics of Slavery*, 43.

44. Joseph G. Rayback, *Free Soil: The Election of 1848* (University Press of Kentucky, 2021).

45. Michael Fitzgibbon Holt, *The Fate of Their Country: Politicians, Slavery Extension, and the Coming of the Civil War* (Macmillan, 2004).

46. Ellis and Kirk, "Presidential Mandates in the Nineteenth Century."

47. Riley, *The Presidency and the Politics of Racial Inequality*, 68.

48. Paul Finkelman, "James Buchanan, Dred Scott, and the Whisper of Conspiracy," in Michael J. Birkner and John W. Quist, eds., *James Buchanan and the Coming of the Civil War*, 25 (University Press of Florida, 2013).

49. O'Reilly, *Nixon's Piano*, 37; Holt, *The Fate of Their Country*, 83–84.

50. Holt, *The Fate of Their Country*, 54.

51. Riley, *The Presidency and the Politics of Racial Inequality*, 69.

52. O'Reilly, *Nixon's Piano*, 38.

53. Birkner and Quist, *James Buchanan and the Coming of the Civil War*.

54. Stephen E. Maizlish, *A Strife of Tongues: The Compromise of 1850 and the Ideological Foundations of the American Civil War* (University of Virginia Press, 2018), 35; Sean Wilentz, *The Rise of American Democracy: Jefferson to Lincoln* (W. W. Norton & Co., 2006), 638. Webster saw extremists "on both sides" as a problem, and he viewed Free Soilers as a threat to the peace and order of the nation. Taylor evolved in his views: he initially blamed abolitionists but eventually came to see Southern "revolutionaries" as the bigger problem.

55. Maizlish, *A Strife of Tongues*.

56. Skowronek, *The Politics Presidents Make*, 179–80.

57. Michael F. Holt, *Franklin Pierce: The 14th President, 1853–1857* (Macmillan, 2010); Skowronek, *The Politics Presidents Make*.

58. Wilentz, *The Rise of American Democracy*, 672.

59. Holt, *Franklin Pierce*, 72.

60. Holt, *The Fate of Their Country*.

61. Holt, *The Fate of Their Country*, 103.

62. Wilentz, *The Rise of American Democracy*, 672.

63. Wilentz, *The Rise of American Democracy*, 635.

64. Holt, *Franklin Pierce*.

65. Joanne B. Freeman, *The Field of Blood: Violence in Congress and the Road to Civil War* (Farrar, Straus and Giroux, 2018), 222.

66. Finkelman, "James Buchanan, Dred Scott, and the Whisper of Conspiracy."

67. Finkelman, "James Buchanan, Dred Scott, and the Whisper of Conspiracy."

68. Michael Morrison, "President James Buchanan: Executive Leadership and the Crisis of Democracy," in Birkner and Quist, *James Buchanan and the Coming of the Civil War*, 142.

69. Morrison, "President James Buchanan."

70. Nicole Etcheson, "General Jackson Is Dead: James Buchanan, Stephen A. Douglas, and Kansas Policy," in Birkner and Quist, *James Buchanan and the Coming of the Civil War*, 94.

71. Etcheson, "General Jackson in Dead."

72. Morrison, "President James Buchanan."

73. Ellis and Kirk, "Presidential Mandates in the Nineteenth Century."

74. C-SPAN, "Presidential Historians Survey 2021: Abraham Lincoln," https://www.c-span.org/presidentsurvey2021/?personid=34702 (accessed February 7, 2025).

75. This line of questioning became especially prominent after public attention turned to presidential war powers during the George W. Bush presidency. See, for example, Jennifer L. Weber, "Was Lincoln a Tyrant?," *New York Times*, March 25, 2013, https://archive.nytimes.com/opinionator.blogs.nytimes.com/2013/03/25/was-lincoln-a-tyrant/; Elizabeth R. Varon, "An

Indictment of Abraham Lincoln as a 'Constitutional Dictator,'" *Washington Post*, November 12, 2021, https://www.washingtonpost.com/outlook/an-indictment-of-abraham-lincoln-as-a-constitutional-dictator/2021/11/10/99f8cd80-366e-11ec-9bc4-86107e7b0ab1_story.html.

76. Lincoln connected his support for African colonization, which is well documented, to his belief that the races were fundamentally different and would have difficulty coexisting in a post-slavery America. During a White House meeting, Lincoln presented this option as the most advantageous for Black Americans. Dirck, *Abraham Lincoln and White America*, 97.

77. Ellis and Kirk, "Presidential Mandates in the Nineteenth Century," 164.

78. David Herbert Donald, *Lincoln Reconsidered: Essays on the Civil War Era* (Knopf Doubleday, 2001); Skowronek, *The Politics Presidents Make*; Doris Kearns Goodwin, *Team of Rivals: The Political Genius of Abraham Lincoln* (Simon & Schuster, 2006).

79. Matthew Karp, "The People's Revolution of 1856: Antislavery Populism, National Politics, and the Emergence of the Republican Party," *Journal of the Civil War Era* 9, no. 4 (2019): 524–45.

80. Freeman, *The Field of Blood*, 209.

81. Seward biographer Walter Stahr also notes that there were some questions about whether Seward would be appealing to immigrant voters or whether he would be associated with the anti-immigrant sentiments sometimes associated with both the Whig and Republican Parties. Walter Stahr, *Seward: Lincoln's Indispensable Man* (Simon & Schuster, 2012).

82. Adam I. P. Smith, "Beyond the Realignment Synthesis: The 1860 Election Reconsidered," in Gareth Davies and Julian E. Zelizer, eds., *America at the Ballot Box: Elections and Political History* (University of Pennsylvania Press, 2015), 59–74.

83. "Republican Party Platform of 1860," May 17, 1860, The American Presidency Project, https://www.presidency.ucsb.edu/documents/republican-party-platform-1860 (accessed August 8, 2023).

84. "Republican Party Platform of 1860."

85. Michael F. Holt, *The Election of 1860: "A Campaign Fraught with Consequences"* (University Press of Kansas, 2017), 92.

86. Wilentz, *The Rise of American Democracy*.

87. Holt, *The Election of 1860*.

88. Smith, "Beyond the Realignment Synthesis," 70.

89. Allen C. Guelzo, *Lincoln's Emancipation Proclamation: The End of Slavery in America* (Simon & Schuster, 2006), 15.

90. Holt, *The Election of 1860*; Louis P. Masur, *Lincoln's Last Speech: Wartime Reconstruction and the Crisis of Reunion* (Oxford University Press, 2015).

91. David Herbert Donald, *Lincoln* (Simon & Schuster, 1995), 267.

92. Leonard L. Richards, *Who Freed the Slaves? The Fight over the Thirteenth Amendment*, 19 (University of Chicago Press, 2015).

93. Crofts, *Lincoln and the Politics of Slavery*; Lincoln as quoted in Donald, *Lincoln*, 268.

94. David Zarefsky, "Philosophy and Rhetoric in Lincoln's First Inaugural Address," *Philosophy & Rhetoric* 45, no. 2 (June 2012): 165–88, https://doi.org/10.5325/philrhet.45.2.0165; Abraham Lincoln, "Inaugural Address," March 4, 1861, The American Presidency Project, https://www.presidency.ucsb.edu/documents/inaugural-address-34 (accessed August 11, 2023).

95. Lincoln, "Inaugural Address" (1861).

96. Lincoln, "Inaugural Address" (1861).

97. Alexander H. Stephens, "Cornerstone Speech," March 21, 1861, American Battlefield Trust, https://www.battlefields.org/learn/primary-sources/cornerstone-speech (accessed August 11, 2023).

98. Lincoln anticipated that slavery might last for another hundred years. The range of political possibilities for eliminating slavery changed very quickly, however, during the Civil War and under the leadership of Lincoln and congressional Republicans. Crofts, *Lincoln and the Politics of Slavery.*

99. Landy and Milkis, *Presidential Greatness.*

100. Guelzo, *Lincoln's Emancipation Proclamation*, 242.

101. The ideas in the address, such as drawing on the ideals of the Declaration of Independence and the concept of national renewal, drew on many years of abolitionist activism and constitutional thinking. See Elizabeth Beaumont, *The Civic Constitution: Civic Visions and Struggles in the Path Toward Constitutional Democracy* (Oxford University Press, 2014).

3. "The Constitution as It Is": Andrew Johnson's Impeachment

1. Jeffrey K. Tulis and Nicole Mellow, *Legacies of Losing in American Politics* (University of Chicago Press, 2018).

2. Jennifer L. Weber, "The Political Culture of the North: Party Politics in State and Nation," in Stephen Douglas Engle, ed., *The War Worth Fighting: Abraham Lincoln's Presidency and Civil War America* (University Press of Florida, 2015).

3. Jon Meacham, Peter Baker, Timothy Naftali, and Jeffrey A. Engel, *Impeachment: An American History* (Random House, 2018).

4. Matt Speiser, "The Ticket's Other Half: How and Why Andrew Johnson Received the 1864 Vice Presidential Nomination," *Tennessee Historical Quarterly* 65, no. 1 (2006): 42–69.

5. "Republican Party Platform of 1864," June 7, 1864, The American Presidency Project, https://www.presidency.ucsb.edu/documents/republican-party-platform-1864 (accessed December 12, 2023).

6. Eric Foner, in *Forever Free: The Story of Emancipation and Reconstruction* (Knopf Doubleday, 2013, 61), refers to this plan as "extremely lenient."

7. Levine, *The Failed Promise*; David Herbert Donald, *Lincoln* (Simon & Schuster, 1995).

8. Donald, *Lincoln*, 473.

9. Chandra Manning, "The Shifting Terrain of Attitudes Toward Abraham Lincoln and Emancipation," *Journal of the Abraham Lincoln Association* 34, no. 1 (2013): 18–39.

10. Stephen Skowronek, *The Politics Presidents Make: Leadership from John Adams to Bill Clinton*, rev. ed. (Harvard University Press, 1997).

11. Robert S. Levine, *The Failed Promise: Reconstruction, Frederick Douglass, and the Impeachment of Andrew Johnson* (W. W. Norton & Co., 2021); Speiser, "The Ticket's Other Half."

12. Brenda Wineapple, *The Impeachers: The Trial of Andrew Johnson and the Dream of a Just Nation* (Random House, 2020).

13. Eric Foner, *A Short History of Reconstruction*, updated ed. (HarperCollins, 2015), 84.

14. Speiser, "The Ticket's Other Half," 45.

15. Speiser, "The Ticket's Other Half," 58.

16. "Republican Party Platform of 1864."

17. Donald, *Lincoln*, 512.

18. Richard J. Ellis and Stephen Kirk, "Presidential Mandates in the Nineteenth Century: Conceptual Change and Institutional Development," *Studies in American Political Development* 9, no. 1 (1995): 117–86, https://doi.org/10.1017/S0898588X00001188.

19. Levine, *The Failed Promise*, 32.

20. Annette Gordon-Reed, *Andrew Johnson: The 17th President, 1865–1869* (Macmillan, 2011), 124.

21. Andrew Johnson, "Executive Order—To Reestablish the Authority of the United States and Execute the Laws Within the Geographical Limits Known as the State of Virginia," May 9, 1865, The American Presidency Project, https://www.presidency.ucsb.edu/documents/executive-order-reestablish-the-authority-the-united-states-and-execute-the-laws-within (accessed December 28, 2023).

22. Levine, *The Failed Promise*, 61; David O. Stewart, *Impeached: The Trial of President Andrew Johnson and the Fight for Lincoln's Legacy* (Simon & Schuster, 2010), 48.

23. Gordon-Reed, *Andrew Johnson*, 100.

24. Hans Louis Trefousse, *Andrew Johnson: A Biography* (W. W. Norton & Co., 1997), 217.

25. Wineapple, *The Impeachers*, 54–55.

26. Foner, *A Short History of Reconstruction*.

27. Foner, *A Short History of Reconstruction*; Andrew Johnson, "Proclamation 134—Granting Amnesty to Participants in the Rebellion, with Certain Exceptions," May 29, 1865, The American Presidency Project, https://www.presidency.ucsb.edu/documents/proclamation-134-granting-amnesty-participants-the-rebellion-with-certain-exceptions (accessed December 28, 2023).

28. Foner, *A Short History of Reconstruction*, 85.

29. Trefousse, *Andrew Johnson*, 225–26.

30. Foner, *A Short History of Reconstruction*, 89.

31. Foner, *A Short History of Reconstruction*.

32. This complaint was raised by Republican Carl Schurz of Illinois after a tour of the South. Wineapple, *The Impeachers*, 104.

33. Wineapple, *The Impeachers*, 16.

34. Wineapple, *The Impeachers*.

35. Wineapple, *The Impeachers*, chap. 5.

36. Stewart, *Impeached*, 54.

37. Stewart, *Impeached*, 111–12.

38. Wineapple, *The Impeachers*, 151–52.

39. Levine, *The Failed Promise*, 117.

40. Trefousse, *Andrew Johnson*, 259.

41. Wineapple, *The Impeachers*, 176; Garry Boulard, *The Swing Around the Circle: Andrew Johnson and the Train Ride That Destroyed a Presidency* (iUniverse, 2008).

42. Gordon-Reed, *Andrew Johnson*, 123–24.

43. Gordon-Reed, *Andrew Johnson*, 123–24.

44. Levine, *The Failed Promise*, 94–99. This statement by Johnson about Frederick Douglass appears frequently in scholarship about Johnson and race in the Reconstruction period, but as Levine points out, the historical record on his exact words is not entirely clear.

45. Gordon-Reed, *Andrew Johnson*, 115.

46. Gordon-Reed, *Andrew Johnson*, 115–16.

47. Stewart, *Impeached*, 50.

48. Stewart, *Impeached*, 50.

49. Meacham et al., *Impeachment*, 77; Foner, *A Short History of Reconstruction*.

50. Andrew Johnson, "Remarks at a Meeting in Honor of Washington's Birthday," February 22, 1866, The American Presidency Project, https://www.presidency.ucsb.edu/documents/remarks-meeting-honor-washingtons-birthday (accessed February 22, 2024).

51. Gordon-Reed, *Andrew Johnson*, 123.

52. Wineapple, *The Impeachers*, 174.

53. Wineapple, *The Impeachers*, 174.

54. Boulard, *The Swing Around the Circle*, 78–82.

55. Wineapple, *The Impeachers*, 175.

56. Boulard, *The Swing Around the Circle*, 115.

57. Levine, *The Failed Promise*, 124.

58. Boulard, *The Swing Around the Circle*.

59. Gordon-Reed, *Andrew Johnson*, 131.

60. Gordon-Reed, *Andrew Johnson*, 131.

61. Wineapple, *The Impeachers*, 212.

62. Wineapple, *The Impeachers*; Meacham et al., *Impeachment*.

63. Meacham et al., *Impeachment*, 86.

64. Wineapple, *The Impeachers*, 223.

65. Stewart, *Impeached*, 84.

66. Meacham et al., *Impeachment*, 86.

67. Andrew Johnson, "Third Annual Message," December 3, 1867, The American Presidency Project, https://www.presidency.ucsb.edu/documents/third-annual-message-10.

68. Levine, *The Failed Promise*, 176.

69. Stewart, *Impeached*, 208–9.

70. Stewart, *Impeached*.

71. Stewart, *Impeached*, 128.

72. Stewart, *Impeached*, 140.

73. Keith Whittington, "Bill Clinton Was No Andrew Johnson: Comparing Two Impeachments," *University of Pennsylvania Journal of Constitutional Law* 2 (2000): 426.

74. Wineapple, *The Impeachers*, 282.

75. Levine, *The Failed Promise*.

76. Levine, *The Failed Promise*, 160.

77. Stewart, *Impeached*, 213.

78. Stewart, *Impeached*, 171.

79. Jeffrey K. Tulis, *The Rhetorical Presidency* (Princeton University Press, 2017).

80. Jeremy D. Bailey, ed., "Articles of Impeachment of Andrew Johnson," Teaching American History (blog), https://teachingamericanhistory.org/document/articles-of-impeachment-of-andrew-johnson/ (accessed January 7, 2025).

81. Meacham et al., *Impeachment*, 89.

82. Gordon-Reed, *Andrew Johnson*.

83. Tulis and Mellow, *Legacies of Losing in American Politics*. Johnson's political isolation is linked by numerous scholars to his political difficulties. Johnson biographer Hans Trefousse emphasizes that Johnson's stances put him on the outs with Republicans and Democrats alike, and that his efforts to establish a permanent National Union Party undermined his credibility with both parties. Stephen Skowronek ties Johnson to Nixon, Clinton, and John Tyler as "pre-emptive" presidents whose political authenticity came under scrutiny, prompting their opponents to "purge them as threats to the constitutional order." Stephen Skowronek, *Presidential Leadership in Political Time: Reprise and Reappraisal*, 3rd ed. (University Press of Kansas, 2020). But the authenticity problems that Skowronek describes also plagued these presidents' predecessors to some degree, as they were unable to satisfy either those who demanded full transformation of the racial status quo or those who sought preservation and maintenance. For this reason, I argue that the political ambiguity and hybridity of figures like Andrew Johnson is only part of the story behind their impeachment, and that other recurring characteristics of backlash leaders—their lawlessness in service of racially regressive goals and the populism that ties this lawlessness to their larger political projects—are just as important.

84. Ron Chernow, *Grant* (Penguin, 2017), 99. Chernow emphasizes that Grant objected to the practice of slavery in the 1850s, but feared the potential of the issue to split up the nation.

85. Xi Wang, *The Trial of Democracy: Black Suffrage and Northern Republicans, 1860–1910* (University of Georgia Press, 2012), 93.

86. Ulysses S. Grant, "Inaugural Address," March 4, 1873, The American Presidency Project, https://www.presidency.ucsb.edu/documents/inaugural-address-37 (accessed February 20, 2024).

87. Christopher Brian Booker, *The Black Presidential Nightmare: African-Americans and Presidents, 1789–2016* (Xlibris, 2017), 257.

88. Chernow, *Grant*, 654.

89. Black officeholders, as well as white Republican politicians, were also commonly the targets of sometimes lethal violence. Douglas R. Egerton, *The Wars of Reconstruction: The Brief, Violent History of America's Most Progressive Era* (Bloomsbury Publishing USA, 2014), 290–91.

90. Paul Frymer, *Uneasy Alliances: Race and Party Competition in America* (Princeton University Press, 1999), 60.

91. W.E.B. Du Bois, *Black Reconstruction in America: An Essay Toward a History of the Part Which Black Folk Played in the Attempt to Reconstruct Democracy in America, 1860–1880* (Oxford University Press, 2014), 560.

92. Philip A. Klinkner and Rogers M. Smith, *The Unsteady March: The Rise and Decline of Racial Equality in America* (University of Chicago Press, 2002), 81.

93. Frymer, *Uneasy Alliances*.

94. Frymer, *Uneasy Alliances*, 61.

95. Wang, *The Trial of Democracy*, 103–4.

96. Chernow, *Grant*, 584–85.

97. Klinkner and Smith, *The Unsteady March*, 85. A series of Supreme Court decisions also weakened claims about the legitimacy of federal intervention to enforce the provisions of the Fourteenth and Fifteenth Amendments and promoted narrow readings of those amendments.

98. Chernow, *Grant*, 790–93.

99. Chernow, *Grant*, 794.

100. Klinkner and Smith, *The Unsteady March*, 91; Edward O. Frantz, *The Door of Hope: Republican Presidents and the First Southern Strategy, 1877–1933* (University Press of Florida, 2011), 38.

101. See, for example, Nell Irvin Painter, *Standing at Armageddon: The United States, 1877–1919* (W. W. Norton & Co., 1989).

4. "Patience and Moderation": Theodore Roosevelt to Lyndon Johnson

1. Johnson quoted in Linda C. McClain, "The Civil Rights Act of 1964 and 'Legislating Morality': On Conscience, Prejudice, and Whether 'Stateways' Can Change 'Folkways,'" *Boston University Law Review* 95 (2015): 891.

2. Kevin Coe and Anthony Schmidt, "America in Black and White: Locating Race in the Modern Presidency, 1933–2011," *Journal of Communication* 62, no. 4 (August 2012): 609–27, 620, https://doi.org/10.1111/j.1460-2466.2012.01652.x.

3. Kimberley Johnson, *Reforming Jim Crow: Southern Politics and State in the Age Before Brown* (Oxford University Press USA, 2010).

4. Megan Ming Francis, *Civil Rights and the Making of the Modern American State* (Cambridge University Press, 2014).

5. Keneshia N. Grant, *The Great Migration and the Democratic Party: Black Voters and the Realignment of American Politics in the 20th Century* (Temple University Press, 2020).

6. Thomas G. Dyer, *Theodore Roosevelt and the Idea of Race* (Louisiana State University Press, 1992); Kenneth O'Reilly, *Nixon's Piano: Presidents and Racial Politics from Washington to Clinton* (Free Press, 1995).

7. Dewey W. Grantham, "Dinner at the White House: Theodore Roosevelt, Booker T. Washington, and the South," *Tennessee Historical Quarterly* 17, no. 2 (1958): 112–30.

8. Edward O. Frantz, *The Door of Hope: Republican Presidents and the First Southern Strategy, 1877–1933* (University Press of Florida, 2011), 158.

9. O'Reilly, *Nixon's Piano*.

10. O'Reilly, *Nixon's Piano*, 64–65.

11. Kathleen Dalton, *Theodore Roosevelt: A Strenuous Life* (Knopf Doubleday, 2007).

12. Deborah Davis, *Guest of Honor: Booker T. Washington, Theodore Roosevelt, and the White House Dinner That Shocked a Nation* (Simon & Schuster, 2012).

13. Davis, *Guest of Honor*, 211.

14. Frantz, *The Door of Hope*, 165.

15. Thomas Dyer presents this as evidence that Theodore Roosevelt could be principled on race. *Theodore Roosevelt and the Idea of Race*, 103. Edward Frantz is more critical, suggesting that Roosevelt "ended up exhausting precious political capital on issues that were not of his choosing."

The Door of Hope, 165. These efforts, Frantz suggests, raised expectations about what Roosevelt could and would deliver for African Americans, without enhancing his capacity to champion more substantive gains.

16. Dalton, *Theodore Roosevelt*, 236.

17. Frantz, *The Door of Hope*.

18. Dalton, *Theodore Roosevelt*, 321.

19. Dalton, *Theodore Roosevelt*.

20. Mary Stuckey, "Establishing the Rhetorical Presidency Through Presidential Rhetoric: Theodore Roosevelt and the Brownsville Raid," *Quarterly Journal of Speech* 92, no. 3 (August 1, 2006): 287–309, https://doi.org/10.1080/00335630600938716.

21. Francis, *Civil Rights and the Making of the Modern American State*, 95.

22. O'Reilly, *Nixon's Piano*; Frantz, *The Door of Hope*; William Howard Taft, "Inaugural Address," March 4, 1909, The Avalon Project, https://avalon.law.yale.edu/19th_century/taft.asp. (accessed September 19, 2024).

23. Russell L. Riley, *The Presidency and the Politics of Racial Inequality: Nation-Keeping from 1831 to 1965* (Columbia University Press, 1999), 125–27.

24. Frantz, *The Door of Hope*.

25. Francis, *Civil Rights and the Making of the Modern American State*, 79.

26. Francis, *Civil Rights and the Making of the Modern American State*, 81.

27. Christopher Brian Booker, *The Black Presidential Nightmare: African-Americans and Presidents, 1789–2016* (Xlibris, 2017); O'Reilly, *Nixon's Piano*; Boris Heersink and Jeffery A. Jenkins, *Republican Party Politics and the American South, 1865–1968* (Cambridge University Press, 2020), 155–56.

28. Nancy Joan Weiss, *Farewell to the Party of Lincoln: Black Politics in the Age of FDR* (Princeton University Press, 2020).

29. Riley, *The Presidency and the Politics of Racial Inequality*, 128.

30. Boris Heersink and Jeffery A. Jenkins, *Republican Party Politics and the American South, 1865–1968* (Cambridge University Press, 2020), 331–32.

31. Klinkner and Smith, *The Unsteady March*, 110.

32. Alvin B. Tillery and Hanes Walton Jr., "Presidential Greatness in the Black Press: Ranking the Modern Presidents on Civil Rights Policy and Race Relations, 1900–2016," *Politics, Groups, and Identities* 7, no. 1 (January 2, 2019): 71–88, https://doi.org/10.1080/21565503.2017.1318760.

33. Ronald J. Pestritto, *Woodrow Wilson and the Roots of Modern Liberalism* (Rowman & Littlefield, 2005), 44–45.

34. O'Reilly, *Nixon's Piano*, 83; Francis, *Civil Rights and the Making of the Modern American State*.

35. Klinkner and Smith, *The Unsteady March*, 111.

36. O'Reilly, *Nixon's Piano*, 84–85. For a more extensive examination of the relationship between Wilson's Progressivism and racism, see Stephen Skowronek, "The Reassociation of Ideas and Purposes: Racism, Liberalism, and the American Political Tradition," *American Political Science Review* 100, no. 3 (August 2006): 385–401, https://doi.org/10.1017/S0003055406062253.

37. Francis, *Civil Rights and the Making of the Modern American State*, 66–67.

38. Mark E. Benbow, "Birth of a Quotation: Woodrow Wilson and 'Like Writing History with Lightning,'" *Journal of the Gilded Age and Progressive Era* 9, no. 4 (October 2010): 509–33, 511, https://doi.org/10.1017/S1537781400004242.

39. Reaching into and reinterpreting Lincoln's disruption of the racial order was an animating theme in Wilson's presidency and prepresidential writings. Skowronek, "The Reassociation of Ideas and Purposes," 2006.

40. Francis, *Civil Rights and the Making of the Modern American State*, 72.

41. Francis, *Civil Rights and the Making of the Modern American State*.

42. Stephen Skowronek, *The Politics Presidents Make: Leadership from John Adams to Bill Clinton*, rev. ed. (Harvard University Press, 1997).

43. William Edward Leuchtenburg, *The White House Looks South: Franklin D. Roosevelt, Harry S. Truman, Lyndon B. Johnson* (Louisiana State University Press, 2005); Ira Katznelson, *Fear Itself: The New Deal and the Origins of Our Time* (W. W. Norton & Co., 2013).

44. O'Reilly, *Nixon's Piano*, 110.

45. Riley, *The Presidency and the Politics of Racial Inequality*, 138.

46. Leuchtenburg, *The White House Looks South*.

47. Katznelson, *Fear Itself*, 163; Linda Faye Williams, *The Constraint of Race: Legacies of White Skin Privilege in America* (Pennsylvania State University Press, 2003).

48. Klinkner and Smith, *The Unsteady March*, 127.

49. Weiss, *Farewell to the Party of Lincoln*.

50. Weiss, *Farewell to the Party of Lincoln*, 102.

51. Katznelson, *Fear Itself*, 169.

52. Weiss, *Farewell to the Party of Lincoln*.

53. Weiss, *Farewell to the Party of Lincoln*.

54. Weiss, *Farewell to the Party of Lincoln*.

55. Megan Ming Francis, *Civil Rights and the Making of the Modern American State* (Cambridge University Press, 2014), chap. 5.

56. Riley, *The Presidency and the Politics of Racial Inequality*, 139.

57. Riley, *The Presidency and the Politics of Racial Inequality*, 141.

58. O'Reilly, *Nixon's Piano*, 128–29. O'Reilly also notes that FDR had initially considered James Byrnes (D-SC) as a 1940 running mate but decided to take him out of consideration owing to the growing power of African American voters and Byrnes's intractable segregationist views.

59. O'Reilly, *Nixon's Piano*.

60. Kevin J. McMahon, *Reconsidering Roosevelt on Race: How the Presidency Paved the Road to Brown* (University of Chicago Press, 2004), 146.

61. O'Reilly, *Nixon's Piano*, 134.

62. O'Reilly, *Nixon's Piano*, 134.

63. O'Reilly, *Nixon's Piano*, 134.

64. McMahon, *Reconsidering Roosevelt on Race*.

65. Klinkner and Smith, *The Unsteady March*, 206.

66. Riley, *The Presidency and the Politics of Racial Inequality*, 155; Grant, *The Great Migration and the Democratic Party*.

67. Sidney Milkis and Katherine Rader, "The March on Washington Movement, the Fair Employment Practices Committee, and the Long Quest for Racial Justice," *Studies in American Political Development* 38, no. 1 (April 2024): 16–35, 16, https://doi.org/10.1017/S0898588X23000044.

68. William E. Juhnke, "President Truman's Committee on Civil Rights: The Interaction of Politics, Protest, and Presidential Advisory Commission," *Presidential Studies Quarterly* 19, no. 3 (1989): 593–610.

69. Busch, *Ronald Reagan and the Politics of Freedom*, 72.

70. Riley, *The Presidency and the Politics of Racial Inequality*, 155–63; Milkis and Rader, "The March on Washington Movement."

71. Mary L. Dudziak, *Cold War Civil Rights: Race and the Image of American Democracy* (Princeton University Press, 2011), 24.

72. Kari A. Frederickson, *The Dixiecrat Revolt and the End of the Solid South, 1932–1968* (University of North Carolina Press, 2001), 129.

73. Busch, *Ronald Reagan and the Politics of Freedom*, 106; Riley, *The Presidency and the Politics of Racial Inequality*, 163.

74. "1944 Democratic Party Platform," July 19, 1944, The American Presidency Project, https://www.presidency.ucsb.edu/documents/1944-democratic-party-platform (accessed January 6, 2025).

75. Frederickson, *The Dixiecrat Revolt and the End of the Solid South*, 129–30.

76. Julia Azari and Didi Kuo, "Political Parties and Norms in American Political Development," in *Parties, Power, and Change: Developmental Approaches to American Party Politics*, edited by Adam Hilton and Jessica Hejny (forthcoming).

77. Abraham Holtzman, "Party Responsibility and Loyalty: New Rules in the Democratic Party," *Journal of Politics* 22, no. 3 (August 1960): 485–501, https://doi.org/10.2307/2126893; Sam Rosenfeld, *The Polarizers: Postwar Architects of Our Partisan Era* (University of Chicago Press, 2018).

78. Riley, *The Presidency and the Politics of Racial Inequality*, 166.

79. John Robert Greene, *I Like Ike: The Presidential Election of 1952* (University Press of Kansas, 2017); Michael D. Bowen, *The Roots of Modern Conservatism: Dewey, Taft, and the Battle for the Soul of the Republican Party* (University of North Carolina Press, 2011); Timothy Nels Thurber, *Republicans and Race: The GOP's Frayed Relationship with African Americans, 1945–1974* (University Press of Kansas, 2013).

80. Greene, *I Like Ike*.

81. Jean Edward Smith, *Eisenhower: In War and Peace* (Random House, 2012); David A. Nichols, *A Matter of Justice: Eisenhower and the Beginning of the Civil Rights Revolution* (Simon & Schuster, 2007).

82. Nichols, *A Matter of Justice*, 60.

83. Riley, *The Presidency and the Politics of Racial Inequality*.

84. Riley, *The Presidency and the Politics of Racial Inequality*. Attorney General Herbert Brownell eventually wrote a brief expressing the administration view that segregation was unconstitutional, despite Eisenhower's misgivings about whether the South would accept the federal imposition of desegregation.

85. Thurber, *Republicans and Race*.

86. Smith, *Eisenhower*, 714.

87. Thurber, *Republicans and Race*, 63, 74. Eisenhower met with a group of civil rights leaders in 1958.

88. "1956 'Southern Manifesto,'" *Congressional Record*, 84th Cong., 2nd sess., vol. 102, pt. 4 (March 12, 1956), 4459–60, Clemson University, Strom Thurmond Institute, https://web .archive.org/web/20150926013722/http://sti.clemson.edu/component/content/article/192 -general-info/790-1956-qsouthern-manifestoq.

89. Elizabeth Gillespie McRae, *Mothers of Massive Resistance: White Women and the Politics of White Supremacy* (Oxford University Press, 2018).

90. Mark Golub, "Remembering Massive Resistance to School Desegregation," *Law and History Review* 31, no. 3 (August 2013): 491–530, https://doi.org/10.1017/S0738248013000230.

91. Thurber, *Republicans and Race*.

92. Thurber, *Republicans and Race*.

93. Dudziak, *Cold War Civil Rights*, chap. 4.

94. Thurber, *Republicans and Race*.

95. Thurber, *Republicans and Race*, 82.

96. Smith, *Eisenhower*, 718.

97. Richard Neustadt identifies Eisenhower's eventual nationalization of the National Guard as one of his "three cases of command" that demonstrated a failure of persuasion and thus presidential weakness.

98. Smith, *Eisenhower*, 718.

99. Smith, *Eisenhower*; Thurber, *Republicans and Race*.

100. Dwight D. Eisenhower, "Radio and Television Address to the American People on the Situation in Little Rock," September 24, 1957, The American Presidency Project, https://www .presidency.ucsb.edu/documents/radio-and-television-address-the-american-people-the -situation-little-rock (accessed December 3, 2023).

101. Thurber, *Republicans and Race*, 85.

102. O'Reilly, *Nixon's Piano*.

103. Thurber, *Republicans and Race*.

104. O'Reilly, *Nixon's Piano*.

105. O'Reilly, *Nixon's Piano*.

106. O'Reilly, *Nixon's Piano*, 180.

107. Nichols, *A Matter of Justice*, 161.

108. Chas. H. Thompson, "Editorial Comment: 'The Civil Rights Bill of 1957,'" *Journal of Negro Education* 26, no. 4 (1957): 433–34.

109. Nichols, *A Matter of Justice*, 167.

110. Nick Bryant, *The Bystander: John F. Kennedy and the Struggle for Black Equality* (Basic Books, 2007), 127.

111. O'Reilly, *Nixon's Piano*, 195.

112. O'Reilly, *Nixon's Piano*, 196.

113. Dudziak, *Cold War Civil Rights*, 156.

114. Sean J. Savage, *JFK, LBJ, and the Democratic Party* (State University of New York Press, 2012), 100.

115. Savage, *JFK, LBJ, and the Democratic Party*, 102.

116. Bryant, *The Bystander*.

117. Robert Dallek, *An Unfinished Life: John F. Kennedy, 1917–1963* (Little, Brown, 2003), 492.

118. Kennedy White House aide Arthur Schlesinger, quoted in Dudziak, *Cold War Civil Rights*, 156.

119. Private conversation recorded in 1963, cited in Dean Kotlowski, "With All Deliberate Delay: Kennedy, Johnson, and School Desegregation," *Journal of Policy History* 17, no. 2 (April 2005): 155–92, 160, https://doi.org/10.1353/jph.2005.0013.

120. James W. Riddlesperger and Donald W. Jackson, *Presidential Leadership and Civil Rights Policy* (Bloomsbury Academic, 1995), 122.

121. Bryant, *The Bystander*, 331–39.

122. Bryant, *The Bystander*, 347–51.

123. Riddlesperger and Jackson, *Presidential Leadership and Civil Rights Policy*, 122.

124. Dudziak, *Cold War Civil Rights*; Klinkner and Smith, *The Unsteady March*, 256.

125. Dudziak, *Cold War Civil Rights*, 156.

126. For a more extended treatment of this contradiction in the relationship between presidents and social movements, see Sidney Milkis and Daniel Tichenor, *Rivalry and Reform: Presidents, Social Movements, and the Transformation of American Politics* (University of Chicago Press, 2019).

127. Klinkner and Smith, *The Unsteady March*, 259.

128. Dudziak, *Cold War Civil Rights*.

129. Klinkner and Smith, *The Unsteady March*, 264.

130. John F. Kennedy "Radio and Television Report to the American People on Civil Rights," June 11, 1963, The American Presidency Project, https://www.presidency.ucsb.edu/documents /radio-and-television-report-the-american-people-civil-rights (accessed February 16, 2024).

131. Klinkner and Smith, *The Unsteady March*; Dudziak, *Cold War Civil Rights*.

132. Dudziak, *Cold War Civil Rights*, 198–99.

133. For a full examination of the civil rights coalition and its lobbying efforts, see Shamira Gelbman, *The Civil Rights Lobby: The Leadership Conference on Civil Rights and the Second Reconstruction* (Temple University Press, 2021).

134. In an analysis of presidential references to race from 1933 through 2011, Kevin Coe and Anthony Schmidt also find that Johnson's rhetoric about race and inequality stands out from that of his counterparts before and since. Coe and Schmidt, "America in Black and White."

135. Lyndon Johnson, "Address Before a Joint Session of the Congress," November 27, 1963, The American Presidency Project, https://www.presidency.ucsb.edu/documents/address -before-joint-session-the-congress-0.

136. Savage, *JFK, LBJ, and the Democratic Party*, 119.

137. Smith's committee reported the bill with an "open rule" that allowed amendments to be added, and in an effort to ensure failure on the floor, the committee was responsible for adding an alleged "poison pill" amendment incorporating gender discrimination into the bill. Julian E. Zelizer, *The Fierce Urgency of Now: Lyndon Johnson, Congress, and the Battle for the Great Society* (Penguin, 2015).

138. Zelizer, *The Fierce Urgency of Now*; John A. Andrew, *Lyndon Johnson and the Great Society* (I. R. Dee, 1998), 26.

139. O'Reilly, *Nixon's Piano*, 243.

140. Andrew, *Lyndon Johnson and the Great Society*, 28.

141. Zelizer, *The Fierce Urgency of Now*.

142. Savage, *JFK, LBJ, and the Democratic Party*, 162.

143. Milkis and Tichenor, *Rivalry and Reform*, 153.

144. For a more extended explanation of the impact of these changes on the Democratic Party's operations, see Sam Rosenfeld, *The Polarizers: Postwar Architects of Our Partisan Era* (University of Chicago Press, 2018).

145. Sidney Milkis and Daniel Tichenor, *Rivalry and Reform: Presidents, Social Movements, and the Transformation of American Politics* (University of Chicago Press, 2019), 155.

146. Andrew, *Lyndon Johnson and the Great Society*, 34.

147. Andrew, *Lyndon Johnson and the Great Society*.

148. Jesse H. Rhodes, *Ballot Blocked: The Political Erosion of the Voting Rights Act* (Stanford University Press, 2017), 35.

149. Lyndon Johnson, "Special Message to Congress: The American Promise," March 15, 1965, The American Presidency Project, https://www.presidency.ucsb.edu/documents/special-message-the-congress-the-american-promise.

150. O'Reilly, *Nixon's Piano*.

151. Steven Goldzwig, "LBJ, the Rhetoric of Transcendence, and the Civil Rights Act of 1968," *Rhetoric and Public Affairs* (Spring 2003): 32, https://epublications.marquette.edu/comm_fac/170.

152. Goldzwig, "LBJ, the Rhetoric of Transcendence, and the Civil Rights Act of 1968," 41.

153. Lyndon B. Johnson, "The President's Address to the Nation Announcing Steps to Limit the War in Vietnam and Reporting His Decision Not to Seek Reelection," March 31, 1968, The American Presidency Project, https://www.presidency.ucsb.edu/documents/the-presidents-address-the-nation-announcing-steps-limit-the-war-vietnam-and-reporting-his (accessed January 7, 2025).

5. Law and Order: Nixon and Watergate

1. Stephen Skowronek, *The Politics Presidents Make: Leadership from John Adams to Bill Clinton*, rev. ed. (Harvard University Press, 1997). Nixon is identified as a "preemptive" president whose political success depended on his ability to exploit fissures within the dominant coalition and forge a "middle course" that lacked authentic roots in any particular political tradition.

2. Joseph E. Lowndes, *From the New Deal to the New Right: Race and the Southern Origins of Modern Conservatism* (Yale University Press, 2008). Lowndes challenges the idea that Watergate was "external to" the racial politics that Nixon navigated on his way to the presidency, arguing that Nixon's actions helped consolidate liberal opposition to him and create powerful enemies within the liberal-dominated institutions of the time.

3. Hans Noel, *Political Ideologies and Political Parties in America* (Cambridge University Press, 2014); Eric Schickler, *Racial Realignment: The Transformation of American Liberalism, 1932–1965* (Princeton University Press, 2016).

4. Edward G. Carmines and James A. Stimson, *Issue Evolution: Race and the Transformation of American Politics* (Princeton University Press, 1990).

5. Lilliana Mason, *Uncivil Agreement: How Politics Became Our Identity* (University of Chicago Press, 2018).

6. Numerous scholars of parties and ideologies have noted this ideological marriage of anti–New Deal conservatism and anti–civil rights conservatism, though they disagree about the timeline. See Hans Noel, *Political Ideologies and Political Parties in America* (Cambridge University Press, 2014); Eric Schickler, *Racial Realignment: The Transformation of American Liberalism, 1932–1965* (Princeton University Press, 2016).

7. The Gallup poll during this period listed "general unrest in the nation" as an option when respondents were asked to identify the most important problem facing the nation. Gallup Organization, "Gallup Poll 1968-0756: 1968 Presidential Election, Survey Question 7, USGALLUP.756.Q007" (Cornell University, Roper Center for Public Opinion Research, 1968), https://doi.org/10.25940/ROPER-31087737.

8. Louis Harris & Associates, "Louis Harris & Associates Poll: April 1967, Survey Question 2, USHARRIS.052267.R2" (Cornell University, Roper Center for Public Opinion Research, 1967), https://doi.org/10.25940/ROPER-31107526.

9. Survey Research Center, University of Michigan, "Justifying Violence: Attitudes of American Men Survey, Survey Question 3, USSRC.45379A.QA01A3," (Cornell University, Roper Center for Public Opinion Research, 1969), https://doi.org/10.25940/ROPER-31108270.

10. John W. Finney, "Republicans Plan a Terse Platform," *New York Times*, July 28, 1969.

11. "A Poll Finds Nixon Holds Lead on Law and Order," *New York Times*, September 13, 1968; "Nixon, Wallace Alike on Law and Order—Thurmond," *Los Angeles Times*, September 15, 1968; "Nixon Backs Agnew on Law and Order," *Los Angeles Times*, September 18, 1968.

12. Nicole Hemmer, *Partisans: The Conservative Revolutionaries Who Remade American Politics in the 1990s* (Basic Books, 2022), 202.

13. As Boris Heersink and Jeffery Jenkins observe, Nixon lacked a "clear constituency" in the party but was able to position himself between influential conservatives in the party and a public that was generally "wary of the right." *Republican Party Politics and the American South, 1865–1968* (Cambridge University Press, 2020), 184; see also Lowndes, *From the New Deal to the New Right*.

14. Timothy Nels Thurber, *Republicans and Race: The GOP's Frayed Relationship with African Americans, 1945–1974* (University Press of Kansas, 2013), 265. Michael Nelson's extensive study of the 1968 election also notes that moderates were ready to unite around Nixon. *Resilient America: Electing Nixon in 1968, Channeling Dissent, and Dividing Government* (University Press of Kansas, 2017).

15. Joseph A. Aistrup, *The Southern Strategy Revisited: Republican Top-Down Advancement in the South* (University Press of Kentucky, 1996), 18.

16. Leah Wright Rigueur, *The Loneliness of the Black Republican: Pragmatic Politics and the Pursuit of Power* (Princeton University Press, 2016), 116.

17. Rigueur, *The Loneliness of the Black Republican*, 131.

18. Rigueur, *The Loneliness of the Black Republican*, 131.

19. Rick Perlstein, *Nixonland: The Rise of a President and the Fracturing of America* (Simon & Schuster, 2010), 192, 343.

20. Thurber, *Republicans and Race*; Rigueur, *The Loneliness of the Black Republican*.

21. Lowndes, *From the New Deal to the New Right*, 109.

22. For a full explanation of the mechanisms by which Nixon and his political associates concluded that outreach to Black voters would damage their coalition-building efforts, see Paul Frymer and John David Skrentny, "Coalition-Building and the Politics of Electoral Capture During the Nixon Administration: African Americans, Labor, Latinos," *Studies in American Political Development* 12, no. 1 (April 1998): 131–61, https://doi.org/10.1017/S0898588X9800131X. This account explains how Nixon continued to pursue other traditionally Democratic constituencies, such as labor and Mexican Americans, while "distancing" from African American voters (137).

23. Lowndes, *From the New Deal to the New Right*, 115–16.

24. Kevin J. McMahon, *Nixon's Court: His Challenge to Judicial Liberalism and Its Political Consequences* (University of Chicago Press, 2011), 38.

25. The campaign's use of imagery—such as burning cities—allowed race and disorder to be invoked without using specific words or even images of African Americans. Carol Anderson, *White Rage: The Unspoken Truth of Our Racial Divide* (Bloomsbury Publishing, 2020), 273.

26. Dan T. Carter, *The Politics of Rage: George Wallace, the Origins of the New Conservatism, and the Transformation of American Politics* (Louisiana State University Press, 2000), 348.

27. Lowndes, *From the New Deal to the New Right*, 115–16.

28. "Law and Disorder," *Washington Post*, September 15, 1968.

29. "Nixon on Integration," *New York Times*, September 16, 1968; Roy Wilkins, "No Time For Yes But," *Los Angeles Times*, September 30, 1968.

30. "The Same Old Nixon," *Chicago Daily Defender*, September 17, 1968.

31. See, for example, Joseph A. Aistrup, *The Southern Strategy Revisited: Republican Top-Down Advancement in the South* (University Press of Kentucky, 2014).

32. Nelson, *Resilient America*, 185.

33. Nelson, *Resilient America*, 208.

34. Lowndes, *From the New Deal to the New Right*, 107; Nelson, *Resilient America*, 185. See also Anna Grzymala-Busse, "Global Populisms and Their Impact," *Slavic Review* 76 (August 2017): S3–8, https://doi.org/10.1017/slr.2017.152; Cas Mudde and Cristobal Rovira Kaltwasser, *Populism: A Very Short Introduction* (Oxford University Press, 2017).

35. Perlstein, *Nixonland*, 342.

36. For more on veneration of the ordinary, see John Gerring, *Party Ideologies in America, 1828–1996* (Cambridge University Press, 1998).

37. Hugh Davis Graham, "Richard Nixon and Civil Rights: Explaining an Enigma," *Presidential Studies Quarterly* 26, no. 1 (1996): 93–106, 94.

38. Graham, "Richard Nixon and Civil Rights," 94.

39. Lowndes, *From the New Deal to the New Right*, 127; Graham, "Richard Nixon and Civil Rights", 94; John D. Skrentny, *The Ironies of Affirmative Action: Politics, Culture, and Justice in America* (University of Chicago Press, 2018), 178.

40. Robert Lieberman, *Shaping Race Policy: The United States in Comparative Perspective* (Princeton University Press, 2011).

41. Dean J. Kotlowski, *Nixon's Civil Rights: Politics, Principle, and Policy* (Harvard University Press, 2001), 99.

42. Kotlowski, *Nixon's Civil Rights*, 108.

43. Kotlowski, *Nixon's Civil Rights*.

44. Lieberman, *Shaping Race Policy*, 181.

45. John D. Skrentny, *The Ironies of Affirmative Action: Politics, Culture, and Justice in America* (University of Chicago Press, 2018), 194.

46. Skrentny, *The Ironies of Affirmative Action*, 209–10, 221.

47. Frymer and Skrentny, "Coalition-Building and the Politics of Electoral Capture," 153; Skrentny, *The Ironies of Affirmative Action*, 179, 211.

48. Elizabeth Hinton, *From the War on Poverty to the War on Crime: The Making of Mass Incarceration in America* (Harvard University Press, 2016), 181.

49. Hinton, *From the War on Poverty to the War on Crime*, 142.

50. Hinton, *From the War on Poverty to the War on Crime*, 135.

51. Jesse H. Rhodes, *Ballot Blocked: The Political Erosion of the Voting Rights Act* (Stanford University Press, 2017), 61.

52. Seth Blumenthal, *Children of the Silent Majority: Young Voters and the Rise of the Republican Party, 1968–1980* (University Press of Kansas, 2019).

53. Perlstein, *Nixonland*; Robert Mason, *Richard Nixon and the Quest for a New Majority* (University of North Carolina Press, 2005).

54. Bruce Miroff, *The Liberals' Moment: The McGovern Insurgency and the Identity Crisis of the Democratic Party* (University Press of Kansas, 2009), 49.

55. As Daniel Galvin points out, Nixon's "antipathy" toward his own party and his decision not to help the campaigns of down-ticket Republicans probably reflected strategic considerations at the time, as parties in general and the Republican Party in particular were not very popular with the electorate. Daniel J. Galvin, "Presidential Partisanship Reconsidered: Eisenhower, Nixon, Ford, and the Rise of Polarized Politics," *Political Research Quarterly* 66, no. 1 (March 1, 2013): 46–60, 52, https://doi.org/10.1177/1065912911427452. The scrambling of party politics also cut both ways for Nixon: His campaign also attracted support from Democrats unhappy with developments in their own party, including prominent members of Congress like John Connally. Mason, *Richard Nixon and the Quest for a New Majority*.

56. Bruce Miroff notes that probably only the "amnesty" part was correct. Miroff, *The Liberals' Moment*, 138.

57. Beverly Gage, "Deep Throat, Watergate, and the Bureaucratic Politics of the FBI," *Journal of Policy History* 24, no. 2 (April 2012): 157–83, https://doi.org/10.1017/S0898030612000012.

58. Gage, "Deep Throat, Watergate, and the Bureaucratic Politics of the FBI," 158.

59. Ruth P. Morgan, "Nixon, Watergate, and the Study of the Presidency," *Presidential Studies Quarterly* 26, no. 1 (1996): 217–38.

60. Daniel S. Chard, *Nixon's War at Home: The FBI, Leftist Guerrillas, and the Origins of Counterterrorism* (University of North Carolina Press, 2021), 126.

61. Gage, "Deep Throat, Watergate, and the Bureaucratic Politics of the FBI," 168.

62. Seymour Hersh, "A Broad Program," *New York Times*, May 24, 1973.

63. Paul Delaney, "NAACP Ponders Nixon Ouster Bid," *New York Times*, July 6, 1973.

64. "Wilkins Hits Nixon on Law and Order," *Washington Post*, July 4, 1973.

65. "Black Solons Agree on Proof of Nixon's Guilt," *Chicago Defender*, May 14, 1974.

66. Representative Parren Mitchell, press release calling for the impeachment of President Nixon, Avoice: Congressional Black Caucus Foundation (blog), May 10, 1974, https://avoice

.cbcfinc.org/exhibits/fair-housing/attachment/rep-parren-mitchell-calls-for-impeachment-of
-president-nixon-1974/ (accessed August 16, 2024).

67. "Articles of Impeachment Adopted by the House of Representatives Committee on the Judiciary," July 27, 1974, The American Presidency Project, https://www.presidency.ucsb.edu/documents/articles-impeachment-adopted-the-house-representatives-committee-the-judiciary (accessed January 9, 2023).

68. Jon Meacham, Peter Baker, Timothy Naftali, and Jeffrey A. Engel, *Impeachment: An American History* (Random House, 2018), 103.

69. Timothy Naftali, panel remarks, "American Political History Conference: Presidential Scandals," C-SPAN, June 11, 2022, https://www.c-span.org/video/?520136-5/american-political-history-conference-presidential-scandals (accessed February 22, 2024).

70. Stanley I. Kutler, *The Wars of Watergate: The Last Crisis of Richard Nixon* (W. W. Norton & Co., 1992), 127.

71. Michael Koncewicz, *They Said No to Nixon: Republicans Who Stood Up to the President's Abuses of Power* (University of California Press, 2018), 8.

72. See Julia Azari, *Delivering the People's Message: The Changing Politics of the Presidential Mandate* (Cornell University Press, 2014).

73. Garrett M. Graff, *Watergate: A New History* (Simon & Schuster, 2022).

74. Gage, "Deep Throat, Watergate, and the Bureaucratic Politics of the FBI"; Graff, *Watergate*.

75. Gage, "Deep Throat, Watergate, and the Bureaucratic Politics of the FBI."

76. Naftali, panel remarks, "Presidential Scandals," 111.

77. Kutler, *The Wars of Watergate*; Meacham et al., *Impeachment*.

78. Daniel P. Franklin, Stanley M. Caress, Robert M. Sanders, and Cole D. Taratoot, *The Politics of Presidential Impeachment* (State University of New York Press, 2020).

79. Stephen Skowronek, *Presidential Leadership in Political Time: Reprise and Reappraisal*, 3rd ed. (University Press of Kansas, 2020).

80. Koncewicz, *They Said No to Nixon*.

81. Naftali, panel remarks, "Presidential Scandals"; Kutler, *The Wars of Watergate*.

82. Naftali, panel remarks, "Presidential Scandals," 125.

83. Lawrence J. McAndrews, "Missing the Bus: Gerald Ford and School Desegregation," *Presidential Studies Quarterly* 27, no. 4 (1997): 791–804.

84. Angie Maxwell and Todd Shields, *The Long Southern Strategy: How Chasing White Voters in the South Changed American Politics* (Oxford University Press, 2019).

85. Skowronek, *The Politics Presidents Make*, 59.

86. Robert A. Strong, "Politics and Principle: Jimmy Carter in the Civil Rights Era," *IJAS Online*, no. 3 (2014): 14–22; Philip A. Klinkner and Rogers M. Smith, *The Unsteady March: The Rise and Decline of Racial Equality in America* (University of Chicago Press, 2002).

87. Burton Ira Kaufman and Scott Kaufman, *The Presidency of James Earl Carter, Jr.* (University Press of Kansas, 2006), 90.

88. "The Clubs Griffin Bell Had to Quit," *New York Times*, February 6, 1977, https://www.nytimes.com/1977/02/06/archives/the-clubs-griffin-bell-had-to-quit-our-club-is-an-extension-of-our.html (accessed December 20, 2022).

89. Edward R. Kantowicz, "Reminiscences of a Fated Presidency: Themes from the Carter Memoirs," *Presidential Studies Quarterly* 16, no. 4 (1986): 651–65.

90. Rigueur, *The Loneliness of the Black Republican*, 276.

91. Paul Delaney, "NAACP Aide Says Carter Disappoints Blacks," *New York Times*, June 28, 1977, https://www.nytimes.com/1977/06/28/archives/naacp-aide-says-carter-disappoints -blacks.html.

92. Rigueur, *The Loneliness of the Black Republican*, 291.

93. Rigueur, *The Loneliness of the Black Republican*, 283.

6. "The Content of Their Character": Ronald Reagan to Barack Obama

1. Tali Mendelberg, *The Race Card: Campaign Strategy, Implicit Messages, and the Norm of Equality* (Princeton University Press, 2017).

2. Paul Frymer, *Uneasy Alliances: Race and Party Competition in America* (Princeton University Press, 1999); LaFleur Stephens-Dougan, *Race to the Bottom: How Racial Appeals Work in American Politics* (University of Chicago Press, 2020).

3. Daniel Schorr, "A New, 'Post-Racial' Political Era in America," *NPR*, January 28, 2008, https://www.npr.org/templates/story/story.php?storyId=18489466.

4. See, for example, the viral video that featured a Black woman talking about "Obama phones" for low-income social program recipients. Although the implied message was essentially misinformation—the program supplying subsidized telephones dated back to the Reagan administration—the phrase and its implications about wasteful social spending, long a racialized topic, gained political traction and became a target of legislative criticism when Republicans took control of the House of Representatives. Karen Tumulty, "'Obama Phones' Subsidy Program Draws New Scrutiny on the Hill," *Washington Post*, April 9, 2023, https://www .washingtonpost.com/politics/obama-phones-subsidy-program-draws-new-scrutiny-on-the -hill/2013/04/09/50699d04-a061-11e2-be47-b44febada3a8_story.html.

5. Eduardo Bonilla-Silva, *Racism Without Racists: Color-Blind Racism and the Persistence of Racial Inequality in America* (Rowman & Littlefield, 2017).

6. Bonilla-Silva, *Racism Without Racists*; Daniel HoSang, *Racial Propositions: Ballot Initiatives and the Making of Postwar California* (University of California Press, 2010).

7. Christopher D. DeSante and Candis Watts Smith, *Racial Stasis: The Millennial Generation and the Stagnation of Racial Attitudes in American Politics* (University of Chicago Press, 2019).

8. Desmond King and Rogers M. Smith, *Still a House Divided: Race and Politics in Obama's America* (Princeton University Press, 2013), 23.

9. HoSang, *Racial Propositions*.

10. HoSang, *Racial Propositions*, 91.

11. DeSante and Smith, *Racial Stasis*.

12. Mendelberg, *The Race Card*.

13. For Republican efforts to change their racial image, see Tasha Philpot, *Race, Republicans, and the Return of the Party of Lincoln* (University of Michigan Press, 2009).

14. Frymer, *Uneasy Alliances*; Stephens-Dougan, *Race to the Bottom*.

15. Ian Haney Lopez, *Dog Whistle Politics: How Coded Racial Appeals Have Reinvented Racism and Wrecked the Middle Class* (Oxford University Press, 2014).

16. Hank Klibanoff, "In This Corner: Old Friends and Oratory a Fair Mix," *Boston Globe*, August 7, 1980.

17. William Endicott, "Ham, Grits and Oratory: Reagan Opens Campaign at a Dixie County Fair," *Los Angeles Times*, August 4, 1980.

18. Andrew Young, "Chilling Words in Neshoba County," *Washington Post*, August 11, 1980.

19. Mendelberg, *The Race Card*, 7.

20. David Edgar, "Reagan's Hidden Agenda: Racism and the New American Right," *Race and Class* 22, no. 3 (January 1, 1981): 221–38, https://doi.org/10.1177/030639688102200301.

21. King and Smith, *Still a House Divided*; Douglas Kneeland, "A Summary of Reagan's Issue Positions on the Major Issues of This Year's Campaign," *New York Times*, July 16, 1980.

22. Kyle Longley, Jeremy Mayer, Michael Schaller, and John W. Sloan, *Deconstructing Reagan: Conservative Mythology and America's Fortieth President* (Routledge, 2015).

23. "The 'Racism' Issue—What Record Shows," *US News & World Report*, September 29, 1980.

24. Jimmy Carter, "The President's News Conference," September 18, 1980, The American Presidency Project, https://www.presidency.ucsb.edu/documents/the-presidents-news-conference-969; Josh Levin, "Being Right About Reagan's Racism Was Bad for Jimmy Carter," *Slate*, August 1, 2019, https://slate.com/news-and-politics/2019/08/ronald-reagan-richard-nixon-racism-monkeys-tape-jimmy-carter.html.

25. "October Surprise: 3 Civil Rights Leaders Back Reagan," *Chicago Defender*, October 18, 1980; Lou Cannon, "Abernathy Endorses Reagan, Raps Carter's Empty Promises," *Washington Post*, October 17, 1980.

26. Alfreda Madison, "Reagan Dims the Lights for Black Justice and Equality," *Washington Informer*, November 25, 1980.

27. "Civil Rights Under the Gun" (editorial), *Philadelphia Tribune*, November 18, 1980.

28. UPI, "Jordan to Let Reagan Act, Then Judge Him on Rights," *New York Times*, December 1, 1980.

29. Kenneth O'Reilly, *Nixon's Piano: Presidents and Racial Politics from Washington to Clinton* (Free Press, 1995), 355.

30. Longley et al., *Deconstructing Reagan*; O'Reilly, *Nixon's Piano*.

31. Josh Levin, *The Queen: The Forgotten Life Behind an American Myth* (Little, Brown, 2020), 57.

32. Levin, *The Queen*.

33. Ange-Marie Hancock, *The Politics of Disgust: The Public Identity of the Welfare Queen* (New York University Press, 2004), 57.

34. Jill Quadagno links the racialization of welfare to cultural arguments about Black poverty dating back to the 1960s. *The Color of Welfare: How Racism Undermined the War on Poverty* (Oxford University Press, 1994).

35. Martin Gilens, *Why Americans Hate Welfare: Race, Media, and the Politics of Antipoverty Policy* (University of Chicago Press, 2009), 181; Quadagno, *The Color of Welfare*.

36. King and Smith, *Still a House Divided*.

37. Robert Pear, "Reagan's Choice for Civil Rights Post," *New York Times*, June 8, 1981; O'Reilly, *Nixon's Piano*.

38. Kenneth Osgood and Derrick E. White, *Winning While Losing: Civil Rights, the Conservative Movement, and the Presidency from Nixon to Obama* (University Press of Florida, 2017).

39. Drew S. Days III, "Turning Back the Clock: The Reagan Administration and Civil Rights," *Harvard Civil Rights–Civil Liberties Law Review* 19, no. 2 (1984): 309.

40. King and Smith, *Still a House Divided*.

41. Days, "Turning Back the Clock."

42. Frymer, *Uneasy Alliances*; Longley et al., *Deconstructing Reagan*.

43. Ronald Reagan, "Remarks and a Question-and-Answer Session During an Administration Briefing in Chicago, Illinois, for Editors from the Midwestern Region," May 10, 1982, The American Presidency Project, https://www.presidency.ucsb.edu/documents/remarks-and-question-and-answer-session-during-administration-briefing-chicago-illinois (accessed October 22, 2023).

44. Denise M. Bostdorff and Steven R. Goldzwig, "History, Collective Memory, and the Appropriation of Martin Luther King, Jr.: Reagan's Rhetorical Legacy," *Presidential Studies Quarterly* 35, no. 4 (2005): 661–90, 668, https://doi.org/10.1111/j.1741-5705.2005.00271.x.

45. Political communication scholars Bostdorff and Goldzwig also note Reagan's lack of enthusiasm for the King holiday bill even as he signed it in 1983.

46. Steven Roberts, "King Holiday: Balky Minority in GOP," *New York Times*, October 21, 1983.

47. Roberts, "King Holiday."

48. Thomson, a member of the John Birch Society and a vocal conservative, had contacted Reagan to urge him to veto the bill. Frances X. Cline, "Reagan's Doubts on Dr. King Disclosed," *New York Times*, October 22, 1983.

49. Bostdorff and Goldzwig, "History, Collective Memory, and the Appropriation of Martin Luther King, Jr.," 669.

50. Mike Feinsilber, "Conservatives Urge Reagan to Veto Holiday Bill," *Associated Press*, October 20, 1983; see also James F. Clarity and Warren Weaver Jr., "BRIEFING; Dr. King Holiday Opposed," *New York Times*, September 29, 1983, https://www.nytimes.com/1983/09/29/us/briefing-dr-king-holiday-opposed.html.

51. Ronald Reagan, "Remarks on Signing the Bill Making the Birthday of Martin Luther King, Jr., a Holiday," November 3, 1983, The American Presidency Project, https://www.presidency.ucsb.edu/documents/remarks-signing-the-bill-making-the-birthday-martin-luther-king-jr-national-holiday.

52. For example, during a news conference Reagan responded to a question from journalist Helen Thomas about his opposition to "flexible hiring goals" for women and minorities by invoking King's legacy of colorblindness. Ronald Reagan, "President's News Conference," February 11, 1986, Ronald Reagan Presidential Library & Museum, https://www.reaganlibrary.gov/archives/speech/presidents-news-conference-27; see also Bostdorff and Goldzwig, "History, Collective Memory, and the Appropriation of Martin Luther King, Jr."

53. As political communication scholar Mary Stuckey explains, Bush's presidency was characterized by the contradictions between his belief in the system and the status quo and

the diversifying and "fragmented" political world around him. His rhetoric about racial minorities "took their experiences out of context" by "placing the national government on their side instead of in opposition to them." Yet while embracing this form of colorblind erasure, Bush also used racial minorities in symbolic contexts that were "othering." Mary E. Stuckey, *Defining Americans: The Presidency and National Identity* (University Press of Kansas, 2004), 298, 324.

54. According to Stuckey, Marshall's retirement constituted a "nightmare" for Bush, who appointed Black conservative Clarence Thomas to the bench. Because Thomas's character and politics were controversial, Bush was in the position of having to defend his choice on multiple and conflicting grounds. To respond to liberal criticisms, Bush highlighted Thomas's support among African Americans. However, the inclusion of race as a selection criterion was political poison with conservatives. Stuckey, *Defining Americans*, 316–17.

55. Haney Lopez, *Dog Whistle Politics*. Although the Bush campaign seized on the issue of Horton and Dukakis's record in Massachusetts, the most infamous of the crime-related ads was not released by the Bush campaign but by a pro-Bush political action committee. Peter Baker, "Bush Made Willie Horton an Issue in 1988, and the Racial Scars Are Still Fresh," *New York Times*, December 4, 2018, https://www.nytimes.com/2018/12/03/us/politics/bush-willie -horton.html.

56. "Message to the Senate Returning Without Approval the Civil Rights Act of 1990," October 22, 1990, The American Presidency Project, https://www.presidency.ucsb.edu/documents /message-the-senate-returning-without-approval-the-civil-rights-act-1990 (accessed October 27, 2023); David Lauter, "Civil Rights Bill Vetoed by Bush: Job Bias: Congress Is Not Likely to Muster the Votes Needed for an Override. The Measure's Supporters Accuse the President of Playing to White Conservatives," *Los Angeles Times*, October 23, 1990, https://www.latimes .com/archives/la-xpm-1990-10-23-mn-2961-story.html.

57. William Welch, "Bush Signs Race Bill, Withdraws Proposed Racial Preferences Ban," Associated Press, November 21, 1991.

58. King and Smith, *Still a House Divided*, 128.

59. Andrew Rosenthal, "Bush Calls Policy Beating 'Sickening,'" *New York Times*, March 22, 1991.

60. O'Reilly, *Nixon's Piano*, 401.

61. Jack Germond and Jules Witcover, "The Ball Is in Bush's Court in Response to LA Riots," *Baltimore Sun*, May 5, 1992.

62. Mary McGrory, "Bush a No-Show on Los Angeles," *Washington Post*, May 5, 1992. McGrory, while critical of Bush's response, falls into a cultural racism trap herself when she cites inadequate Black family formation as a reason for the situation in Los Angeles and compares Blacks unfavorably to Korean immigrants.

63. Nicole Hemmer, *Partisans: The Conservative Revolutionaries Who Remade American Politics in the 1990s* (Basic Books, 2022).

64. Jeanne Cummings, "Separating Fact from Fiction in Campaign Ads," *Atlanta Journal-Constitution*, March 1, 1992.

65. Robin Toner, "The 1992 Campaign: New Hampshire; Bush Jarred in First Primary; Tsongas Wins Democratic Vote," *New York Times*, February 19, 1992, https://www.nytimes.com

/1992/02/19/us/1992-campaign-new-hampshire-bush-jarred-first-primary-tsongas-wins
-democratic.html.

66. Peter Applebome, "The 1992 Campaign: Racial Politics; Perot Speech Gets Cool Reception at NAACP," *New York Times*, July 12, 1992, https://www.nytimes.com/1992/07/12/us/the
-1992-campaign-racial-politics-perot-speech-gets-cool-reception-at-naacp.html.

67. Frymer, *Uneasy Alliances*, 91.

68. Claire Jean Kim, "Managing the Racial Breach: Clinton, Black-White Polarization, and the Race Initiative," *Political Science Quarterly* 117, no. 1 (2002): 55–79, https://doi.org/10.2307/798094.

69. Kim, "Managing the Racial Breach."

70. Noam Biale, Elizabeth Hinton, and Elizabeth Ross, "The Discriminatory Purpose of the 1994 Crime Bill," *Policy Review* 16 (1994): 116–58, 141.

71. DeWayne Wickham, *Bill Clinton and Black America* (Random House, 2004).

72. David Lauter, "Clinton Withdraws Guinier as Nominee for Civil Rights Job: Justice Department: The President Says He Only Lately Read Her Legal Writings. He Decided She Stood for Principles He Could Not Support in a Divisive Confirmation Battle," *Los Angeles Times*, June 4, 1993, https://www.latimes.com/archives/la-xpm-1993-06-04-mn-43290-story.html.

73. Kim, "Managing the Racial Breach," 65–66.

74. Kim, "Managing the Racial Breach."

75. Kim, "Managing the Racial Breach"; Biale et al., "The Discriminatory Purpose of the 1994 Crime Bill."

76. Biale et al., "The Discriminatory Purpose of the 1994 Crime Bill"; Elizabeth Hinton, Julilly Kohler-Hausmann, and Vesla M. Weaver, "Did Blacks Really Endorse the 1994 Crime Bill?," *New York Times*, April 13, 2016, https://www.nytimes.com/2016/04/13/opinion/did
-blacks-really-endorse-the-1994-crime-bill.html.

77. Martin Carcasson, "Ending Welfare as We Know It: President Clinton and the Rhetorical Transformation of the Anti-Welfare Culture," *Rhetoric and Public Affairs* 9, no. 4 (2006): 655–92.

78. Stephen Skowronek, *The Politics Presidents Make: Leadership from John Adams to Bill Clinton*, rev. ed. (Harvard University Press, 1997).

79. Gilens, *Why Americans Hate Welfare*.

80. Carcasson, "Ending Welfare as We Know It."

81. Carcasson, "Ending Welfare as We Know It," 673.

82. Sanford F. Schram, Joe Brian Soss, and Richard Carl Fording, *Race and the Politics of Welfare Reform* (University of Michigan Press, 2010).

83. Daniel P. Franklin, Stanley M. Caress, Robert M. Sanders, and Cole D. Taratoot, *The Politics of Presidential Impeachment* (State University of New York Press, 2020).

84. Toni Morrison, "On the First Black President," *The New Yorker*, https://www.newyorker
.com/magazine/1998/10/05/comment-6543 (accessed January 31, 2024).

85. Peter Baker and Helen Dewar, "The Senate Acquits President Clinton," *Washington Post*, February 13, 1999, https://www.washingtonpost.com/politics/clinton-impeachment/senate
-acquits-president-clinton/ (accessed January 31, 2024).

86. Anthony Sparacino, "Compassionate Conservatism in the Spiral of Politics," *American Political Thought* 7, no. 3 (June 2018): 480–513, 489. https://doi.org/10.1086/698602.

87. Pearl K. Ford Dowe, "Wading in the Water: George W. Bush's Civil Rights Agenda," in Donald R. Kelley and Todd G. Shields, eds., *Taking the Measure: The Presidency of George W. Bush* (Texas A&M University Press, 2013).

88. Sparacino, "Compassionate Conservatism in the Spiral of Politics," 497.

89. George W. Bush, "Address to the Nation on the Terrorist Attacks," September 11, 2001, The American Presidency Project, https://www.presidency.ucsb.edu/documents/address-the -nation-the-terrorist-attacks (accessed October 20, 2022).

90. Avi Selk, "'Not the America I Know': George W. Bush's Daughter Wants You to Remember His Speech on Islam," *Washington Post*, February 1, 2017, https://www.washingtonpost.com /news/the-fix/wp/2017/02/01/not-the-america-i-know-george-w-bushs-daughter-wants-you -to-remember-his-speech-on-islam/ (accessed October 19, 2022).

91. Aymann Ismail, "Why It Matters That George W. Bush Paid Lip Service to Muslims After 9/11," *Slate*, September 11, 2020, https://slate.com/human-interest/2020/09/bush-muslims-lip -service-911-attacks.html (accessed October 19, 2022).

92. Nadeem Muaddi, "The Bush-Era Muslim Registry Failed. Yet the US Could Be Trying It Again," CNN, December 22, 2016, https://www.cnn.com/2016/11/18/politics/nseers-muslim -database-qa-trnd/index.html (accessed October 11, 2023); Audie Cornish, Ashley Brown, and Ashish Valentine, "How Surveillance Programs Developed After 9/11—And How Those Targeted Pushed Back," NPR, September 10, 2021, https://www.npr.org/2021/09/10/1036039849/how -surveillance-programs-developed-after-9-11-and-how-those-targeted-pushed-bac.

93. Research belies this denial and shows that old-fashioned biological forms of racism also underlie white attitudes toward Muslims. See, for example, Nazita Lajevardi and Kassra A. R. Oskooii, "Old-Fashioned Racism, Contemporary Islamophobia, and the Isolation of Muslim Americans in the Age of Trump," *Journal of Race, Ethnicity, and Politics* 3, no. 1 (March 2018): 112–52, https://doi.org/10.1017/rep.2017.37.

94. Michael Eric Dyson, *Come Hell or High Water: Hurricane Katrina and the Color of Disaster* (Basic Books, 2007).

95. Kristen Lavelle and Joe Feagin, "Hurricane Katrina: The Race and Class Debate," *Monthly Review* 58, no. 3 (July/August 2006), https://doi.org/10.14452/MR-058-03-2006-07_6.

96. Frazier Moore, Associated Press, "NBC Disavows Rant by West at Benefit," *Pittsburgh Post-Gazette*, September 7, 2005; Jim DeRogatis, "A Flood of Words; Context Is Required to Understand Kanye West's Latest Outburst—Criticizing President Bush on National TV During Telethon," *Chicago Sun-Times*, September 5, 2005.

97. Dyson, *Come Hell or High Water*, 164.

98. "Two-In-Three Critical of Bush's Relief Efforts," Pew Research Center, September 8, 2005, https://www.pewresearch.org/politics/2005/09/08/two-in-three-critical-of-bushs -relief-efforts/.

99. Ismail K. White, Tasha S. Philpot, Kristin Wylie, and Ernest McGowen, "Feeling the Pain of My People: Hurricane Katrina, Racial Inequality, and the Psyche of Black America," *Journal of Black Studies* 37, no. 4 (March 1, 2007): 523–38, https://doi.org/10.1177 /0021934706296191.

100. White et al., "Feeling the Pain of My People."

101. Robert C. Lieberman, "'The Storm Didn't Discriminate': Katrina and the Politics of Color Blindness," *Du Bois Review: Social Science Research on Race* 3, no. 1 (March 2006): 7–22, https://doi.org/10.1017/S1742058X06060024.

102. Kathryn A. Sweeney, "The Blame Game: Racialized Responses to Hurricane Katrina," *Du Bois Review* 3, no. 1 (2006): 161–74, https://www.cambridge.org/core/journals/du-bois-review-social-science-research-on-race/article/abs/blame-game-racialized-responses-to-hurricane-katrina/961890A95E29427E2C1E54110D5ACD42 (accessed October 9, 2023).

103. "Biden: 'Obama Is Clean & Articulate'.mov," available at YouTube, https://www.youtube.com/watch?v=vJSfBKQA_KQ.

104. Julie Bosman, "Bill Clinton Says Critics Distorted Remarks About Obama," *New York Times*, March 18, 2008, https://www.nytimes.com/2008/03/18/us/politics/18bill.html.

105. Joshua Gunn and Mark Lawrence McPhail, "Coming Home to Roost: Jeremiah Wright, Barack Obama, and the (Re)Signing of (Post) Racial Rhetoric," *Rhetoric Society Quarterly* 45, no. 1 (January 1, 2015): 1–24, https://doi.org/10.1080/02773945.2014.973612.

106. Gunn and McPhail, "Coming Home to Roost," 8.

107. Carly Fraser, "Race, Postblack Politics, and the Candidacy of Barack Obama," in Manning Marable and Kristen Clarke, eds., *Barack Obama and African American Empowerment: The Rise of Black America's New Leadership* (Springer, 2009).

108. Melanye T. Price, *The Race Whisperer: Barack Obama and the Political Uses of Race* (New York University Press, 2016).

109. Stephens-Dougan, *Race to the Bottom.*

110. "Transcript: Barack Obama's Speech on Race," NPR, March 18, 2008, https://www.npr.org/templates/story/story.php?storyId=88478467.

111. Rachel Sklar, "Jon Stewart Gets All Earnest on Us! Obama Race Speech 'Spoke to Americans as Though They Were Adults,'" *HuffPost*, March 28, 2008, https://www.huffpost.com/entry/jon-stewart-gets-all-earn_n_92448 (accessed February 15, 2024).

112. LaFleur Stephens-Dougan places the speech in the category she identifies as "racial distancing" and notes that, while commentators saw the speech as starting a conversation on race, Obama was returning to a favorite theme that he linked to "negative stereotypes" about African Americans: the need for personal responsibility among Black Americans. Stephens-Dougan, *Race to the Bottom*, 68.

113. Valeria Sinclair-Chapman and Melanye Price, "Black Politics, the 2008 Election, and the (Im)Possibility of Race Transcendence," *PS: Political Science and Politics* 41, no. 4 (2008): 739–45, 740.

114. Linda Beail and Rhonda Kinney Longworth, *Framing Sarah Palin: Pit Bulls, Puritans, and Politics* (New York: Routledge, 2012).

115. Alessandra Stanley, "Cheers, Tears, and a Sense of the Historic Moment," *New York Times*, November 6, 2008, https://www.nytimes.com/2008/11/06/us/politics/06watch.html.

116. James A. Bacon, "Election Underscores New Hope for a Colorblind Society," *Richmond Times-Dispatch*, November 13, 2008.

117. William McKenzie, "Inaugural Begins a Discussion About Post-Racial Society," *Dallas Morning News*, January 19, 2009.

118. "Is This the Birth of Post-Racial America?" *Chicago Daily Herald,* January 23, 2009.

119. "Photos: Inside *Black Enterprise*'s Exclusive Interview with President Barack Obama," *Black Enterprise,* April 13, 2012, https://www.blackenterprise.com/inside-black-enterprise -exclusive-oval-office-interview-with-president-barack-obama/ (accessed October 11, 2023); Pavielle E. Haines, Tali Mendelberg, and Bennett Butler, "'I'm Not the President of Black America': Rhetorical Versus Policy Representation," *Perspectives on Politics* 17, no. 4 (December 2019): 1038–58, https://doi.org/10.1017/S1537592719000963.

120. Andra Gillespie, *Race and the Obama Administration: Substance, Symbols, and Hope* (Manchester University Press, 2019).

121. Barack Obama, "The President's News Conference," July 22, 2009, The American Presidency Project, https://www.presidency.ucsb.edu/documents/the-presidents-news-conference -1121 (accessed October 11, 2023).

122. Jamelle Bouie, "The Professor, the Cop, and the President," *Slate,* September 21, 2016, https://slate.com/news-and-politics/2016/09/the-henry-louis-gates-beer-summit-and-racial -division-in-america.html.

123. Bouie, "The Professor, the Cop, and the President."

124. "South Carolina Rep Wilson Shouts, 'You Lie' at Obama," available at YouTube, https:// www.youtube.com/watch?v=XBKAHRYkGVQ.

125. Theda Skocpol and Vanessa Williamson, *The Tea Party and the Remaking of Republican Conservatism* (Oxford University Press, 2016); Christopher S. Parker and Matt A. Barreto, *Change They Can't Believe In: The Tea Party and Reactionary Politics in America,* updated ed. (Princeton University Press, 2014).

126. Skocpol and Williamson, *The Tea Party and the Remaking of Republican Conservatism.*

127. "Politics: Polling the Tea Party," *New York Times,* April 14, 2010, https://archive.nytimes .com/www.nytimes.com/interactive/2010/04/14/us/politics/20100414-tea-party-poll -graphic.html (accessed April 6, 2023).

128. Parker and Barreto, *Change They Can't Believe In,* 161.

129. Rage has been an important frame for understanding the Tea Party. See Steven W. Webster, *American Rage: How Anger Shapes Our Politics* (Cambridge University Press, 2020); Carol Anderson, *White Rage: The Unspoken Truth of Our Racial Divide* (Bloomsbury Publishing, 2020).

130. Michael Tesler, *Post-Racial or Most-Racial? Race and Politics in the Obama Era* (University of Chicago Press, 2016).

131. "Dissecting the 2008 Electorate: Most Diverse in US History," Pew Research Center, April 30, 2009, https://www.pewresearch.org/hispanic/2009/04/30/dissecting-the-2008 -electorate-most-diverse-in-us-history/.

132. Gene Demby, "Who Is the White Vote?," *All Things Considered,* NPR, November 5, 2020, https://www.npr.org/2020/11/05/931836604/who-is-the-white-vote.

133. Michael Tesler, "President Obama and the Emergence of Islamophobia in Mass Partisan Preferences," *Political Research Quarterly* 75, no. 2 (June 1, 2022): 394–408, https://doi.org/10 .1177/10659129211007211.

134. These myths persisted throughout Obama's time in office, and the perception that African Americans and "illegal immigrants" benefit disproportionately from the Affordable Care

Act has shaped white attitudes about the law. Daniel J. Hopkins, *Stable Condition: Elites' Limited Influence on Health Care Attitudes* (Russell Sage Foundation, 2023).

135. Keeanga-Yamahtta Taylor, *From #BlackLivesMatter to Black Liberation* (Haymarket Books, 2016). Taylor also identifies the Bush and Obama presidencies as "the end of colorblindness," even while acknowledging the persistence of economic disparities under Obama. Keeanga-Yahmatta Taylor, "From Colorblind to Black Lives Matter: Race, Class, and Politics Under Trump," in Julian E. Zelizer, ed., *The Presidency of Donald J. Trump: A First Historical Assessment* (Princeton University Press, 2022).

136. Bryan Monroe, "How Obama's Comments on Race Sparked Very Different Reactions," CNN, July 19, 2013, https://www.cnn.com/2013/07/19/politics/obama-race-comments -reaction/index.html.

137. Abigail Thernstrom, "Obama's Mistake on Trayvon Martin Case," CNN, July 15, 2013, https://www.cnn.com/2013/07/15/opinion/thernstrom-trayvon-martin-obama/index.html.

138. Letitia Stein, "Zimmerman Blames Obama for Racial Tensions After Trayvon Martin Shooting," *Reuters*, March 23, 2015, https://www.reuters.com/article/us-usa-florida-zimmerman -idUSKBN0MJ2DD20150323.

139. Denise M. Bostdorff and Steven R. Goldzwig, "Barack Obama's Eulogy for the Reverend Clementa Pinckney, June 26, 2015: Grace as the Vehicle for Collective Salvation and Obama's Agency on Civil Rights," *Rhetoric and Public Affairs* 23, no. 1 (March 1, 2020): 107–52, https://doi .org/10.14321/rhetpublaffa.23.1.0107.

7. "Hostile Takeover": The Two Impeachments of Donald Trump

1. Later analyses of the 2016 election would reveal a more complicated picture. A Pew Research Center study showed that Trump in 2016 and Mitt Romney in 2012 had won white voters by the same margin, and that the real shift in 2016 was between voters with a college degree and those without: the latter group had swung toward Trump. White noncollege voters had been a significant part of the New Deal coalition, and Trump's 2016 coalition represented a major turn away from that historical pattern. Alec Tyson and Shiva Maniam, "Behind Trump's Victory: Divisions by Race, Gender, Education," Pew Research Center, November 9, 2016, https://www .pewresearch.org/short-reads/2016/11/09/behind-trumps-victory-divisions-by-race-gender -education/ (accessed September 20, 2023); Alan I. Abramowitz, "The Transformation of the American Electorate—Sabato's Crystal Ball," Center for Politics, March 23, 2023, https:// centerforpolitics.org/crystalball/articles/the-transformation-of-the-american-electorate/; Adam Harris, "America Is Divided by Education," *The Atlantic*, November 7, 2018, https://www .theatlantic.com/education/archive/2018/11/education-gap-explains-american-politics /575113/.

2. *Saturday Night Live*, "Election Night—SNL," November 12, 2016, https://www.youtube .com/watch?v=SHG0ezLiVGc.

3. The commonly reported number associated with the claim that "white women voted for Trump" is 52 percent, which is cited in numerous authoritative studies of the intersection between race and gender in contemporary politics. Political scientist Jane Junn wrote, "But, in the end, a majority of white female voters chose Trump's 'velvet glove' over the extended hand of a

white woman," referring to the protective paternalism associated with some depictions of white womanhood. Jane Junn, "The Trump Majority: White Womanhood and the Making of Female Voters in the US," *Politics, Groups, and Identities* 5, no. 2 (April 3, 2017): 343–52, https://doi.org/10.1080/21565503.2017.1304224. Similarly, Charles Tien uses the 52 percent statistic from exit polls to inform a study in which he finds that racial resentment and attitudes toward minorities help to explain the variation in white women's evaluations of Trump. Charles Tien, "The Racial Gap in Voting Among Women: White Women, Racial Resentment, and Support for Trump," *New Political Science* 39, no. 4 (October 2, 2017): 651–69, https://doi.org/10.1080/07393148.2017.1378296.

4. Jenée Desmond-Harris, "To Understand the Women's March on Washington, You Need to Understand Intersectional Feminism," *Vox*, January 21, 2017, https://www.vox.com/identities/2017/1/17/14267766/womens-march-on-washington-inauguration-trump-feminism-intersectionaltiy-race-class (accessed September 20, 2023).

5. Tali Mendelberg, *The Race Card: Campaign Strategy, Implicit Messages, and the Norm of Equality* (Princeton University Press, 2017); Ian Haney Lopez, *Dog Whistle Politics: How Coded Racial Appeals Have Reinvented Racism and Wrecked the Middle Class* (Oxford University Press, 2014).

6. Ashley Parker and Steve Eder, "Inside the Six Weeks Donald Trump Was a Nonstop 'Birther,'" *New York Times*, July 2, 2016, https://www.nytimes.com/2016/07/03/us/politics/donald-trump-birther-obama.html.

7. John Blake, "Who Will You Blame Once Obama's Gone?," CNN, November 27, 2015. https://www.cnn.com/2015/11/27/us/obama-race-cnn-kff-poll/index.html.

8. Theda Skocpol and Vanessa Williamson, *The Tea Party and the Remaking of Republican Conservatism* (Oxford University Press, 2016); Christopher S. Parker and Matt A. Barreto, *Change They Can't Believe In: The Tea Party and Reactionary Politics in America*, updated ed. (Princeton University Press, 2014).

9. Ashley Killough, "Jeb Bush on Immigration: My Plan Is 'Dignified,'" CNN, September 21, 2015, https://www.cnn.com/2015/09/21/politics/jeb-bush-immigration-election/index.html.

10. Manu Raju and Seun Min Kim, "Immigration Debacle Dogs Rubio," *Politico*, April 14, 2015, https://www.politico.com/story/2015/04/marco-rubio-2016-immigration-116926.

11. The nativist wing of the Republican Party, associated at the time with figures like Pat Buchanan and Representative Duncan Hunter (R-CA), had been a consistent presence in right-wing politics for decades.

12. John Sides, Michael Tesler, and Lynn Vavreck, *Identity Crisis: The 2016 Presidential Campaign and the Battle for the Meaning of America* (Princeton University Press, 2019), 81.

13. Sides et al., *Identity Crisis*, 86.

14. Ashley Jardina, *White Identity Politics* (Cambridge University Press, 2019), 252. Studies looking to explain Trump support in the 2016 primaries yielded a variety of findings. At least one analysis reported findings broadly similar to those of Sides and his colleagues, finding that Trump's 2016 primary campaign appeared to appeal to a wide variety of "anxieties" about cultural and racial change. Michael Lee, "Multiple Baskets: Diverse Racial Frames and the 2016 Republican Primary," *New Political Science* 39, no. 4 (October 2, 2017): 631–50, https://doi.org/10.1080/07393148.2017.1378788. A study of a panel of voters conducted over the course of the primary season found that anti-Muslim sentiment and authoritarianism were more important

than economic or populist attitudes, and that anti-Muslim voters may have moved toward Trump over the course of the campaign; anti-Black and anti-Latino attitudes were found to have a more constant impact over time. Patrick D. Tucker, Michelle Torres, Betsy Sinclair, and Steven S. Smith, "Pathways to Trump: Republican Voters in 2016," *Electoral Studies* 61 (October 2019): 102035, https://doi.org/10.1016/j.electstud.2019.03.011. Other studies have emphasized the importance of authoritarian attitudes and anti-establishment attitudes. Matthew C. MacWilliams, "Who Decides When the Party Doesn't? Authoritarian Voters and the Rise of Donald Trump," *PS: Political Science and Politics* 49, no. 4 (October 2016): 716–21, https://doi.org/10.1017/S1049096516001463; Joshua J. Dyck, Shanna Pearson-Merkowitz, and Michael Coates, "Primary Distrust: Political Distrust and Support for the Insurgent Candidacies of Donald Trump and Bernie Sanders in the 2016 Primary," *PS: Political Science and Politics* 51, no. 2 (April 2018): 351–57, https://doi.org/10.1017/S1049096517002505.

15. J. Eric Oliver and Wendy M. Rahn, "The Rise of the Trumpenvolk: Populism in the 2016 Election," *Annals of the American Academy of Political and Social Science* 667, no. 1 (2016): 189–206.

16. Joseph Lowndes, "Populism and Race in the United States from George Wallace to Donald Trump," in Carlos de la Torre, ed., *Routledge Handbook of Global Populism* (Routledge, 2018).

17. Indeed, comparisons between Goldwater and Trump were drawn throughout the 2016 campaign—on the basis of their divisiveness, the perceptions that they were temperamentally unfit to be president, and the assumption that both would suffer significant electoral defeat.

18. Jessica Taylor, "Dumpster Fires, Fishing and Travel: These Republicans Are Sitting Out the RNC," NPR, July 18, 2016, https://www.npr.org/2016/07/18/486398726/dumpster-fires-fishing-and-travel-these-republicans-are-sitting-out-the-rnc.

19. Jonathan Martin and Patrick Healy, "Rancor Reigns as Bitterly Divided Republicans Begin Their Convention," *New York Times*, July 18, 2016, https://www.nytimes.com/2016/07/19/us/politics/republican-convention-donald-trump.html.

20. Sides et al., *Identity Crisis*, 113.

21. Anne Gearan and Abby Phillip, "Clinton Regrets 1996 Remark on 'Super-Predators' After Encounter with Activist," *Washington Post*, February 25, 2016, https://www.washingtonpost.com/news/post-politics/wp/2016/02/25/clinton-heckled-by-black-lives-matter-activist/.

22. Michelle Alexander, "Why Hillary Clinton Doesn't Deserve the Black Vote," *The Nation*, February 10, 2016, https://www.thenation.com/article/archive/hillary-clinton-does-not-deserve-black-peoples-votes/; John Wagner and Vanessa Williams, "Cornel West Joins Bernie Sanders on the Campaign Trail in South Carolina," *Washington Post*, September 12, 2015, https://www.washingtonpost.com/politics/cornel-west-joins-bernie-sanders-on-the-campaign-trail-in-south-carolina/2015/09/12/bc9b4236-58c2-11e5-b8c9-944725fcd3b9_story.html.

23. Mark Murray, Andrew Rafferty, and Marianna Sotomayor, "Congressional Black Caucus PAC Endorses Clinton," *NBC News*, February 10, 2016, https://www.nbcnews.com/politics/2016-election/congressional-black-caucus-endorse-clinton-n516216.

24. Seth Masket, "Race Is Still the Central Dividing Line in the Democratic Party," *Vox*, August 26, 2018, https://www.vox.com/mischiefs-of-faction/2018/8/26/17782102/race-dnc-superdelegates (accessed January 26, 2023); Ismail K. White and Chryl N. Laird, *Steadfast Democrats: How Social Forces Shape Black Political Behavior* (Princeton University Press, 2020).

25. Gregory Krieg, "How Did Trump Win? Here Are 24 Theories," CNN, November 10, 2016, https://www.cnn.com/2016/11/10/politics/why-donald-trump-won/index.html (accessed February 23, 2024).

26. James E. Campbell, Helmut Norpoth, et al., "A Recap of the 2016 Election Forecasts," *PS: Political Science and Politics* 50, no. 2 (April 2017): 331–38, https://doi.org/10.1017/S1049096516002766.

27. Jenna Johnson and Abigail Hauslohner, "'I Think Islam Hates Us': A Timeline of Trump's Comments About Islam and Muslims," *Washington Post*, May 20, 2017, https://www.washingtonpost.com/news/post-politics/wp/2017/05/20/i-think-islam-hates-us-a-timeline-of-trumps-comments-about-islam-and-muslims/; Olivia Nuzzi, "Trump: Make America Scared Again," *The Daily Beast*, September 20, 2016, https://www.thedailybeast.com/articles/2016/09/19/donald-trump-s-pitch-feel-terrified-and-vote-for-me.

28. Nazita Lajevardi and Kassra A. R. Oskooii, "Old-Fashioned Racism, Contemporary Islamophobia, and the Isolation of Muslim Americans in the Age of Trump," *Journal of Race, Ethnicity, and Politics* 3, no. 1 (March 2018): 112–52, https://doi.org/10.1017/rep.2017.37.

29. Jennifer Mercieca, *Demagogue for President: The Rhetorical Genius of Donald Trump* (Texas A&M University Press, 2020), 90.

30. Joshua P. Darr, "*Polls and Elections*: Abandoning the Ground Game? Field Organization in the 2016 Election," *Presidential Studies Quarterly* 50, no. 1 (2020): 163–75, https://doi.org/10.1111/psq.12612.

31. Mark Murray, "'Not Who We Are' Group Highlights Trump Insults, Controversies," *NBC News*, October 4, 2016, https://www.nbcnews.com/politics/2016-election/not-who-we-are-group-highlights-trump-insults-controversies-n658891.

32. Rebecca Hersher, "At Susan B. Anthony's Grave, Visiting Hours Extended for Election Day Crowds," NPR, November 8, 2016, https://www.npr.org/sections/thetwo-way/2016/11/08/501167896/hours-of-susan-b-anthonys-gravesite-extended-to-accommodate-election-day-visits.

33. See Seth Masket, *Learning from Loss: The Democrats, 2016–2020* (Cambridge University Press, 2020), for a full accounting of the different explanations of the 2016 election result and how they changed over time. Lawrence Grossback, David A. M. Peterson, and James Stimson, in *Mandate Politics* (New York: Cambridge University Press, 2006), have also demonstrated that surprising election results can stoke media attention to the question of whether the election was a "mandate." For an extended analysis of the impact of election narratives on the Republican Party, see Julia R. Azari, "Leadership by Dilemma," in Julia R. Azari, Bert Rockman and Andrew Rudalevige, eds., *The Trump Legacy* (forthcoming from University Press of Kansas).

34. Jennifer Senior, "Review: In 'Hillbilly Elegy,' a Tough Love Analysis of the Poor Who Back Trump," *New York Times*, August 10, 2016, https://www.nytimes.com/2016/08/11/books/review-in-hillbilly-elegy-a-compassionate-analysis-of-the-poor-who-love-trump.html.

35. Arlie Russell Hochschild, *Strangers in Their Own Land: Anger and Mourning on the American Right* (New Press, 2018).

36. Laura C. Bucci, "White Working-Class Politics and the Consequences of Declining Unionization in the Age of Trump," *Politics, Groups, and Identities* 5, no. 2 (April 3, 2017): 364–71, https://doi.org/10.1080/21565503.2017.1310118.

37. Sides et al., *Identity Crisis*; Brian F. Schaffner, Matthew Macwilliams, and Tatishe Nteta, "Understanding White Polarization in the 2016 Vote for President: The Sobering Role of Racism and Sexism," *Political Science Quarterly* 133, no. 1 (March 1, 2018): 9–34, https://doi.org/10.1002/polq.12737; Diana C. Mutz, "Status Threat, Not Economic Hardship, Explains the 2016 Presidential Vote," *Proceedings of the National Academy of Sciences* 115, no. 19 (May 8, 2018): E4330–39, https://doi.org/10.1073/pnas.1718155115.

38. Kevin Mattson, "President Trump's 'American Carnage' Speech Fit into a Long American Tradition," *Vox*, January 28, 2017, https://www.vox.com/the-big-idea/2017/1/26/14393288/trump-inaugural-american-carnage-speech; Bart Bonikowski, "Trump's Populism: The Mobilization of Nationalist Cleavages and the Future of US Democracy." In Kurt Weyland and Raúl L. Madrid, eds., *When Democracy Trumps Populism: European and Latin America Lessons for the United States* (Cambridge University Press, 2019): 110–31.

39. James Pfiffner, "The Contemporary Presidency: Organizing the Trump Presidency," *Presidential Studies Quarterly* 48, no. 1 (2018): 153–67.

40. Jenna Johnson, "Trump Calls for 'Total and Complete Shutdown of Muslims Entering the United States,'" *Washington Post*, December 7, 2015, https://www.washingtonpost.com/news/post-politics/wp/2015/12/07/donald-trump-calls-for-total-and-complete-shutdown-of-muslims-entering-the-united-states/.

41. Richard Wolf, "Travel Ban Lexicon: From Candidate Donald Trump's Campaign Promises to President Trump's Tweets," *USA Today*, April 24, 2018, https://www.usatoday.com/story/news/politics/2018/04/24/travel-ban-donald-trump-campaign-promises-president-tweets/542504002/ (accessed September 25, 2023); Alan Gomez, "What President Trump Has Said About the Travel Ban," *USA Today*, June 11, 2017, https://www.usatoday.com/story/news/politics/2017/06/11/what-president-trump-has-said-about-muslims-travel-ban/102565166/ (accessed September 25, 2023).

42. Manu Raju and Theodore Schleifer, "Schiff: New Evidence Shows Possible Trump-Russia Collusion," CNN, March 23, 2017, https://www.cnn.com/2017/03/23/politics/adam-schiff-trump-russia-grand-jury/index.html; Jo Becker, Adam Goldman, and Matt Apuzzo, "Russian Dirt on Clinton? 'I Love It,' Donald Trump Jr. Said," *New York Times*, July 11, 2017, https://www.nytimes.com/2017/07/11/us/politics/trump-russia-email-clinton.html.

43. Peter Baker, "In Trump's Firing of James Comey, Echoes of Watergate," *New York Times*, May 9, 2017, https://www.nytimes.com/2017/05/09/us/politics/trump-fbi-investigation-nixon.html.

44. "61 Percent Say Trump Fired Comey to Protect Himself (Poll)," *ABC News*, June 7, 2017, https://abcnews.go.com/Politics/61-percent-trump-fired-comey-protect-poll/story?id=47864899 (accessed February 23, 2024).

45. Mark Murray, "NBC/WSJ Poll: Just 29 Percent Approve of Trump's Firing of James Comey," *NBC News*, May 14, 2017, https://www.nbcnews.com/politics/donald-trump/nbc-wsj-poll-just-29-percent-approve-trump-s-firing-n759196.

46. Samuel Perry, "President Trump and Charlottesville: Uncivil Mourning and White Supremacy." *Journal of Contemporary Rhetoric* 8, nos. 1/2 (2018): 57–71.

47. LaFleur Stephens-Dougan, *Race to the Bottom: How Racial Appeals Work in American Politics* (University of Chicago Press, 2020).

48. Azari, "Leadership by Dilemma."

49. Andrew Kaczynski and Christopher Massie, "A Running List of Democrats Who Have Discussed Impeachment," CNN, May 12, 2017, https://www.cnn.com/2017/05/12/politics/kfile-democrats-impeach-trump/index.html.

50. Stacy M. Brown, "Maxine Waters and the Call for Trump's Impeachment," *Washington Informer*, April 20, 2017.

51. Michael Collins and Daniel Connolly, "Rep. Steve Cohen Seeks to Impeach President Trump After Charlottesville," *The Tennessean*, August 17, 2017, https://www.tennessean.com/story/news/2017/08/17/steve-cohen-impeach-president-trump-charlottesville/575764001/ (accessed May 29, 2023).

52. Chandelis R. Duster, "Black Caucus Vows to 'Root Out Racism' in Federal Policy, White House," *NBC News*, August 21, 2017, https://www.nbcnews.com/news/nbcblk/black-caucus-vows-root-out-racism-federal-policy-white-house-n794221.

53. Jonathan Martin and Alexander Burns, "Democratic Leaders Try to Slow Calls to Impeach Trump," *New York Times*, May 18, 2017, https://www.nytimes.com/2017/05/18/us/politics/democrats-trump-impeachment.html (accessed September 27, 2023).

54. Jonathan Martin, "Republicans Seize on Impeachment for Edge in 2018 Midterms," *New York Times*, April 8, 2018, https://www.nytimes.com/2018/04/08/us/politics/trump-impeachment-midterms.html.

55. Martin, "Republicans Seize on Impeachment for Edge in 2018 Midterms."

56. Darren Samuelsohn, Burgess Everett, and Kyle Cheney, "Democrats Struggle with Midterm Message on Impeachment," *Politico*, May 30, 2018, https://www.politico.com/story/2018/05/30/impeachment-trump-midterms-warner-615250.

57. "US Voters Believe Comey More than Trump, Quinnipiac University National Poll Finds; Support for Marijuana Hits New High," Quinnipiac University Poll, April 26, 2018, https://poll.qu.edu/Poll-Release-Legacy?releaseid=2539.

58. One of the anti-Trump resistance organizations that emerged was Indivisible, which played an active role in candidate recruitment and strategizing for the 2018 midterms. David S. Meyer and Sidney G. Tarrow, *The Resistance: The Dawn of the Anti-Trump Opposition Movement* (Oxford University Press, 2018), 181–82.

59. Kathryn Watson, "Rashida Tlaib Twitter Video: Michigan's New Congresswoman on Trump: 'We're Going to Impeach the Motherfucker,'" *CBS News*, January 4, 2019, https://www.cbsnews.com/news/congresswoman-rashida-tlaib-trump-profanity-curse-says-impeach-the-motherf-twitter-video/.

60. Peter Baker and Susan Glasser, *The Divider: Trump in the White House, 2017–2021* (Knopf Doubleday, 2023).

61. Bryan Armen Graham, "Donald Trump Blasts NFL Anthem Protesters: 'Get That Son of a Bitch off the Field,'" *The Guardian*, September 23, 2017, https://www.theguardian.com/sport/2017/sep/22/donald-trump-nfl-national-anthem-protests.

62. Betsy Klein, "Trump Greenville Rally: Crowd Chants 'Send Her Back' as Trump Escalates Attacks on Ilhan Omar and 'The Squad,' CNN, July 18, 2019, https://www.cnn.com/2019/07/17/politics/donald-trump-greenville-rally/index.html (accessed September 13, 2023).

63. Lisa Mascaro, "Dems Debate Next Steps," *Chicago Daily Herald*, April 20, 2019.

64. Kevin Breuninger and Mike Calia, "Special Counsel Mueller's Report Has Been Released to the Public—Read Key Findings Here," CNBC, April 18, 2019, https://www.cnbc.com/2019/04/18/special-counsel-muellers-report-has-been-released-to-the-public.html.

65. Lawrence J. Trautman, "Impeachment, Donald Trump, and the Attempted Extortion of Ukraine," *Pace Law Review* 40, no. 2 (2020): 141–225.

66. Gil Cisneros et al., "Seven Freshman Democrats: These Allegations Are a Threat to All We Have Sworn to Protect," *Washington Post*, September 23, 2019, https://www.washingtonpost.com/opinions/2019/09/24/seven-freshman-democrats-these-allegations-are-threat-all-we-have-sworn-protect/.

67. Rachael Bade and Karoun Demirjian, *Unchecked: The Untold Story Behind Congress's Botched Impeachments of Donald Trump* (HarperCollins, 2022), 276–77.

68. P. R. Lockhart, "How Russia Exploited Racial Tensions in America During the 2016 Elections," *Vox*, December 17, 2018, https://www.vox.com/identities/2018/12/17/18145075/russia-facebook-twitter-internet-research-agency-race.

69. By June 2019, when the phone call between Trump and Zelenskyy took place, the press had covered Biden's popularity with Black Democratic voters and their importance to his lead in the presidential nomination contest. Harry Enten, "Joe Biden's Challenge: Sustaining Support from Black Voters," CNN, June 22, 2019, https://www.cnn.com/2019/06/22/politics/joe-biden-2020-black-voters-poll/index.html.

70. Bade and Demirjian, *Unchecked*, 259.

71. "Romney Delivers Remarks on Impeachment Vote," KUTV, February 5, 2020, https://kutv.com/news/local/full-text-romney-delivers-remarks-on-impeachment-vote/.

72. Yasmeen Abutaleb and Damien Paletta, *Nightmare Scenario: Inside the Trump Administration's Response to the Pandemic That Changed History* (New York: HarperCollins, 2021), 13.

73. The first US case was reported on January 20, 2020. John Sides, Chris Tausanovitch, and Lynn Vavreck, *The Bitter End: The 2020 Presidential Campaign and the Challenge to American Democracy* (Princeton University Press, 2022), 134.

74. Don Bambino, Geno Tai, Aditya Shah, Chyke A. Doubeni, Irene G. Sia, and Mark L. Wieland, "The Disproportionate Impact of COVID-19 on Racial and Ethnic Minorities in the United States," *Clinical Infectious Diseases* 72, no. 4 (February 15, 2021): 703–6, https://doi.org/10.1093/cid/ciaa815.

75. Abutaleb and Paletta, *Nightmare Scenario*, 191–92.

76. "Trump: Asian-Americans Not Responsible for Virus, Need Protection," *Reuters*, March 24, 2020, https://www.reuters.com/article/idUSKBN21A3V6/.

77. Katie Rogers, Lara Jakes, and Ana Swanson, "Trump Defends Using 'Chinese Virus' Label, Ignoring Growing Criticism," *New York Times*, March 18, 2020, https://www.nytimes.com/2020/03/18/us/politics/china-virus.html (accessed January 9, 2024); Colby Itkowitz, "Trump Again Uses Racially Insensitive Term to Describe Coronavirus," *Washington Post*, June 23, 2020, https://www.washingtonpost.com/politics/trump-again-uses-kung-flu-to-describe-coronavirus/2020/06/23/0ab5a8d8-b5a9-11ea-aca5-ebb63d27e1ff_story.html (accessed January 9, 2024).

78. Christina Maxouris, Holly Yan, and Ralph Ellis "Cities Extend Curfews for Another Night in an Attempt to Avoid Violent Protests over George Floyd's Death," CNN, May 31, 2020,

https://www.cnn.com/2020/05/31/us/george-floyd-protests-sunday/index.html (accessed February 23, 2024).

79. Bob Woodward and Robert Costa, *Peril* (Simon & Schuster, 2023), 114–19.

80. Perry Bacon and Julia Azari, "Trump's Use of Tear Gas to Break Up a Protest Undermined Three Core Values of American Democracy," *FiveThirtyEight,* June 2, 2020, https://fivethirtyeight.com/features/trumps-use-of-tear-gas-to-break-up-a-protest-undermined-three-core-values-of-american-democracy/; Caitlin Oprysko, "Trump Threatens to End Protests with Military," *Politico,* June 1, 2020, https://www.politico.com/news/2020/06/01/trump-slams-governors-as-weak-crackdown-on-protests-294023.

81. Jonathan Allen and Amie Parnes, *Lucky: How Joe Biden Barely Won the Presidency* (Crown, 2021).

82. Lara Bazelon, "Kamala Harris Was Not a 'Progressive Prosecutor,'" *New York Times,* January 17, 2019, https://www.nytimes.com/2019/01/17/opinion/kamala-harris-criminal-justice.html.

83. William A. Galston, "New 2020 Voter Data: How Biden Won, How Trump Kept the Race Close, and What It Tells Us About the Future," Brookings, July 6, 2021, https://www.brookings.edu/articles/new-2020-voter-data-how-biden-won-how-trump-kept-the-race-close-and-what-it-tells-us-about-the-future/ (accessed January 10, 2024).

84. Kathleen Belew, "Militant Whiteness in the Age of Trump," in Julian E. Zelizer, ed., *The Presidency of Donald J. Trump: A First Historical Assessment* (Princeton University Press, 2022).

85. Sides et al., *The Bitter End,* 179, 220.

86. David T. Canon and Owen Sherman, "Debunking the 'Big Lie': Election Administration in the 2020 Presidential Election," *Presidential Studies Quarterly* 51, no. 3 (2021): 546–81, https://doi.org/10.1111/psq.12721.

87. Michael D. Shear and Stephanie Saul, "Trump, in Taped Call, Pressured Georgia Official to 'Find' Votes to Overturn Election," *New York Times,* January 3, 2021, https://www.nytimes.com/2021/01/03/us/politics/trump-raffensperger-call-georgia.html.

88. Derek T. Muller, "Democrats Have Been Shameless About Your Presidential Vote Too," *New York Times,* January 6, 2021, https://www.nytimes.com/2021/01/06/opinion/democrat-republican-electoral-votes.html.

89. Brian Naylor, "Read Trump's Jan. 6 Speech, a Key Part of Impeachment Trial," NPR, February 10, 2021, https://www.npr.org/2021/02/10/966396848/read-trumps-jan-6-speech-a-key-part-of-impeachment-trial (accessed January 10, 2024).

90. Lyman Trumbull, who voted against Johnson's conviction in the Senate, explained that he did not think Johnson was a fit president, but was bound to cast his impeachment vote on the basis of the actions presented by the impeachment leaders. Brenda Wineapple, *The Impeachers: The Trial of Andrew Johnson and the Dream of a Just Nation* (Random House, 2020), 398.

91. Matt A. Barreto, Claudia Alegre, et al., "Black Lives Matter and the Racialized Support for the January 6th Insurrection," *Annals of the American Academy of Political and Social Science* 708, no. 1 (2023): 6, https://doi.org/10.1177/00027162241228395.

92. *Final Report of the Select Committee to Investigate the January 6 Attack on the US Capitol,* House Report 117-663, 117th Cong., 2nd sess. (US Government Publishing Office, December 22, 2022).

93. Barreto et al., "Black Lives Matter and the Racialized Support for the January 6th Insurrection," 6.

94. David A. Hopkins, "How Trump Changed the Republican Party—and the Democrats, Too," in Steven E. Schier and Todd E. Eberly, eds., *The Trump Effect: Disruption and Its Consequences in US Politics and Government* (Rowman & Littlefield, 2022).

95. Donald R. Kinder and Lynn M. Sanders, *Divided by Color: Racial Politics and Democratic Ideals* (University of Chicago Press, 1996).

96. Robert C. Smith, "Presidential Responsiveness to Black Interests from Grant to Biden: The Power of the Vote, the Power of Protest," *Presidential Studies Quarterly* 52, no. 3 (2022): 648–70, https://doi.org/10.1111/psq.12762.

97. Brian Naylor, "Kamala Harris Tells Guatemalans Not to Migrate to the United States," NPR, June 7, 2021, https://www.npr.org/2021/06/07/1004074139/harris-tells-guatemalans -not-to-migrate-to-the-united-states.

98. Julia Ainsley and Frank Thorp V, "Nearly 80 Democrats Send Letter to Biden Blasting Border, Migrant Policy," *NBC News*, January 26, 2023, https://www.nbcnews.com/politics /immigration/77-democrats-criticize-biden-border-asylum-policy-rcna67617.

99. Gerren Keith Gaynor, "Most Black Voters Tell theGrio/KFF Survey They Support Funding or Increased Funding for Police," theGrio, October 25, 2022, https://thegrio.com/2022/10 /25/black-voters-thegrio-kff-funding-police/; Nekima Levy Armstrong, "Black Voters Want Better Policing, Not Posturing by Progressives," *New York Times*, November 9, 2021, https:// www.nytimes.com/2021/11/09/opinion/minneapolis-police-defund.html.

8. Conclusion: The Choices We Face: Rethinking Presidential Impeachment

1. Rogers M. Smith and Desmond King, *America's New Racial Battle Lines: Protect Versus Repair* (University of Chicago Press, 2024).

2. Jennifer L. Hochschild, Vesla M. Weaver, and Traci R. Burch, *Creating a New Racial Order: How Immigration, Multiracialism, Genomics, and the Young Can Remake Race in America* (Princeton University Press, 2012).

3. Ronald L. Hatzenbuehler, "Abraham Lincoln's Evolving Appreciation of the Declaration of Independence," American Nineteenth Century History 21, no. 2 (May 3, 2020): 171–86, https://doi.org/10.1080/14664658.2020.1807697.

Afterword: We Are Going Back

1. Chelsea Bailey, "Nikki Haley in Her Own Words: Why America 'Has Never Been a Racist Country,'" CNN, January 19, 2024, https://www.cnn.com/2024/01/19/politics/nikki-haley -why-america-isnt-racist/index.html (accessed February 23, 2024).

2. Kaia Hubbard, "JD Vance Defends Amplifying False Claims about Immigrants, Saying 'You're Never Going to Get This Stuff Perfect,'" CBS News, September 15, 2024, https://www.cbsnews.com/news/jd-vance-ohio-haitian-immigrants-false-claims-face-the -nation/.

3. Stephen Fowler, "Vance Says Haitian Migrants with Protected Status Are 'Illegal Aliens' to Be Deported," NPR, September 18, 2024, https://www.npr.org/2024/09/18/g-s1-23667 /vance-haiti-migrants-tps-parole-immigration-pets-springfield.

4. Oliver Darcy, "Right-Wing Media Figures Call Kamala Harris a 'DEI' Candidate as Race-Based Attacks Ramp Up," CNN, July 24, 2024, https://www.cnn.com/2024/07/24/media/right-wing-media-kamala-harris-dei-race-attacks/index.html (accessed July 24, 2024); Olivia Beavers and Jordain Carney, "House GOP Leaders Urge Members: Stop Making Race Comments About Harris," *Politico*, July 23, 2024, https://www.politico.com/news/2024/07/23/gop-race-comments-harris-00170735.

5. Amanda Terkel, "Trump and Allies Attack Kamala Harris Based on Race, Gender: 'Dumb' and a 'DEI' Candidate," NBC News, July 24, 2024, https://www.nbcnews.com/politics/2024-election/republican-attacks-kamala-harris-center-race-gender-dumb-dei-candidate-rcna162570 (accessed July 24, 2024).

6. "'We Are Not Going Back' Wasn't Written to Be a Campaign Catchphrase. Kamala Harris Voters Had Other Ideas," *Vanity Fair*, September 6, 2024, https://www.vanityfair.com/news/story/we-are-not-going-back-kamala-harris-campaign (accessed January 21, 2025).

7. August Brown, "Beyoncé and Kendrick Lamar Open the BET Awards with a Rebellious Performance," *Los Angeles Times*, June 26, 2016, https://www.latimes.com/entertainment/music/la-et-ms-beyonce-kendrick-20160626-snap-story.html.

8. "The Campaign Moment" (podcast), *Washington Post*, July 23, 2024, https://www.washingtonpost.com/podcasts/the-campaign-moment/ (accessed July 24, 2024).

9. Shane Goldmacher, Maggie Haberman, and Michael Gold, "Trump at the Garden: A Closing Carnival of Grievances, Misogyny and Racism," *New York Times*, October 28, 2024, https://www.nytimes.com/2024/10/27/us/trump-msg-rally.html.

10. "The 2024 Election Story Is More Complex than 'Racial Realignment,'" Good Authority, November 18, 2024, https://goodauthority.org/news/election-2024-racial-realignment-us-politics/ (accessed January 21, 2025); "Trump Gained Some Minority Voters, but the GOP Is Hardly a Multiracial Coalition," Brookings, December 13, 2024, https://www.brookings.edu/articles/trump-gained-some-minority-voters-but-the-gop-is-hardly-a-multiracial-coalition/ (accessed January 21, 2025).

11. "Proclamation 6677—Announcing the Death of Richard Milhous Nixon," April 22, 1994, The American Presidency Project, https://www.presidency.ucsb.edu/documents/proclamation-6677-announcing-the-death-richard-milhous-nixon (accessed January 21, 2025).

12. Donald Trump, "Inaugural Address," January 20, 2025, The American Presidency Project, https://www.presidency.ucsb.edu/documents/inaugural-address-54 (accessed January 21, 2025).

Abernathy, Ralph, 146
abolitionism/anti-slavery movement: opposition to, 27–28; pre–Civil War actions of, 31
abuses of presidential power: Andrew Johnson, 64; as basis for impeachment, 9, 12, 64, 126–27, 130, 187, 189, 195–96; Nixon, 112, 126–27, 129–32, 135; populist origins of, in attacks on institutions and norms, 12, 135; Trump, 186–87, 189, 195–96. *See also* lawlessness; presidential powers
Adams, Charles Francis, 73
affirmative action, 122–23, 137–38, 142, 145, 147, 148, 151–52, 159, 169, 177. *See also* employment discrimination; individualism; meritocracy; quotas; reverse discrimination/racism
Affordable Care Act, 167–69, 171, 185, 248n134
African Americans: Andrew Johnson and, 55, 57–60, 66–67; Bill Clinton and, 154–55, 158; Carter and, 139; citizenship of, 38–39, 61; and Democratic Party politics, 77, 118, 181; federal positions for, 80, 82, 84, 88, 91, 99; Franklin Roosevelt and, 86; George W. Bush and, 159, 162; Nixon and, 112, 119, 123, 128–30; Northern resentment of, in Reconstruction era, 74; Obama and, 1; political power and influence of, 77, 88; post–Civil War discrimination against, 7; Reagan and, 146, 149; Republican Party and, 115–16; rights of, 39, 59, 71–73, 76 (*see also* voting rights for); stereotypes of, 147, 247n112; Theodore Roosevelt and, 78–80, 230n15; Truman and, 90; Trump's targeting of, 2; violence against, 54, 57–58, 73–74, 76–77, 89, 95, 101–2, 106, 107, 151–53, 198, 229n89; voting rights for, 55–56, 65–67, 73–74, 82, 99, 105–8, 124, 148; whites' sexual fears regarding, 79, 81, 84–85, 95, 99. *See also* colorblind ideology/rhetoric; enslaved persons; Great Migration
Agnew, Spiro, 116
Alexander, Michelle, 180
American Civil Liberties Union, 185
American political development, 14–18
Anthony, Susan B., 183
Anti-Lynching Bill, 82
anti-slavery movement. *See* abolitionism/ anti-slavery movement
Ashley, James, 65, 68
authoritarianism, 179

backlash, racial. *See* racial backlash
backlash presidents: Andrew Johnson, 4, 20, 70–71; congressional opposition to, 14; impact of, 16, 20, 204; Nixon, 5–6, 20; overview of, 5; populism used by, 4, 10–12, 207; themes of, 4; as threat to democracy, 12; Trump, 4, 20, 203
Baio, Scott, 179
Baker, Howard, 126
Barr, William, 107
Belafonte, Harry, Jr., 97
Belew, Kathleen, 199
Bell, Griffin, 138

Bell, John, 43, 45

Bernstein, Carl, 126

Biden, Hunter, 3, 195

Biden, Joe, 3, 12, 163, 188, 195, 199–200, 203–6, 208, 209, 214, 217

birther movement, 176

Birth of a Nation (film), 84

black-and-tan Republicans, 17, 78, 82

Black codes, 57, 70. *See also* Jim Crow era

Black Enterprise (magazine), 1

Black Lives Matter, 2, 171–72, 177, 179–80, 204

Black Panthers, 128

Black Power movement, 128

block grants, 123

Blumenthal, Seth, 124

Bouie, Jamelle, 168

Brazile, Donna, 181

Breckinridge, John, 43, 45

Brooke, Edward, 115

Brooks, Preston, 38

Brown, Michael, 161

Brownell, Herbert, 95, 97, 233n84

Brownsville massacre (1906), 81

Brown v. Board of Education, 94–98

Bucci, Laura, 184

Buchanan, James, 36, 38–40

Buchanan, Pat, 123, 152, 153, 250n11

Bush, George H. W., 151–54, 243n53, 244n54, 244n55

Bush, George W., 141, 159–63, 182, 201, 249n135

Bush, Jeb, 177, 178

Buttigieg, Pete, 203

Byrnes, James, 232n58

Calhoun, John C., 34

California, 33–34

campaigns. *See* presidential campaigns

Carmines, Edward, 113

Carter, Dan, 118

Carter, Jimmy, 136–39, 144–46, 205–6

Cass, Lewis, 31

Castro, Joaquin, 189

Centers for Disease Control and Prevention (CDC), 196–97

Central High School, Little Rock, Arkansas, 96

Central Intelligence Agency (CIA), 130

Chappelle, Dave, 175

Charlottesville, Virginia, "Unite the Right" rally, 187–90, 204

Chicago Daily Defender (newspaper), 119

Chicago Daily News (newspaper), 166

China, 196–97

Christian nationalism, 209

Churchill, John, 65, 66

CIA. *See* Central Intelligence Agency

citizenship, for African Americans, 38–39, 61

Civilian Conservation Corps (CCC), 87

civil rights: of African Americans, 39, 59, 71–73, 76; *Brown v. Board of Education* decision and, 94–98; Democratic Party and, 91–93; Eisenhower and, 93–98, 102; executive actions promoting, 77; federal enforcement of, 89; foreign policy linked to, 100–101; group vs. individual, 148; growing demands for, 77; Kennedy and, 98–102; Lyndon Johnson and, 5, 8, 75–76, 78, 102–9; as moral issue, 78, 85, 88–89, 96–98, 101–3, 106–7; Nixon and, 98, 117–24; Reagan and, 145, 148; Republican Party and, 115; Sanders and, 180; Truman and, 90–93, 102; Vietnam War and, 113–14. *See also* voting rights

Civil Rights Act (1957), 97, 103

Civil Rights Act (1964), 5, 75, 76, 78, 101, 103–4, 106, 145, 150, 152

Civil Rights Act (Fair Housing Act, 1968), 5, 76, 78

civil service, 80, 82, 84, 91

civil unrest. *See* riots and unrest

Civil War: Lincoln and, 40, 42; slavery as cause of, 47–49

The Clansman (film), 84

Clarke, David, 179

Clay, Henry, 22, 30, 34

Clifford, Clark, 91

Clinton, Bill: and African Americans, 154–55, 158; character/personality of, 158;

and crime, 155, 180; impeachment of, 9, 13, 18, 156–59, 190; and Obama, 163; as preemptive president, 17, 229n83; and the South, 137; and welfare, 154–56
Clinton, Hillary, 156, 163–65, 174, 179–83, 204
Clyburn, James, 181
Coates, Ta-Nehisi, 180; "The First White President," 3
Coe, Alexis, 24
Coe, Kevin, 76, 235n134
Cohen, Steve, 189
Cohn, Nate, 174
colonization approach to slavery, 23, 41, 225n76
colorblind ideology/rhetoric: Bill Clinton and, 154; George H. W. Bush and, 151, 153; George W. Bush and, 160–61, 249n135; individualism as component of, 8, 142; meanings of, 142–44; Nikki Haley and, 213; Obama and, 141, 163–69, 172, 249n135; origins of, 137–40; Palin and, 166; precursor of, 60; Reagan and, 145–50, 243n52; societal norm of, 8, 13, 143, 145–46, 162–64, 169, 172, 175
Comey, James, 186–87
Communism, 150
compassionate conservatism, 159
compromise/moderation: in aftermath of Andrew Johnson presidency, 71–74; in aftermath of Nixon presidency, 137; Bill Clinton and, 155–56; Compromise of 1850, 32–37; in the Constitution, 24–25; Eisenhower and, 94–98; following racial transformations, 208–11; Franklin Roosevelt and, 86–90; George H. W. Bush and, 151–53; Kennedy and, 98–102; Lincoln and, 42, 43, 46–48, 51; Lyndon Johnson and, 78, 105; Missouri Compromise, 25–26, 35, 37, 39; negative aspects of, 19; Nixon and, 117–19; Obama and, 2, 17, 165, 167, 171; political role of, 18–19; on racial issues, 6–8, 19, 20; Reagan and, 150; on slavery, 22–40; Theodore Roosevelt and, 81; Three-Fifths Compromise, 25;

Van Buren and, 28–29. *See also* racial backlash; racial transformation
Compromise of 1850, 32–37
Confederate statues, removal of, 188
Congress: Andrew Johnson's relations with, 10, 58–71; Nixon's relations with, 10, 111, 133–36; norms of behavior and actions of, 12–14; presidents' relations with, 9–10, 17–18; and Reconstruction, 58–62, 65; and slavery, 23, 25, 37, 39, 44, 46, 54; Trump's relations with, 10, 190–92, 194–95. *See also* House of Representatives; Senate
Congressional Black Caucus, 14, 129, 155, 180, 189
Connally, John, 239n55
Conservative Caucus, 150
conservative movement: 1968 election and, 113, 115–16; and Clinton's impeachment, 13, 157; and colorblind rhetoric, 8, 140, 142; George W. Bush and, 159; New Deal and civil rights as targets of, 237n6; Nixon and, 120; populism aligned with, 120; Reagan and, 144–50; Republican Party and, 115–16, 120
Constitution: and impeachment, 14, 64, 133, 207; on presidents' role, 6, 23, 68; and slavery, 23, 24–25, 44, 46
Constitutional Convention, 25
Constitutional Union Party, 43
context, political. *See* political environment
convention system, 28
Coolidge, Calvin, 82–83
Copperhead Democrats, 52
Corwin amendment, 46–47
Costigan, Edward, 87
COVID-19, 196–97
Cox, Archibald, 130
Cox, Jacob Dobson, 72
Cox, Minnie, 80
crime: Democratic Party and, 143, 155, 180; Republican Party and, 123, 145, 151; whites' anxieties about, 107, 114, 123, 143, 145, 151, 154. *See also* law-and-order ideology/rhetoric

Crittenden, John J., 46
Crowley, James, 168
culture wars, 112, 126, 161

Dallas Morning News (newspaper), 166
Dallek, Robert, 99
Dalton, Kathleen, 80
Daniels, Jonathan, 89
Davies, Elizabeth Jordan, 172
Davis, Henry Winter, 53
Davis, Jefferson, 52, 57, 63
Days, Drew, 148
Declaration of Independence, 44, 49, 210–11
Deferred Action for Childhood Arrivals (DACA), 176–77
"defund the police," 199, 205
democracy: backlash presidents as threat to, 12; civil rights publicity as reflection on, 101; implications of racial order, racial transformation, and racial backlash for, 18–20; post–Civil War, 62, 71; restoration of, after backlash presidencies, 200, 210; white nationalist threats to, 188
Democratic Party: African Americans' role in, 77, 118, 181; associated with social disorder, 19; and civil rights, 91–93; during Civil War, 52; divisions within, in 1960s and 1970s, 111, 114, 117, 120, 122–23, 125; formation of, 22, 28; Franklin Roosevelt and, 86, 89–90; Nixon's strategy against, 117, 122–23; Northern and Southern interests in, 16–17, 22, 28, 29, 31, 36–37, 86–87, 89–92, 98–99, 102, 105, 111, 118; and populism in 2016, 179–81; post-Obama, 179–81, 188–96, 199, 202–6; and race in civil rights era, 8; and race in post–civil rights era, 143; and race in post–Civil War era, 7; and slavery, 7, 22, 37–38; Van Buren and, 28; and white supremacy, 7, 52. *See also* Congressional Black Caucus; Jacksonian Democrats; New Deal Democrats; New Democrats
DeSante, Christopher, 142

DeSantis, Ron, 205
DeVos, Betsy, 202
Dirksen, Everett, 104
discrimination. *See* affirmative action; employment discrimination; racial discrimination; reverse discrimination/racism
District of Columbia. *See* Washington, DC
"diversity, equity and inclusion" (DEI), 205, 214
Dole, Bob, 149
Douglas, Stephen, 21, 36–39, 43, 62
Douglass, Frederick, 51, 59, 228n44; "Oration in Memory of Abraham Lincoln," 21–22
Dred Scott v. Sandford, 38, 43
Du Bois, W.E.B., 84
Dukakis, Michael, 151, 154, 244n55
Duke, David, 152
Dyer, Leonidas, 82
Dyer, Thomas, 230n15

East St. Louis massacre (1917), 85
economy: African Americans and, 59; Andrew Johnson and, 11, 52–53; Carter and, 139; populism and, 11, 52–53, 85–86; racial inequalities in, 2, 8, 56–58, 76–78, 88–89, 97, 123, 129, 146; Reagan and, 144, 146; Trump and, 11, 184
Eisenhower, Dwight, 7, 18, 77, 93–98, 102, 234n97
election interference: Andrew Johnson and, 4, 12, 208; Nixon and, 6, 12, 135, 208; populism linked to, 12; Trump and, 3, 12, 135, 200–203, 208
Electoral College, 2, 25, 43, 74, 92, 166, 174, 183, 200–201, 208, 215
Electoral Count Act (1887), 200–201
elites: Andrew Johnson and, 11, 62; Democratic Party defections by, 111; Nixon and, 11; as target of populist sentiment, 11–12, 120; Trump and, 11, 178
Emancipation Proclamation, 4, 41, 47–48

employment discrimination, 87, 89, 91–93, 104, 117, 122–23, 148, 151. *See also* affirmative action

enslaved persons, Three-Fifths Compromise on, 25

environment, political. *See* political environment

Equal Employment Opportunity Commission, 104, 148

Ervin, Sam, 136

Esper, Mark, 107

Evers, Charles, 146

Evers, Medgar, 146

Executive Order 8802, 89

executive powers. *See* presidential powers

executive privilege, 131

expansionism, 30–31, 35, 37

Fair Employment Practices Committee, 89, 91

Faubus, Orville, 96

Federal Bureau of Investigation (FBI), 127, 130, 132–33, 150

Federal Emergency Management Agency (FEMA), 161

federalism: Jackson and, 27; and racial hierarchy, 206; and slavery, 23. *See also* states

Felt, Mark, 132–33

Fessenden, William Pitt, 58

Fifteenth Amendment, 73, 76, 230n97

Fillmore, Millard, 33–35

Fitzwater, Marlin, 153

Flake, Jeff, 178

Floyd, George, 198, 203

Foner, Eric, 57, 67

Forbes, Robert Pierce, 26

Ford, Gerald, 136–37

"forgotten man/American," 85–86, 88, 120, 184, 186. *See also* "silent majority;" "true people"

Fourteenth Amendment, 61, 73, 76, 94, 230n97

Francis, Megan Ming, 82, 85, 88

Frantz, Edward, 82, 230n15

Freedmen's Bureau, 59

Freedom Riders, 101

Freeman, Ruby, 203

Free Soil movement/Party, 31–32, 35, 36, 224n54

Frymer, Paul, 118

Fugitive Slave Law (1850), 34–35, 46

Gage, Beverly, 132–33

gag rule, 29

Galvin, Daniel, 239n55

Gates, Henry Louis, 168

gender, and 2016 election, 175, 249n3

Germond, Jack, 153

Gettysburg Address (Lincoln), 44, 47–49

Gingrich, Newt, 1, 157

Goldwater, Barry, 104–6, 111, 115, 178, 251n17

Goldzwig, Steven, 108

Gordon-Reed, Annette, 24, 55, 61, 64–65

Gore, Al, 201

Graham, Billy, 95

Grant, Ulysses S., 67, 72–74, 138, 205–6

Gray, L. Patrick, 132

Great Depression, 83, 87

Great Migration, 77, 90

Great Society, 78, 103, 123, 153

Greeley, Horace, 73

Guinier, Lani, 155

guns, 145

habeas corpus, 41, 48

Haldeman, H. R., 122

Haley, Nikki, 213

Hamer, Fannie Lou, 105

Hancock, Ange-Marie, 147

Hanna, Mark, 79

Harding, Warren G., 82

Harlan, John Marshall, 140, 142

Harris, Kamala, 199, 205, 209, 214–15

Harrison, William Henry, 29–30

Hayes, Rutherford B., 72, 74, 138

Health, Education, and Welfare Department, 119, 122

health-care legislation, 167–71. *See also* Affordable Care Act

Heersink, Boris, 237n13

Helms, Jesse, 146, 149

Hemings, Sally, 24

Hersh, Seymour, 128

Heyer, Heather, 188

high crimes and misdemeanors, 8–9, 64, 190

Hinton, Elizabeth, 123

Hochschild, Arlie Russell, *Strangers in Their Own Land*, 184

Holden, William W., 56

Holt, Michael, 32, 45

Hoover, Herbert, 82–83

Hoover, J. Edgar, 132

Horton, Willie, 151, 244n55

HoSang, Daniel, 142

House Judiciary Committee, 9, 65–66, 112, 126, 129–30, 133, 136, 158

House of Representatives: gag rule on slavery petitions in, 29; presidential elections determined by, 92; role of, in impeachment, 14. *See also* House Judiciary Committee; impeachments

Howard University, 83

Humphrey, Hubert, 91, 107, 116, 118, 120

Hunter, Duncan, 250n11

Hurricane Katrina, 159, 161–63

Hurricane Maria, 192

Huston, Tom, 128

Huston Plan, 112, 127–28, 132, 134

Ickes, Harold, 86

immigrants/immigration, 2, 176–77, 179, 182, 192–93, 205, 210

impeachments: abuse of power as basis for, 9, 12, 64, 126–27, 130, 187, 189, 195–96; Andrew Johnson, 4, 18, 63–71, 208, 229n83, 256n90; Bill Clinton, 9, 13, 18, 156–59, 190; characteristics of presidents subject to, 10; Constitutional guidance lacking for, 14, 64, 133, 207; fallout for Congress of, 14; House of Representatives' crucial role in, 14; legal context for, 8–9, 64–65, 67–70, 157–58, 187, 190, 196, 208, 220n16; legitimacy as issue in, 69, 134–36; Nixon, 6, 9, 18, 110, 112, 126–36, 208; norms of, 13–14, 157, 187, 191–92, 208; parliamentary processes compared to, 64–65; political (vs. legal) context for, 158, 187, 190, 196, 208; political environments for, 9–14, 18, 64–65, 70–71, 111, 131, 133–36, 141, 157, 191–92, 207–8, 220n16; racial transformation linked to, 8–14, 70–71, 134–36, 207; Trump, 3–4, 18, 186–90, 193–96, 202–3, 208

individualism, and racial politics, 8, 15, 74, 140, 142, 148, 162. *See also* affirmative action; meritocracy

Indivisible, 254n58

infamous bargain, 74

institutions: FBI norms, 133; Jackson's attitude toward, 26; Nixon's attitude toward, 131–34; political roles of, 18; populist attacks on, 10–12, 121; Trump's attitude toward, 177–78, 187. *See also* norms

Internal Revenue Service (IRS), 127, 134

ironclad oath, 53

IRS. *See* Internal Revenue Service

Islamophobia, 160–61, 170–71, 182, 185–86, 246n93

Ismail, Aymann, 160

Jackson, Andrew, 19, 22, 26–28, 52, 222n20, 222n23, 223n36

Jackson, Jesse, 154, 163

Jacksonian Democrats, 16–17

January 6, 2021, insurrection, 3, 12, 201–3, 208

Jardina, Ashley, 11

Jefferson, Thomas, 22, 24, 27

Jenkins, Jeffery, 237n13

Jim Crow era: beginning of, 17; ending of, 104; Lyndon Johnson and, 78; racial hierarchy in, 81; status quo in, 7; voting rights in, 203; Wilson and, 84. *See also* Black codes; racial violence

Johnson, Andrew: and African Americans, 55, 57–60, 66–67; aftermath of the presidency of, 71–74; as backlash president, 4, 20, 70–71; congressional relations with, 10, 58–71; Democratic Party and, 4; election interference by, 4, 12; impact of backlash presidency of, 20; impeachment of, 4, 18, 63–71, 208, 229n83, 256n90; Nixon compared to, 110, 115, 122, 134–35; norms challenged, ignored, and broken by, 63; political background of, 50, 52, 54; political environment for, 23; political isolation of, 50, 62–63, 71, 229n83; and populism, 10–11, 52, 61–63, 121; as preemptive president, 17, 229n83; presidential powers wielded by, 4, 55–58, 64; racial issues exploited by, 11, 19; racism of, 4, 59, 66–67, 228n44; and Reconstruction, 4, 11, 52–53, 55–58, 63, 65–66, 70; and slavery, 52; and the South, 19, 50, 52, 54–58, 70–71; Trump compared to, 71, 187, 189, 192, 195–98, 201–3; and the Union's preservation, 19, 50, 52, 56, 61; vice presidential selection of, 4, 50, 53; and white supremacy, 4, 19, 55, 58–59, 62, 66–67

Johnson, Kimberley, 76

Johnson, Lyndon: and civil rights, 5, 8, 75–76, 78, 102–9; and race, 8; and racial transformation, 75–76, 78, 102–9; as transformative president, 5, 76, 78, 211

Jones, Paula, 156–57

Jordan, Barbara, 110, 130, 136

Jordan, Vernon, 146–47

Journal of Negro Education, 97

Judge, Oney, 24

Junn, Jane, 249n3

Justice Department, 89, 94, 97, 100, 138, 148, 186

Kaepernick, Colin, 192

Kansas, 38–39, 43

Kansas-Nebraska Act, 37–39

Kantowicz, Edward, 138

Karp, Matt, 42

Kasich, John, 178

Katznelson, Ira, 87

Kendall, Amos, 27

Kennedy, John F., 7, 8, 77, 98–102

Kennedy, Robert, 98

King, Desmond, 15, 142, 209

King, Martin Luther, Jr., 95, 97, 98, 107–8, 113–14, 149–50

King, Rodney, 151–53

Klinkner, Phil, 83

Know-Nothing Party, 38

Koncewicz, Michael, 131

Kotlowski, Dean, 123

Ku Klux Klan, 69, 73, 74, 84, 146–47

Kutler, Stanley, 131

Lance, Bert, 138

law-and-order ideology/rhetoric: 1968 election and, 113; applied to civil rights questions, 85, 97; Democratic Party and, 118; George H. W. Bush and, 152–53; Humphrey and, 118; Nixon and, 5, 19, 114, 119, 123–24, 238n25; Reagan and, 115; Republican Party and, 114–15; Trump and, 2, 4, 198; Willie Horton ad and, 151, 244n55. *See also* crime

lawlessness: ambiguity and vagueness as invitation to, 19; populism linked to, 10, 12, 130, 207; presidential, 9, 10, 12, 111–12, 130, 183, 196; racial backlash linked to, 9, 112, 117, 183. *See also* abuses of presidential power; norms

Leadership Conference on Civil Rights, 145

Lecompton Constitution, 39, 43

Lee, Robert E., 137, 188

legitimacy: denied to opponents by politicians, 12, 61–62, 112, 121, 134; of impeachments, 69, 134–36; as issue in impeachments, 134–36; presidents', 30, 62–63, 117, 134–36, 169, 175, 189, 191, 194

Levine, Robert, 55, 228n44

Lewinsky, Monica, 157

Lewis, John, 180, 181

lily-white Republicans, 17, 81–83

Limbaugh, Rush, 1

Lincoln, Abraham: 1860 election, 42–45; 1864 election, 50–53; assassination of, 65; Gettysburg Address, 44, 47–49; and Johnson's vice presidency nomination, 50, 53; and Mexican-American War (1846–48), 30; moderation of, 42, 43, 46–48, 51; political background of, 42; political context for, 23, 41–42; presidential powers wielded by, 40–41, 47–48; Proclamation of Amnesty and Reconstruction, 51; and race, 21, 40–41, 49, 225n76; and racial transformation, 21–22, 44–45, 47–49; and Reconstruction, 53–54; and slavery, 4, 21–22, 24, 41, 43, 48–49, 54, 226n98; as transformative president, 4, 21–24, 40, 48–49, 211

Louis Harris and Associates, 113

Louisiana Purchase, 36

Lowndes, Joe, 116, 178, 236n2

lynching, 76–77, 79, 81–83, 85, 87–89, 91, 103

Manchin, Joe, 191

March on Washington (1963), 102

Marshall, Thurgood, 151, 153, 244n54

Martin, Trayvon, 172

Marxism-Leninism, 128

masculinity, 178, 188

Mason, Lilliana, 113

McCain, John, 2, 165–66, 174

McCarthy, Eugene, 108

McClellan, George, 4, 51

McConnell, Mitch, 202

McGovern, George, 125

McGrath, Howard, 91

McGrory, Mary, 153, 244n62

McKinley, William, 79, 80

Meacham, Jonathan, 65, 70

Mellow, Nicole, 71

Memphis riot (1866), 58

Mercieca, Jennifer, 182

Meredith, James, 100

meritocracy, 142, 162, 184. *See also* affirmative action; individualism

Mexican Cession, 31

Mexican War (1846–48), 30–31, 34

Mfume, Kwesi, 155

Military Reconstruction Act, 66

Milkis, Sidney, 90, 105

Miller, Stephen, 107, 186

Milley, Mark, 107

Mississippi Freedom Democratic Party, 105

Missouri Compromise, 25–26, 35, 37, 39

Mitchell, Clarence, 123, 129, 145

Mitchell, Parren, 129

moderation. *See* compromise/moderation

Mondale, Walter, 154

Monroe, James, 25–26

morality and moral leadership: Bill Clinton and, 158–59; civil rights issues and, 78, 85, 88–89, 96–98, 101–3, 106–7; Kennedy and, 101–2; Lincoln and, 21, 44–45, 48–49; Lyndon Johnson and, 102–3, 106–7; moral status of slavery, 17, 25, 27, 34, 40, 44–45, 47–49; presidents' avoidance of, 26, 36, 72, 78, 85, 89, 96–98; sexual anxieties linked to, 95; welfare linked to, 60

Morgan, Ruth, 127

Morrison, Toni, 157–58

Morrow, E. Frederic, 95

Moss, Shaye, 203

Mueller, Robert, and the Mueller report, 193–94

Muslims. *See* Islamophobia

Myers, Mike, 162

NAACP. *See* National Association for the Advancement of Colored People

Naftali, Timothy, 130

National Association for the Advancement of Colored People (NAACP), 77, 82–85, 87–88, 90–91, 97, 122, 128–29, 159

National Football League (NFL), 192

nationalism, 11, 54, 74, 177, 182, 185, 188, 192, 209

national security, 130–31, 182, 195

National Union Party, 50, 53, 60–61, 63, 229n83

National Youth Administration (NYA), 86

Native Americans, 26, 222n20

Nebraska, 36–37

Nelson, Michael, 237n14

neo-Nazis, 187–88

Neustadt, Richard, 234n97

New College of Florida, 205

New Deal, 17, 86–89

New Deal Democrats, 17, 137

New Democrats, 154–55

New Left, 128

New Mexico, 33–34

New Orleans massacre (1866), 58

The New Republic (magazine), 156

New Yorker (magazine), 157

New York Times (newspaper), 169, 176

Nixon, Richard: 1968 campaign, 117–21; abuses of power by, 112, 126, 129–32, 135; and African Americans, 112, 119, 123, 128–30; Andrew Johnson compared to, 110, 115, 122, 134–35; as backlash president, 5–6, 20; character/personality of, 127, 135; and civil rights, 98, 117–24; congressional relations with, 10, 111, 133–36; election interference by, 6, 12, 135 (*see also* Watergate scandal); impact of backlash presidency of, 20; impeachment proceedings against, 6, 9, 18, 110, 112, 126–36, 208; law-and-order rhetoric of, 5, 19, 114, 119, 123–24, 238n25; nomination of, 111, 114–17; norms/institutions challenged, ignored, and broken by, 131–34; opponents/"enemies" of, 111, 112, 116–17, 120, 127–30, 132–34; and populism, 10–11, 116, 120–21, 131–32, 135, 184; as preemptive president, 17, 123, 229n83, 236n1; and race, 11, 19, 123–24, 134; racial issues exploited by, 11, 19, 111–12, 116; racism of, 121–22, 129; and the Republican Party, 111–12, 114–17, 125, 237n13, 239n55; and the South, 11, 115–16, 119–21, 136; Trump compared to, 110, 115, 122, 134–35, 187, 192, 195–98. *See also* Watergate scandal

Noel, Hans, 113

norms: Andrew Johnson's challenging, ignoring, and breaking of, 63; challenging of, as invitation to ignoring/breaking of, 13; of congressional behavior and actions, 13, 132–34; decline of, in politics from the 1970s on, 112; FBI's, 133; Franklin Roosevelt's challenging, ignoring, and breaking of, 86; of impeachment, 13–14, 157, 187, 191–92, 208; Nixon's challenging, ignoring, and breaking of, 131–34; populist attacks on, 10, 12, 121; of presidential behavior and actions, 12–13; pros and cons of, 12–13; racial transformation leading to uncertainty about, 13, 132, 136, 141; Republican Party's challenging, ignoring, and breaking of, 13–14; Trump's challenging, ignoring, and breaking of, 2–3, 4, 174, 177–78, 184–87, 193, 203. *See also* institutions; lawlessness

North Carolina, 56

Obama, Barack: on campaign trail, 163–65; criticisms of, 2, 171, 176–77, 179–80; moderation of, 2, 17, 165, 167, 171; "otherness" of, 169–70, 177; political impact of, 17; and race, 1–2, 140–41, 144, 163–73, 247n112, 249n135; racial backlash against, 176–77; and racial transformation, 163–73; racist attacks on, 1–2, 176; as transformative president, 4, 211; Trump's reversal of policies and accomplishments of, 185

O'Malley, Martin, 180
Omar, Ihlan, 192
O'Reilly, Kenneth, 232n58

Palin, Sarah, 165–66
Panetta, Leon, 122
Parker, John J., 83
partisan polarization: 1968 election and, 113;
    2016 election and, 181; compromise vs.,
    18, 33; impeachments in relation to, 9, 141;
    racial factors in, 113, 209
party system, 22, 27, 28. *See also* partisan
    polarization
Pelosi, Nancy, 193, 195
Perkins, Frances, 86
Perlstein, Rich, 116
Perot, H. Ross, 153
Perry, Samuel, 188
Personal Responsibility and Work
    Opportunity Reconciliation Act
    (PRWORA; 1996), 155–56
Philadelphia Plan, 117, 122–23
Philadelphia Tribune (newspaper), 146
Phillips, Kevin, 123
Phillips, Wendell, 61, 63
Pierce, Franklin, 36–38
Pinckney, Clementa, 173
Plessy v. Ferguson, 94, 140
polarization. *See* partisan polarization
police violence, 89, 107, 151–53, 198
political development. *See* American
    political development
political environment: Andrew Johnson and,
    50, 71; for impeachments, 14, 70, 111, 131,
    133–36, 141, 190–92, 194, 207; Nixon and,
    111, 122, 125, 127, 131, 135; racial factors in, 14,
    144, 191–92, 203, 210–11; in Reagan-
    Clinton years, 156; Trump and, 71, 203
political parties. *See* Constitutional Union
    Party; Democratic Party; Free Soil
    movement/Party; Know-Nothing Party;
    National Union Party; partisan
    polarization; party system; Republican
    Party; Whig Party

political polarization. *See* partisan
    polarization
political time, 15–18
Polk, James K., 29–31
popular sovereignty, 37
populism: Andrew Johnson and, 10–11, 52,
    61–63, 121; backlash presidents and, 4,
    10–12, 207; conservative movement
    aligned with, 120; defined, 10; delegitimi-
    zation of the opposition by forces of,
    12, 61–62, 121; Democratic Party in 2016
    and, 179–81; flexibility of, 121; Franklin
    Roosevelt and, 85–86; institutions and
    norms under attack by, 10–12, 121;
    lawlessness linked to, 10, 12, 130, 207;
    Nixon and, 10–11, 116, 120–21, 131–32, 135,
    184; Palin and, 165–66; Pat Buchanan
    and, 152, 153; Perot and, 154; and racial
    backlash, 207; racial hierarchy reinforced
    by, 120; "true people" as ideological
    foundation of, 10, 12; Trump and, 4, 10–11,
    121, 178, 183–85; victimhood associated
    with, 10–11, 116, 120–21; Wallace and, 120.
    See also "forgotten man/American;"
    "silent majority;" "true people"
postal service, 27
postracial rhetoric, 166–68,
    173
preemption, politics of, 17–18, 123, 229n83,
    236n1
presidential campaigns: Nixon, 5, 19, 117–21;
    pre–Civil War, 33; Trump, 2, 176–79,
    181–82
presidential powers: Andrew Johnson's use
    of, 4, 55–58; civil rights advanced
    through, 77; expansion of, 70, 77, 131;
    Jackson and, 26, 222n23; Lincoln's use of,
    40–41, 47–48; Polk and, 31; populist
    support of, 131–32; Trump and, 198;
    Whig Party's position on, 33. *See also*
    abuses of presidential power
presidential prerogative, 131
presidents: congressional relations with,
    9–10, 17–18; constitutional framing of

the role of, 6, 23, 68; evaluation of, 22–23; historical idealization of, 24; lawless behavior and rhetoric of, 9, 10, 12, 111–12; limitations on, 77, 92–93; norms of behavior and actions of, 12–13; political and policy impact of, 16; "political time" theory of, 15–18; and the politics of race, 6–8, 16; preemptive, 17–18, 229n83; as slave owners, 22, 24, 25, 27, 29, 31–32, 72. *See also* abuses of presidential power; presidential powers

President's Committee on Civil Rights, 90–91

Price, Melanye, 165

Proclamation of Amnesty and Reconstruction (Lincoln), 51

Progressivism, 84, 86, 87

Proud Boys, 199–200

Public Works Administration (PWA), 86–87

Puerto Rico, 128, 192

PWA. *See* Public Works Administration

quotas, 117, 123, 138, 145, 147–48, 150–53

race: 1968 election and, 113–14, 118; 2016 election and, 174–75, 177, 179, 181–84, 186, 195, 249n1, 249n3; 2020 election and, 199–200; Andrew Johnson and, 11, 19; Biden and, 204–5, 255n69; Charlottesville, Virginia, "Unite the Right" rally and, 187–90, 204; COVID-19 and, 197; and diversification of political voices, 210; and election fraud allegations, 200–201, 203; Franklin Roosevelt and, 86–90; Kennedy and, 7, 8; Lincoln and, 21, 40–41, 49, 225n76; Lyndon Johnson and, 8, 235n134; Nixon and, 11, 19, 123–24, 134; Obama and, 1–2, 140–41, 144, 163–73, 247n112, 249n135; polarization based on, 113, 209; in post–civil rights era, 140–41, 144–50; presidents and the politics of, 6–8, 16; Republican Party and, 7, 8, 17, 42, 78–83, 114–17; Trump and, 2–3, 19, 174–75, 177, 179, 181–84, 186, 188–90, 192–93, 199, 202–4; Watergate scandal in relation to, 110–11, 126, 128–30, 236n2. *See also* African Americans; colorblind ideology/rhetoric; Jim Crow era; racial backlash; racial discrimination; racial hierarchy; racial order; racial transformation; racism; segregation

racial backlash: 1992 election and, 153–54; aims or targets of, 19; American political development in relation to, 14–18; Andrew Johnson and, 19, 70–71; criticisms of the concept, 19–20; defined, 19; early-twentieth-century presidents subject to, 79–80, 82; Lyndon Johnson and, 102–3, 108–9, 216; Nixon and, 11, 19, 111–12, 116, 128, 216; Obama as victim of, 1–2, 141; political impact of, 2; politics of, 9; populism and, 10, 207; presidential lawlessness linked to, 9, 112, 117, 183; Republican Party and, 115; Trump and, 19, 176; Wallace and, 118. *See also* compromise/moderation; racial hierarchy; racial order; racial transformation; racism

racial discrimination, 89, 91. *See also* Black codes; civil rights; Jim Crow era; quotas; segregation

racial hierarchy: in civil rights era, 76; colorblind rhetoric and, 140; as foundational to America, 20; in Jim Crow era, 81, 88; populist reinforcement of, 120; in the South during Reconstruction, 57. *See also* Jim Crow era; racial backlash; racial order; racial transformation; racism; white supremacy

racial order: defined, 15; following racial transformations, 208–11; impeachments as diversion from addressing, 71; maintenance/avoidance of, 6–8, 15, 16, 20, 81, 86–87, 92, 105, 141, 156, 165, 167; norms rooted in, 132; tacit character of, 19, 20. *See also* compromise/moderation; Jim Crow era; racial backlash; racial hierarchy; racial transformation racial transformation: American political development in relation to, 14–18; basic features of, 45; congressional advocates for, 14; impeachment linked to, 8–14, 70–71, 134–36, 207; Lincoln and, 21–22, 44–45, 47–49; Lyndon Johnson and, 75–76, 78, 102–9; norms challenged and overturned in, 13, 132, 136, 141; Obama and, 163–73; populism as response to, 10–11; presidential resistance to (maintenance of status quo), 6–8, 15, 16; racial order following, 208–11. *See also* compromise/moderation; race; racial backlash; racial hierarchy; racial order; transformative presidents

racial violence: in civil rights era, 95, 100–102, 106; in early twentieth century, 76–77, 87–88; in Reconstruction era, 54, 57–58, 73–74, 229n89; school integration as spark for, 100. *See also* lynching; violence

racism: alleged demise of, 150; Andrew Johnson's, 4, 59, 66–67, 228n44; Charlottesville, Virginia, "Unite the Right" rally and, 187–90; colorblind rhetoric as denial of, 142; individual vs. systemic conceptions of, 168, 172–73, 180; Islamophobia as form of, 161, 246n93; legacy of, 140, 142; Lyndon Johnson's statements against, 76; Nixon's, 121–22, 129; Obama subjected to, 1–2; of pre–Civil War Republicans, 42; presidents' espousal of, 22; Reagan's, 145, 147; in Reconstruction era, 57; "scientific," 84; sexual anxieties linked to, 79, 81, 84–85, 99; Theodore Roosevelt's, 78; Trump's, 176, 183, 188, 189, 192; underlying slavery, 40; Wilson's, 83–85, 232n39. *See also* colorblind ideology/rhetoric; Jim Crow era; racial backlash; racial discrimination; racial hierarchy; reverse discrimination/racism; segregation; white supremacy

Rader, Katherine, 90

radical Republicans, 14, 53, 58, 64

Raffensperger, Brad, 200

Rainbow-PUSH, 154

Ramaswamy, Vivek, 213

Rangel, Charles, 129

Raskin, Jamie, 196

Rauh, Joseph, 105

Reagan, Ronald, 115, 139, 140, 142, 144–50, 243n52

Reconstruction: Andrew Johnson and, 4, 11, 52–53, 55–58, 63, 65–66, 70; Black suffrage and, 55–56; Congress and, 58–62, 65; Lincoln and, 53–54; radical Republican vision for, 53; Southern white supremacy during, 54; Wilson on, 84

Republican Party: 1860 election, 43; and African Americans, 115–16; black-and-tan faction of, 17, 78, 82; and control of Congress from late twentieth century on, 155–57, 171; divisions within, in 2016, 178; divisions within post–Civil War, 73; divisions within pre–Civil War, 35; formation of, 35, 38; and immigration, 177; law-and-order rhetoric of, 114–15; lily-white faction of, 17, 81–83; Lincoln and, 40–42; nativism in, 250n11; Nixon and, 111–12, 114–17, 125, 237n13, 239n55; norms challenged, ignored, and broken by, 13–14; and race in civil rights era, 8, 114–17; and race in early twentieth century, 78–83; and race in post–civil rights era, 143; and race in post–Civil War era, 7, 17; and race in pre–Civil War era, 42; and slavery, 35, 38, 42, 44–45, 51, 54; in the South from mid-twentieth century, 105, 114–16; Theodore Roosevelt and, 78–80; Trump and, 177–78. *See also* radical Republicans

reverse discrimination/racism, 145, 148, 151, 154, 164, 169

Reynolds, William Bradford, 148

Rhodes, Jesse, 106

Richardson, Elliot, 130

Richmond, Cedric, 189

Richmond Times-Dispatch (newspaper), 166

rights. *See* civil rights

Rigueur, Leah Wright, 116

Riley, Russell, 6, 16

riots and unrest: in civil rights era, 107–8, 113–14; in post–civil rights era, 152–53, 198; post–Civil War, 58

Rock, Dave, 175

Romney, George, 115

Romney, Mitt, 176, 196, 249n1

Roof, Dylann, 173

Roosevelt, Eleanor, 88

Roosevelt, Franklin, 7, 17, 85–90, 232n58

Roosevelt, Theodore, 7, 78–79, 230n15

Ross, Edmund, 70

Rubio, Marco, 177, 178

Ruckelshaus, William, 130

Russian interference in 2016 election, 183, 186–87, 193–94, 196

Rustin, Bayard, 123

Sanders, Bernie, 180–81

Saturday Night Live (television show), 175

Saturday Night Massacre, 127, 130, 186

Schickler, Eric, 113

Schmidt, Anthony, 76, 235n134

Schurz, Carl, 73

Scott, Tim, 213

secession, of Southern states, 45–47

sectional crisis, 31–35, 37–40, 45

segregation: educational, 94–100, 119, 122; residential, 87, 98, 108. *See also* racial discrimination

Select Committee to Investigate the January 6th Attack on the United States Capitol, 201, 203

Senate: filibuster in, 87, 88, 103–4, 149; impeachment proceedings in, 68–70, 159, 195, 196, 202, 208; and Watergate, 126, 128, 131, 136

September 11, 2001, terrorist attacks, 159–61, 164

Seward, William, 42, 225n81

Sides, John, 177, 200

"silent majority," 11, 124, 131–32, 134, 184. *See also* "forgotten man/American;" "true people"

Sinclair-Chapman, Valeria, 165

Skowronek, Stephen, 15–18, 134, 229n83

slave owners: compensation of, 47; presidents as, 22, 24, 25, 27, 29, 31–32, 72

slavery: Andrew Johnson and, 10–11, 52; as cause of Civil War, 47–49; colonization approach to, 23, 41, 225n76; compromise/ moderation on, 22–40; Congress and, 23, 25, 37, 39, 44, 46, 54; Constitution and, 23, 24–25, 44, 46; Democratic Party and, 7, 22, 37–38; Lincoln and, 4, 21–22, 24, 41, 43, 48–49, 54, 226n98; moral status of, 17, 25, 27, 34, 40, 44–45, 47; norms protecting, 12–13; political context for addressing, 23, 37–38; pre-Lincoln presidents' handling of, 6–7, 22, 24–40; Republican Party and, 35, 38, 42, 44–45, 51, 54; Thirteenth Amendment abolishing, 4, 47, 49, 54. *See also* abolitionism/anti-slavery movement; enslaved persons; slave owners

Smith, Candis Watts, 142

Smith, Howard, 103, 235n137

Smith, Robert, 204

Smith, Rogers, 15, 83, 142, 209

Social Security Act, 87

social unrest. *See* riots and unrest

South: accommodations made by politicians to ideology and politics of, 7, 11, 12–13, 19, 22, 25–40, 53–62, 71–74, 80–81, 86–88, 91–93, 97, 99, 137; Andrew Johnson and, 19, 50, 52, 54–58, 70–71; Bill Clinton and, 137; Democratic courting of, in late twentieth century, 137; Franklin Roosevelt and, 86; Nixon and, 11, 115–16, 119–21, 136; political power and influence of, 25, 40, 92, 103–4; Reagan and, 144–45; Republican Party from mid-twentieth century in, 105, 114–16; and school desegregation, 95–98, 100; secession of, 45–47; sectional crisis and, 1–35, 37–40, 45; states' rights and powers in, 27; Theodore Roosevelt and, 79–81. *See also* Jim Crow era; Reconstruction; white supremacy

Southern Manifesto, 95, 104

Southern strategy, 120–21, 145

the Squad, 191, 192

Stanbery, Henry, 65

Stanley, Alessandra, 166

Stanton, Edwin, 66–68

State Department, 100, 102

states: backlash presidents' impact on
politics of, 20; federal power over, during
Reconstruction, 55–59, 66, 74; federal
power over, in civil rights era, 95–96, 100,
104, 107, 115, 120, 122, 123; federal power
over, in early twentieth century, 87–88,
90; federal power over, in post–civil
rights era, 147; racial backlash policies
enacted by, 205–6; rights and powers of,
27, 55–59, 66, 74, 88, 92, 146

States' Rights Party, 92

status quo. *See* racial order; racial
transformation

Stephens, Alexander, 22, 32, 47, 57

Stephens-Dougan, LaFleur, 247n112

Stevens, Thaddeus, 56, 61, 63, 67

Stewart, David O., 58

Stewart, Jon, 165

Stimson, James, 113

Strong, Cecily, 175

Stuckey, Mary, 243n53

Sullivan, Bill, 128

Sumner, Charles, 38, 56, 61

Supreme Court, on Fourteenth and
Fifteenth Amendments, 230n97. *See also
individual decisions by name*

Sweet, Lynn, 167

Taft, Robert, 93

Taft, William Howard, 81–82

Taney, Roger, 39

Tausanovich, Chris, 200

Taylor, Keeanga-Yamahtta, 171, 249n135

Taylor, Zachary, 18, 31–35, 42, 224n54

Tea Party movement, 169, 171, 177

Ten Percent Plan, 53

Tenure of Office Act, 66–69, 196

Tesler, Michael, 2, 170, 177

Texas, 30

Thirteenth Amendment, 4, 47, 49, 54

Thomas, Clarence, 148, 244n54

Thomas, Helen, 243n52

Thomas, Lorenzo, 67–68

Thomas Proviso, 26

Thompson, Bennie, 203

Thomson, Meldrim, 150, 243n48

Three-Fifths Compromise, 25

Thurmond, Strom, 92, 104, 115, 119, 146

Tichenor, Dan, 105

Tien, Charles, 249n3

Tilden, Samuel, 74

Till, Emmett, 95

Tillman, Benjamin, 79, 81

Tlaib, Rashida, 191

transformative presidents: grounding of, in
American history, 210–11; impact of, 6,
16; Kennedy, 102; Lincoln, 4, 21–24,
40–41, 48–49, 211; Lyndon Johnson, 5,
76, 78, 211; Obama, 4, 211; overview of, 5;
racial order reconfigured by, 6. *See also*
racial transformation

Treaty of Versailles, 17

Trefousse, Hans, 229n83

"true people," 10, 12, 131–32, 175, 185–86, 207.
See also "forgotten man/American;"
"silent majority"

Truman, Harry, 7, 77, 90–93, 102, 167

Trumbull, Lyman, 58, 256n90

Trump, Donald: 2018 midterm elections
and, 190–92; 2024 campaign of, 214;
abuses of power by, 186–87, 189, 195–96;
Andrew Johnson compared to, 71, 187,
189, 192, 195–98, 201–3; as backlash
president, 4, 20, 203; campaign of, 2,
176–79, 181–82; congressional relations
with, 10, 190–92, 194–95; and COVID-19,
196–97; election interference by, 3, 12, 135,
200–203, 208; Goldwater compared to,
251n17; and immigration, 2, 177, 182,

192–93; impact of backlash presidency of, 20, 204; impeachments of, 3–4, 18, 186–90, 193–96, 202–3, 208; and January 6, 2001, insurrection, 3, 12, 201–3, 208; law-and-order rhetoric of, 2, 4, 198; "make America great again" slogan of, 2, 19; nationalist ideology/rhetoric of, 2, 11, 19, 185, 192, 209; Nixon compared to, 110, 115, 122, 134–35, 187, 192, 195–98; nomination of, 176–79, 250n14; norms/institutions challenged, ignored, and broken by, 2–3, 4, 174, 177–78, 184–87, 193, 203; and populism, 4, 10–11, 121, 178, 183–85; and race, 2–3, 19, 174–75, 177, 179, 181–84, 186, 188–90, 192–93, 199, 202–4; racism of, 176, 183, 188, 189, 192; reelection of, 3; and the Republican Party, 177–78; and white supremacy, 3, 188–89, 195, 199–200, 204
Tulis, Jeffrey, 71
Twelfth Amendment, 92
Twenty-Fifth Amendment, 202
Twenty-Second Amendment, 108
Tyler, John, 17, 29–30, 223n36, 229n83

Ukraine, 3, 194–96, 255n69
Union/national unity, preservation of: Andrew Johnson and, 19, 50, 52, 56–57, 61; compromises over slavery aimed at, 27–29, 31; Franklin Roosevelt and, 89; Jackson and, 27–28; Lincoln and, 46, 51, 53; Van Buren and, 29; Wade-Davis Bill and, 53
University of California Regents v. Bakke case, 137–38
University of Mississippi, 100
Urban League, 146

Van Buren, Martin, 22, 28–29, 30, 223n29, 223n30
Vance, J. D., 213–14; Hillbilly Elegy, 184, 214
Vardaman, James, 80–81
Vavreck, Lynn, 177, 200
victimhood: Andrew Johnson and, 11, 61; populist exploitation of a sense of, 10–11,

116, 120–21; whites' claims of, 11, 59–60, 153–54, 169. See also reverse discrimination/racism
Vietnam War, 107–9, 113–14, 125
vigilantism, 27
Vindman, Alexander, 195
violence: Charlottesville, Virginia, "Unite the Right" rally and, 187–88; against politicians, 229n89; Trump's and Republican Party's advocacy of, 179, 199–200. See also lynching; police violence; racial violence
Virginia, 55–56
voting rights, for African Americans, 55–56, 65–67, 73–74, 82, 99, 105–8, 124, 148
Voting Rights Act (1965), 5, 76, 78, 106–8, 124, 145, 148

Wade, Benjamin, 53, 56
Wade-Davis Bill, 53
Wagner, Robert, 87
Walker, Scott, 178
Wallace, George, 11, 105, 114, 116, 118–20, 179
Wards Cove Packing Co. v. Antonio, 151
War on Poverty, 103
War on Terror, 159–61
Warren, Earl, 94
Washington, Booker T., 79, 82
Washington, DC, slavery in, 28–29, 33
Washington, George, 22, 24, 61
Washington Post (newspaper), 119, 126
Watergate scandal: aftermath of, 136–39; cover-up of, 12, 126–27, 130–32, 196; impeachment linked to, 6, 9, 110; interpretations of, 111, 126–36; race in relation to, 110–11, 126, 128–30, 236n2
Waters, Maxine, 189
Weaver, Robert, 99
Weaver, Vesla, 19
Weber, Jennifer, 52
Webster, Daniel, 35, 224n54
welfare, 145, 147, 154–56

welfare, opposition to, 60
West, Cornel, 180
West, Kanye, 162
Whig Party: demise of, 43; divisions within, 32–34, 37; Lincoln and, 40, 42; and Mexican-American War (1846–48), 30–31; and slavery, 7, 22, 32–33
White, Walter, 88
White Citizens' Councils, 95
White League, 74
white nationalism, 188
whites: and culture wars, 161; discrimination against, 145; Palin and, 166; racial identity of, 177, 184, 203; Trump support from, 174–75, 177, 183–84, 249n1, 249n3; and victimhood, 11, 59–60, 153–54, 169; voter behavior of, 170, 174, 175; working-class, 183–84, 249n1. *See also* colorblind ideology/rhetoric; racism; white supremacy
white supremacy: Andrew Johnson and, 4, 19, 55, 58–59, 62, 66–67; Democratic Party during Civil War and, 52; Democratic Party in post–Civil War era and, 7; opposition to George H. W. Bush and, 152; political and economic aspects of, 76; in Reconstruction era, 19, 54, 73; Republican Party in pre–Civil war era and, 42, 45; Theodore Roosevelt and, 79, 81; Trump and, 3, 188–89, 195, 199–200, 204; Wilson and, 84. *See also* Jim Crow era; racial backlash; racial hierarchy; racism
Whittington, Keith, 68, 158
Wilentz, Sean, 36
Wilkins, Roy, 97, 119
Williams, Hosea, 146
Wilmot, David, and the Wilmot Proviso, 31–35, 44
Wilson, Joe, 168
Wilson, Woodrow, 7, 17, 83–85, 232n39
Witcover, Jules, 153
Women's March (2017), 175
Woodward, Bob, 126
World War I, 83
Wright, Fielding, 92
Wright, Jeremiah, 164

Xi Jinping, 197

Young, Andrew, 129, 146

Zelenskyy, Volodymyr, 194, 255n69
Zelizer, Julian, 103

The Unsolid South: Mass Politics and National Representation in a One-Party Enclave, Devin Caughey

Southern Nation: Congress and White Supremacy After Reconstruction, David A. Bateman, Ira Katznelson, and John S. Lapinsky

California Greenin': How the Golden State Became an Environmental Leader, David Vogel

Building an American Empire: The Era of Territorial and Political Expansion, Paul Frymer

Racial Realignment: The Transformation of American Liberalism, 1932–1965, Eric Schickler

Paths Out of Dixie: The Democratization of Authoritarian Enclaves in America's Deep South, 1944–1972, Robert Mickey

When Movements Anchor Parties: Electoral Alignments in American History, Daniel Schlozman

Electing the Senate: Indirect Democracy Before the Seventeenth Amendment, Wendy J. Schiller and Charles Stewart III

Looking for Rights in All the Wrong Places: Why State Constitutions Contain America's Positive Rights, Emily Zackin

The Substance of Representation: Congress, American Political Development, and Lawmaking, John S. Lapinski

Fighting for the Speakership: The House and the Rise of Party Government, Jeffery A. Jenkins and Charles Stewart

Three Worlds of Relief: Race, Immigration, and the American Welfare State from the Progressive Era to the New Deal, Cybelle Fox

Building the Judiciary: Law, Courts, and the Politics of Institutional Development, Justin Crowe

Still a House Divided: Race and Politics in Obama's America, Desmond King and Rogers M. Smith

Reputation and Power: Organizational Image and Pharmaceutical Regulation at the FDA, Daniel Carpenter

The Litigation State: Public Regulation and Private Lawsuits in the US, Sean Farhang

Why Is There No Labor Party in the United States?, Robin Archer

Presidential Party Building: Dwight D. Eisenhower to George W. Bush, Daniel J. Galvin

Fighting for Democracy: Black Veterans and the Struggle Against White Supremacy in the Postwar South, Christopher S. Parker

The Fifth Freedom: Jobs, Politics, and Civil Rights in the United States, 1941–1972, Anthony S. Chen